T0358353

Fintech for Finance Professionals

Global Fintech Institute - World Scientific Series on Fintech

Print ISSN: 2737-5897
Online ISSN: 2737-5900

Series Editors: David LEE Kuo Chuen *(Global Fintech Institute, Singapore &*
Singapore University of Social Sciences, Singapore)
Joseph LIM *(Singapore University of Social Sciences, Singapore)*
PHOON Kok Fai *(Singapore University of Social Sciences, Singapore)*
WANG Yu *(Singapore University of Social Sciences, Singapore)*

In the digital era, emerging technologies such as artificial intelligence, big data, and blockchain have revolutionized people's daily lives and brought many opportunities and challenges to industries. With the increasing demand for talents in the fintech realm, this book series serves as a good guide for practitioners who are seeking to understand the basics of fintech and the applications of different technologies. This book series starts with fundamental knowledge in finance, technology, quantitative methods, and financial innovation to lay the foundation for the fundamentals of fintech, and understanding the trending issues related to fintech such as regulation, applications, and global trends. It is a good starting point to the fintech literature and is especially useful for people who aspire to become fintech professionals.

Published:

Forthcoming:

More information on this series can also be found at https://www.worldscientific.com/series/gfiwssf

(Continued at end of book)

Global Fintech Institute - World Scientific
Series on Fintech : **3**

Fintech for Finance Professionals

Editors

David LEE Kuo Chuen
Global Fintech Institute, Singapore
Singapore University of Social Sciences, Singapore

Joseph LIM
Singapore University of Social Sciences, Singapore

PHOON Kok Fai
Singapore University of Social Sciences, Singapore

WANG Yu
Singapore University of Social Sciences, Singapore

Published by

World Scientific Publishing Co. Pte. Ltd.

5 Toh Tuck Link, Singapore 596224

USA office: 27 Warren Street, Suite 401-402, Hackensack, NJ 07601

UK office: 57 Shelton Street, Covent Garden, London WC2H 9HE

and

Global Fintech Institute Ltd.

80 Robinson Road, #08-01, Singapore 068898

Library of Congress Cataloging-in-Publication Data

Names: Lee, David (David Kuo Chuen), editor. | Lim, Joseph, editor. |
  Phoon, Kok Fai, editor. | Wang, Yu, editor.
Title: Fintech for finance professionals / editors, David Lee Kuo Chuen
  (Global Fintech Institute, Singapore, Singapore University of Social Sciences, Singapore),
  Joseph Lim (Singapore University of Social Sciences, Singapore),
  Phoon Kok Fai (Singapore University of Social Sciences, Singapore),
  Wang Yu (Singapore University of Social Sciences, Singapore).
Description: Singapore ; Hackensack, NJ : World Scientific, [2022] |
  Series: Global Fintech Institute - World Scientific series on fintech, 2737-5897 ; vol. 3 |
  Includes bibliographical references.
Identifiers: LCCN 2021041940 | ISBN 9789811241079 (hardcover) |
  ISBN 9789811241864 (paperback) | ISBN 9789811241086 (ebook) |
  ISBN 9789811241093 (ebook other)
Subjects: LCSH: Finance--Technological innovations. | Finance--Technological innovations--
  Problems, exercises, etc. | Financial engineering. | Finance.
Classification: LCC HG173 .F5375 2022 | DDC 332--dc23
LC record available at https://lccn.loc.gov/2021041940

British Library Cataloguing-in-Publication Data

A catalogue record for this book is available from the British Library.

Copyright © 2022 by Global Fintech Institute

All rights reserved.

For any available supplementary material, please visit
https://www.worldscientific.com/worldscibooks/10.1142/12390#t=suppl

Desk Editors: Balasubramanian Shanmugam/Yulin Jiang

Typeset by Stallion Press
Email: enquiries@stallionpress.com

Printed in Singapore

Preface

The Fintech for Finance Professionals Volume provides a significant underpinning to the CFtP qualification. It covers important concepts in technologies for professionals in the finance and fintech areas. Technologies such as artificial intelligence, big data, and data science have been applied to various areas in finance and there is an increasing demand for the skills and knowledge related to fintech. It is high time for finance professionals to know about the basics of these technologies and fundamentals of subjects like data structure and computer network. This will give finance professionals a better idea of how to explore the potentials of applying emerging technologies in solving issues in the financial industries. The knowledge will be useful for anyone that would like to have a solid understanding of the Fintech.

This book covers the main concepts and theories of the technologies in Fintech which consist of four parts. Part I is Data Structure, Algorithms, and Programming in Python and it covers the basics of Python programming and the fundamentals in data structure and algorithms. Part II covers the big data and data science, including their architecture, applications, as well as the comparison of the two. It is the first module of Data Management. Part III is the second module of Data Management: Artificial Intelligence and Machine Learning, where the evolution and concepts of artificial intelligence and the common algorithms in machine learning and deep learning are introduced. Finally, Part IV includes Computer Network and Network Security.

This book is a companion volume to the book titled *Finance for Fintech Professionals* that covers the fundamental concepts in Finance. Together, these two books form the foundation for a good understanding of finance and fintech applications which will be covered in subsequent volumes.

About the Editors

Professor David LEE Kuo Chuen is a professor at the Singapore University of Social Sciences and Adjunct Professor at the National University of Singapore. He is also the founder of BlockAsset Ventures, the Chairman of Global Fintech Institute, Vice President of the Economic Society of Singapore, Co-founder of Blockchain Association of Singapore, and Council Member of British Blockchain Association. He has 20 years of experience as a CEO and an independent director of listed and tech companies and is a consultant and advisor to international organizations on food supply chain, blockchain, fintech, and digital currency.

Associate Professor Joseph LIM is with the Singapore University of Social Sciences where he teaches finance. He has also taught at the National University of Singapore and the Singapore Management University. Joseph obtained his MBA from Columbia University and PhD from New York University. In between his stints in academia, he worked in various advisory positions in the areas of private equity and valuation. Joseph, who is a CFA charter holder, has served in various committees at the CFA Institute and as President of CFA Singapore. In addition, he was on the board and committees of various investment industry associations. In the non-profit sector, he was on the board of a pension fund and several endowment funds. He is a coauthor of several popular college finance textbooks.

Associate Professor Kok Fai PHOON teaches finance at the School of Business, Singapore University of Social Sciences (SUSS). He received his PhD in finance from Northwestern University, MSc in Industrial Engineering from the National University of Singapore, and BASc in Mechanical Engineering (Honours) from the University of British Columbia. His research interests focus on the use of technology in portfolio management, wealth management, and risk and complexity of financial products. In addition to his current position at SUSS, Kok Fai has taught at other universities in Singapore and at Monash University in Australia. He has worked at Yamaichi Merchant Bank, at GIC Pte Ltd, and as Executive Director at Ferrell Asset Management, a Singapore hedge fund. He has published in academic journals including the *Review of Quantitative Finance and Accounting* and the *Pacific Basin Finance Journal* as well as practice journals like the *Financial Analyst Journal*, the *Journal of Wealth Management*, and the *Journal of Alternative Investments*.

Ms Yu WANG (Cheryl) is a fintech research fellow at the Singapore University of Social Sciences FinTech and Blockchain Group. Her main research interests are fintech, machine learning, and asset pricing. Prior to SUSS, she worked at the National University of Singapore, Business School as a research associate on corporate governance and sustainability. She graduated with an MSc in Applied Economies from Nanyang Technological University and BSc in Financial Engineering from Huazhong University of Sciences of Technologies. She has multiple journal papers, including an empirical study on sustainability reporting and firm value published on an SSCI journal, *Sustainability*, and one investigating cryptocurrency as a new alternative investment published on *Journal of Alternative Investments* that has been cited for over 200 times and recommended by *CFA Institute Journal Review*. She also serves as referee for various journals such as *Singapore Economic Review*, *Quarterly Review of Economics and Finance*, and *Journal of Alternative Investments*.

Contents

Part I

Data Structures

Chapter 1

Python Programming Basics

1.1 Introduction

1.1.1 *Getting Started*

Developed by Guido van Rossum in the late eighties and early nineties at the National Research Institute for Mathematics and Computer Science in the Netherlands, Python has grown into Python 3. Today, all of the most important libraries in the Python mainstream run on Python 3. The most prominent Python programmers in the world are also programming in Python 3. Python has been widely used in search engines, gravitational wave analysis, and many other fields.[1]

Learning Objectives
- Understand Python's main features and the reasons why it is widely used.
- Learn about the integrated development environment (IDE) to choose between interactive and script mode in the practical application scenario.
- Learn to write simple statements and understand what Python can do.

---

[1]Song Tian, Huang Tianyu, & Li Xin. Python Programming. Python 语言程序设计. Beijing Institute of Technology. Retrieved from https://www.icourse163.org/learn/BIT-268001?tid=1460270441#/learn/content?type=detail&id=1236349063&cid=1256098128&replay=true (accessed July 14, 2020).

Main Takeaways

Main Points
- Python is an interpreted, interactive, object-oriented, and beginner-friendly language.
- Python programs executed by the interpreter can be written in either interactive mode or script mode.

Main Terms
- **Python interpreter:** A program that reads and executes instructions written in the Python language.
- **IDE:** An application for a provider development environment that typically includes tools such as code editors, compilers, debuggers, and graphical user interfaces.

(a) Python Features
Several factors are contributing to the popularity of Python 3.

- **Interpreted:** Users do not need to compile their program before executing Python.
- **Intuitive:** Compared to other programming languages, Python code is more clearly defined and readable.
- **Extendable:** Users can add low-level modules to the interpreter.
- **Extensible:** The Python interpreter is easily extended with new functions and data types implemented in C or C++, and it can be easily integrated with C, C++, COM, ActiveX, CORBA, and JAVA.
- **Object-oriented:** Python supports an object-oriented style or programming technique that encapsulates code within objects.
- **Friendly to beginners:** Beginner-level programmers find Python relatively user-friendly and find themselves accessible to a wide range of applications from simple text processing to some complicated game browsers.

(b) Python Applications
In recent years, the financial industry has witnessed lots of changes. Fintech is one of the most important trends, which incorporates emerging technologies such as big data, blockchain, and artificial intelligence. Products developed in the fintech market need high-level security and functionality, which means that fintech practitioners need appropriate

technical tools to achieve their goals. This technology tool needs to have the following properties: fast development speed to face the changing market, suitable for financial big data processing and analysis, and convenient interactive operation and testing process. Fortunately, Python can meet these requirements, making it the preferred technical tool for financial workers.

One of Python's features is that it can help financial workers digitize their work. Python's rich built-in data types enable analysts and programmers to focus more on the problems they solve without spending too much time on low-level machine structure settings. Financial practitioners are using Python to simplify and accelerate their analysis process and get more reliable and diverse analysis results in financial analysis. Python is omnipotent in the field of financial analysis, including option pricing, trading strategy, value at risk measurement, investment evaluation of the bond market and stock market, etc. In the past, financial data analysis required weeks or even months of data collection, calculation, and visualization of results. However, with Python, all these can be completed with only a few lines of code. Besides, compared with other languages such as C++, Python has lower learning cost, higher development efficiency, and lower difficulty building models. So, it is very suitable for the needs of financial workers.

Another one of Python's characteristics is its rich third-party libraries and API interfaces. This extensible feature makes it a good combination with new technology. A good training framework is necessary for artificial intelligence, and Python has tensorflow and pytorch to implement. In big data processing and analysis, data needs to be batch pre-processed and visualized, and Python has pandas and matplotlib to implement. In mathematical computing, complex financial problems need advanced digital operation and modeling, and Python has numpy and SciPy to implement. Python currently has tens of thousands of third-party libraries, covering almost everything the financial sector needs. Also, Python can be integrated with nearly all other technologies without worrying about the underlying technology implementation, allowing users to focus more on the analysis field. Therefore, compared with other languages such as MATLAB and C++, Python can significantly speed up the degree of automation of research and use the rich tools provided by the third-party library to complete almost all other languages' functions. With Python, analysts can react quickly, provide valuable insights in almost real-time, and ensure that they are one step ahead of their competitors.

This improvement in efficiency can easily be translated into measurable financial results.

(c) Python Interpreter

Python interpreter is a program that reads and executes instructions written in the Python language. Python programs run by the interpreter can be written in either interactive mode or script mode. In interactive mode, users can execute single lines of code and get the results immediately. In script mode, users can write a batch of statements in source files and produce the final result through one-time execution.

For interactive mode, the user will first need to find and run their computer's command-line interface called terminal in Mac or Linux OS, or the DOS prompt in Windows OS. There will be a command line where users can type code. After installing Python, users can access the Python shell by typing "python". The ">>>" indicates that the shell is ready to execute and send commands to the interpreter. To execute code, users can type their commands and hit enter.[2] Another popular software where both interactive and script mode can be used is Jupyter Notebook.

Users can carry out simple calculations using mathematical operators using Python. In the following example, the area of a circle can be calculated with a given radius in interactive mode.

```
>>>r=25
>>>area=3.1415*r*r
>>>print(area)
1963.4375000000002
>>>print("{:.2f}".format(area))
1963.44
```

We can write these statements to a Python file in script mode, save it as CalCircle.py and run it.

---

[2]Samuel, N. (2020). Python Programming in Interactive vs Script Mode. Retrieved from https://stackabuse.com/python-programming-in-interactive-vs-script-mode/.

```
r=25
area=3.1415*r*r
print(area)
print("{:.2f}".format(area))

======================= D:/CalCircle.py =======================
1963.4375000000002
1963.44
```

Moreover, you may come across some **IDEs** when using Python in the future. An IDE is an application that provides a development environment, which typically includes tools such as a code editor, compiler, debugger, and graphical user interface. It integrates code writing, analysis, compilation, debugging functions, and other integrated development software service sets. There are many outstanding python IDEs such as PyCharm, Eclipse with PyDev, Sublime Text.

(d) Statements
Python's syntax is specific in terms of the statement structure. On most occasions, statements are contained in a single line of the text file. However, there are exceptions when we wish to split a single statement across several lines:

- Using backslash (\) at the end of the line so that you can continue the statement on the following line.
- In pairs of parentheses (contained by function calls or method invocations), the Python interpreter can recognize the content across lines until the closing parenthesis, even if there is no backslash.
- In a compound statement, the interpreter begins the parsing of the statement block with the following line and ends with the next blank line or the first statement whose indentation level is shorter than in the code block. The following example shows a crossline compound statement. In such cases, it is necessary to identify the header (followed by a colon) and the statement blocks marked out by indentation. Generally, four whitespaces or a single tab are used for indentation.

```
while a>2:
    year += a
    a += 1
```

In Python IDEs, we can add comments or notes to the code (this part will be not be run with the command lines) by starting the sentence with "#" or using a pair of three quotation marks ("""" """"").

(e) Standard Input and Output
There is a built-in function, *input([prompt])*, with the parameter prompt to prompt for user input. The input() function in Python 3 takes a standard input and returns a string.

```
>>>s = input("Now, please input a string: ")
Now, please input a string: "hello world"
>>>print(s)
hello world
```

The print() function can display information to the terminal. We find that the print() function can only output strings from previous cases. However, Python can implicitly convert any of the built-in types to strings and display the standard result. In the following example, the integer value stored in *gap* is converted to a string and outputs the result shown below.

```
age1, age2= map(int,input("Please key in the ages of two people :").
split())
gap=age1-age2
print("Your age gap is:")
print(gap)
================= D:/AgeGap.py =================
Please key in the ages of two people (separated by space):20 14
Your age gap is:
6
```

To improve the code, we can output the result on the same line by using multiple arguments in the print() function with a comma to separate, or by including a keyword argument *end* to the argument list: print("Your age gap is", gap).

Furthermore, some escape sequences are frequently used in codes to insert some space (e.g., "\t" is to insert a tab) or start a new line (e.g., "\n" is used to start a new line). To output the original symbol of a specific character, we add a backslash before it, as shown in the example below.

```
>>> print("Here is a double quotation mark(\")")
Here is a double quotation mark(")
```

Escape sequences also have some fixed combinations to encode new lines, tabs, and even the quote characters. Table 1.1 shows some quote characters and their meanings.

Besides, Python uses C-style string formatting to create new, formatted strings. The "%" operator is used to format a set of variables enclosed in a "tuple" (a fixed-size list), together with a format string, which contains normal text together with "argument specifiers", special symbols like "%s" and "%d". For example, in the code "%-10.2s", the *[flag]* "-" represents "left alignment"; the *[width]* "10" means that the length of the whole output is 10; the *[.precision]* means that only two characters will be displayed in the output; the *code s* means the type of the output is a string.

```
>>> print('%-10.2s' % ('Fintech_intro'))
Fi
```

Table 1.2 summarizes the common code and corresponding variable types.

Table 1.1: Quote characters and their meanings.

Quote characters	Description
\	Backslash
\n	New line
\"	Double quote
\'	Single quote
\t	Horizontal tab

Table 1.2: Codes and their description.

Code	Description
%s	String
%d	Integers
%i	Floating point numbers
%o	Octal
%x	Hexadecimal
%e	Displayed as a scientific counting method
%f	Displayed as a floating-point value

1.1.2 *Variables*

In Python, all data are stored in objects, and we must have some means to access the object after it has been created. Variables are used for this purpose. A variable is a storage location that associates a name with an object.

Learning Objectives
- Understand the essence and meaning of variables, grasp techniques of assigning values to variables, and multiple assignments.
- Learn about the seven standard data types.

Main Takeaways

Main Points
- A variable is a storage location that allows us to access the object after it has been created.
- When assigning variables, the right-hand side of the equal sign is the value to be stored in the variable on the left-hand side. Assigning new values to the same variable replaces the old values.

Main Terms
- **Variable:** A storage location that associates a name with an object.
- **Mutable:** Objects whose value can change are said to be mutable.

(a) Standard Data Types
Integer: The concept of **integer** in Python is consistent with the one in mathematics. An integer can be positive or negative and has no value

range limit. It has four base representations, of which the decimal is the most commonly used, such as 1000 and –99. Binary representations start with 0b or 0B, such as 0b011 and –0B1010, while octal representation starts with 0o or 0O, and hexadecimal representation starts with 0x or 0X.

Floating Point: Floating point number refers to the number with decimal point. Though usually ignored in conventional calculation, its value range and decimal precision are limited (range of 10^{-308}–10^{308} and precision of 10^{-16}). Besides, there will be uncertain mantissa in the calculation between floating-point numbers, which is a common problem in many programming languages. With function round(), we can cope with uncertain mantissa in simple cases:

```
print(0.1+0.2)
print(round(0.1+0.2,2))
======================= D:/Floating.py =======================
0.30000000000000004
0.3
```

Boolean: Boolean is the most basic type of data. It is the embodiment of the binary computer world, where everything is 0 and 1. Boolean types in Python have only two values: True and False (the initial letters are capitalized, which is different from the lower case used in C++ and JavaScript). The *bool()* function can convert integers and floating-point numbers to a Boolean type. An integer, float, or complex number will return False if set to zero and True if set to any other positive or negative number. Boolean arithmetic is the arithmetic of true and false logic and is very helpful in writing code, such as while-loops when certain conditions need to be met. The following example shows how Boolean is used to determine whether a value is in a sequence:

```
>>> a=(1,2,3,4)
>>> 3 in a
True
>>> b=[5,6,7,8]
>>> 3 in b
False
```

Boolean values can also be manipulated and combined using logical operators such as AND, OR, and NOT. Do note that such statements apply for both tuples (i.e., *a*) and lists (i.e., *b*).

```
>>> a=(1,2,3,4)
>>> 1 not in a
False
>>> b=[5,6,7,8]
>>> 5 and 6 in b
True
```

String: A **string** is an ordered sequence of characters with zero or more characters in quotation marks. Characters in a string can be accessed using the standard [ ] syntax. Python uses zero-based indexing, so if s is "hello" s[1] is "e". The characters in a string can be sorted either forward (from 0 to n) or backward (from -n–1 to –1). This means that the first character can be indexed by either 0 or -n–1. Based on these orders, we can use [M] and [M:N] to realize indexing or slicing and obtain a single character or a substring, respectively, as indicated by the following example. Do note that we can also store the string in a variable a= "Please say your name:" and a[0] and a[0:6] (or a[:6]) will do the same as the following codes.

```
>>> "Please say your name:"[0]
'P'
>>> "Please say your name:"[0:6]
'Please'
```

Furthermore, Python has some functions to process strings, as shown in Table 1.3.

List: Another built-in collection type, **list**, stores an ordered sequence of mixed types. A list comprises square brackets, together with a comma-separated sequence. Utilizing its sequence, users can either obtain a single element or search an element in the list using indexing or slicing, as mentioned above. The following example shows a few functions such as *index()*, *append()*, and *pop()* that can be used with a list as the input.

Table 1.3: Functions and their description.

Function	Description
len(x)	Output the length of string x
str(x)	Generate the string corresponding to any type x
hex(x) or oct(x)	Generate hexadecimal or octal string of the integer x
chr(u)	Return the character corresponding to unicode u
ord(x)	Return the Unicode corresponding to character x

```
>>> agelist=[10,24,33,7,52,12,48]
>>> agelist[2]
33
>>> agelist[-2]
12
>>> agelist.index(33) # Returns the index of where the parameter
first appeared
2
>>> agelist.append(23) # Add the parameter at the end of the list
>>>agelist
[10,24,33,7,52,12,48,23]
>>>b = agelist.pop() #Remove the last element of the list and return
the removed element
>>>agelist
[10,24,33,7,52,12,48]
>>>b
23
```

Indexing and slicing are used frequently for lists and strings. The full notation is *[start:stop:step]*. In the following example, if no index is listed for any of the *start, stop* or *step,* they will take on their default values, which are 0, n, and 1, respectively. The following example shows how indexing is used.

```
>>> agelist[0:3] # Equivalent of agelist[:3]
[10,24,33]
>>> agelist[5:]
[12,48]
```

Table 1.4:　Frequently used functions and methods.

Function or Method	Description
len(list)	Return the number of the elements
max(list)	Return the maximum value of the list
min(list)	Return the minimum value of the list
list.append(obj)	Add an object to the end of the list
list.count(obj)	Counts the number of times an element appears in the list
list.insert(index,obj)	Insert the object to the list
list.pop([index=-1])	Remove an element from the list (the last element by default)
list.remove(obj)	Remove the object that first appeared in the list
list.reverse()	Reverse the elements in the list

```
>>> agelist[:2]
[10,24]
>>> agelist[:-2]
[10,24,33,7,52]
>>> agelist[:-2:2]
[10,33,52]
```

Table 1.4 shows some frequently used functions and methods.

Tuple: In general, string, list, and tuple are three built-in sequence types in Python, among which tuples and strings are **immutable**, and lists are **mutable**. If a sequence is mutable, it means the user can change the sequence's value once it is created. **Tuples** are very similar to lists, except that tuples are immutable. A tuple is created using a pair of parentheses. Many operators used for lists can also be used on tuples.

The elements in tuples are obtained in the same way as lists. Users can convert tuples to lists using the function *list(tuple)*. Tuples can also perform some other operations as shown in the example below:

```
>>> len((1,2,3))
3
>>>(1,2,3,4) + (5,6,7,8)
(1,2,3,4,5,6,7,8)
```

```
>>>(1,2) * 5
(1,2,1,2,1,2,1,2,1,2)
>>>3 in (1,2)
False
```

Dictionary: Dictionary in Python is a built-in class that stores a mapping between a set of keys and values. Keys in dictionaries can be any immutable type, and values can be any type. Thus, a single dictionary can store values of several different types. Users can execute five operations to dictionaries, which are define, modify, view, lookup, and delete key-value pairs in the dictionary. In the following example, the keys are "name" and "color" before the colon, while the values are "rose", "red", and so on.

```
>>> d1={'name':'rose',
      'color':'red'}
>>> d1['name']
'rose'
>>> d1['name']='lily' # To change the value of a key
>>> d1
{'name': 'lily', 'color': 'red'}

>>> d1['year']=1.5 # To add a new key-value pair
>>> d1
{'name': 'lily', 'color': 'red', 'year': 1.5}

>>> del d1['color'] # To delete the key-value pair
>>> d1
{'name': 'lily', 'year': 1.5}

>>> d1.keys() # To see all the keys in the dictionary d1
dict_keys(['name', 'year'])
>>> d1.items() # To see all the keys and values in d1
dict_items([('name', 'lily'), ('year', 1.5)])
```

Note that the same key is not allowed to appear twice in Python. If the same key is assigned twice when created, the latter value will be stored.

```
>>>dict = {'Name' : 'Nancy' , 'Age' : 18 , 'Name' : 'Tom'}
>>>dict['Name']
Tom
```

Table 1.5 summarizes the built-in methods of dictionary in Python as follows.

(b) Assignment

A variable itself does not have a type and can store a reference to any type of object. A variable is created by simply using it. That is, Python variables are dynamic, untyped, and are references to objects. With a single equal sign (=), a reference to the right-hand side's resulting value will be stored in the variable on the left-hand side. When a new reference is assigned to an existing variable, the old reference is replaced. Do note that in an *if* statement, we need to use double equal signs (==) to see if a variable or an element equals something instead of the single equal sign (because the latter is used to assign values).

```
>>>a=70
>>>b=40
>>>c=a+b
>>>print(c)
110
```

Table 1.5: Built-in methods of dictionary in Python.

Method	Description
dict.clear()	Clear all the elements in the dictionary
dict.has_key(key)	If the key is in the dictionary, return True, or return False
dict.items()	Return a list of traversable array of (keys, values) tuples
dict.keys()	Return a list of keys in the dictionary
dict.values()	Return a list of values in the dictionary
dict.pop(key[,default])	Deletes the value corresponding to the key given by the dictionary and returns the deleted value
dict.popitem()	Returns and deletes the last pair of keys and values in the dictionary

Also, Python allows for multiple assignments, and users can assign values to multiple variables in a single line of code using the values in the list. The following example shows how values can be assigned to multiple variables at once:

```
>>>names=['Jack','Peter','Leslie']
>>>a, b, c=names
>>>print(a, b, c)
Jack Peter Leslie
```

1.2 Python Programming

1.2.1 *Operators*

The interpreter can act as a simple calculator where users can type an expression into it and obtain the evaluated value. Operators in Python mainly include arithmetic operators, relational (comparison) operators, logical operators, assignment operators, and identity operators.

Learning Objectives
• Understand each kind of operator's meaning and perform basic calculations using these operators.
• Learn to perform basic operations using expressions, operators, and statements.

Main Takeaways

Main Points
• Operators in Python mainly include arithmetic operators, relational (comparison) operators, logical operators, assignment operators, and identity operators.
• When carrying out associative operations with different operators, there is a pre-defined order called operator precedence, which tells the interpreter which operators are executed first.

Main Terms
• **Operator:** A symbol used to perform operations on variables and values.
• **Logical (Boolean) operators:** Operators that are applied to Boolean values.

(a) Arithmetic Operators

Users can type expressions into the interpreter to perform common mathematical operations. Table 1.6 shows basic arithmetic operators.

The following examples show how arithmetic operators are used in Python.

```
>>> 6*4-2+5
27
>>> print(13/4,13//4,13%4)
3.25 3 1
>>>2**6
64
```

The difference between the three kinds of division operations should be noted — division (/) always returns a float, floor division (//) returns a quotient, and the modulo operator (%) returns the remainder.

It is also important to note the three distinct numeric types in Python: integer, floating-point, and complex numbers. Python supports mixed arithmetic — this means that mathematical operations can be carried out when the operands are of different numeric types. The operand with the "narrower" type is widened to that of the other, with integer being the narrowest type and complex numbers being the widest.[3] The following example illustrates this mixed arithmetic.

Table 1.6:   Basic arithmetic operators.

Operator	Name
+	Addition
–	Subtraction
*	Multiplication
/	Division
%	Modulus
**	Exponentiation
//	Floor division

---

[3] Built-in Types — Python 3.8.6rc1 Documentation (2020). Retrieved from https://docs.python.org/3/library/stdtypes.html#numeric-types-int-float-complex (accessed September 14, 2020).

```
>>> 33-5.0
28.0
```

(b) Assignment Operators
In addition to the basic assignment operator (=), we can also modify variables in place by using the assignment operator in combination with most arithmetic operators. Table 1.7 shows some examples of how operators can be combined.

Compared to normal assignment statements, these assignment operators make the code look more compact and readable, which is one of Python's key advantages.

(c) Relational (Comparison) Operators
Relational (comparison) operators return an answer of True or False. The operands on either side must be of types that can be compared to relational operators. Python might surface an error when comparing illogical types, so it is good to test conditional expressions thoroughly and check the values being compared. Table 1.8 lists the relational operators used in Python.

The following example illustrates the simplest form of how relational operators can be used.

```
>>> x=1
>>> y=3
>>> x!=y
True
```

(d) Logical (Boolean) Operators
Logical (Boolean) operators are applied to Boolean values. With logical operators, users can combine multiple Boolean expressions and execute more complicated logical expressions (Table 1.9).

Table 1.7: List of operators.

Operator	Example	Meaning
=	x = 1	x = 1
+=	x += 1	x = x+1
−=	x −= 2	x = x−2
*=	x *= 5	x = x*5

Table 1.8:   Relational operators.

Operator	Name
==	Equal
!=	Not equal
>	Greater than
<	Less than
>=	Greater than or equal to
<=	Less than or equal to

Table 1.9:   Boolean operators and their description.

Operator	Description
and	Returns True if both statements are true
or	Returns True if one of the statements is true
not	Reverses the result, i.e., returns False if the result is True

Logical operators are handy for conditional statements and are often used in loops. A simple example of logical operators is shown below.

```
>>> x=6
>>> x>5 or x<10
True
>>> not (x>5 or x<10)
False
```

(e) Identity Operators
Identity operators can be used to compare the identity of two objects. Table 1.10 lists the operators and their descriptions.

This operator is similar to the relational operators "==" and "!=". It is essential to understand the difference. While the "==" relational operator compares the *objects' value*s, the "is" identity operator compares if both objects belong to the same memory location.[4] Simply put, it compares the

---

[4]Sudhakar, K. (2020). Learn Python Identity Operator and Difference Between "==" and "IS" Operator. Retrieved from https://www.tecmint.com/learn-python-identity-operator/#:~:text=Identity%20operator%20(%20%E2%80%9Cis%E2%80%9D%20and,compare

Table 1.10: Identity operators and their description.

Operator	Description
Is	Returns True if both variables are the same object
is not	Returns True if both variables are not the same object

ID of the objects. This difference is more clearly illustrated in the example below. The ID of objects *a* and *b* is different, while the ID of objects *a* and *c* is the same. Objects with the same ID are the same.

```
>>> a=[1,2,3]
>>> b=a[:]
>>> print(b is a)
False
>>> print(b==a)
True
>>> print(id(b))
60987312
>>> print(id(a))
60987032
>>> c=a
>>> print(c is a)
True
>>> print(c==a)
True
>>> print(id(c))
60987032
```

(f) Membership Operators

Membership operators are used to testing whether a sequence is present in an object. *in* and *not in* are the two main membership operators:

- *in*: Returns True if sequence with a specified value is present in the object.

%20the%20object's%20memory%20location.&text='%3D%3D'%20compares%20if%20both%20the,to%20the%20same%20memory%20location.

Table 1.11:   Operator precedence.

Operator	Name
x**y	Exponentiation
+x, -x	Positive, negative
x*y, x/y, x//y, x%y	Multiplication, division, floor division, modulus
x+y, x-y	Addition, subtraction
x<y, x<=y, x>y, x>=y, x==y, x!=y	Relational (comparison)
x is y and x is not y	Identity IS
x in y and x not in y	Membership IN
not x	Boolean NOT
x and y	Boolean AND
x or y	Boolean OR

- *not in*: Returns True if sequence with a specified value is not present in the object.

(g) Summary and Operator Precedence
Operators are evaluated in the following order unless there are inner brackets. In general, arithmetic operators have higher precedence over comparison operators, which have higher precedence over logical (boolean) operators. The operator precedence is shown in Table 1.11 in descending order.

1.2.2 *Selection and Loops*

In many cases, users use *if* and *if-else* statements to choose whether to execute some statements based on logical expressions and/or to repeat one process over a range of different values. This is more efficient for both the user and the computer. To make codes more compact, we can use a loop to ensure certain statements are executed repeatedly. In Python, either the *while* or *for* statements can create a loop.

Learning Objectives
- Learn about the fundamental control structures for decision making and be able to write *if* and *if-else* statements.

- Understand the basic structure of *while* and *for* loop, learn about writing a loop, and exit a clause using *break*, *continue* and *pass*.

Main Takeaways

Main Points
- As selection statements, *if* and *if-else* statements allow us to choose whether to execute a statement based on a logical expression.
- The *while* and *for* loop help you repeat the same process over a range of different values.
- The *break* statement breaks out the innermost enclosing *for* or *while* loop. The continue statement continues with the next iteration of the loop. The *pass* statement results in no operation without Python raising any execution errors.

Main Terms
- **Loop:** A code construction that repeats.
- **Loop body:** The indented statements after the *while* or *for* keyword and the colon.

(a) *if* Statement
The *if* statement is a selection statement that allows you to choose whether to execute a statement based on the result of a logical expression (Necaise, 2010). The following example shows a simple *if* statement. The third line is executed if the user inputs a negative number. If the user inputs a positive number, nothing will be printed.

```
a= int(input("Please enter a number:"))
if a<0:
    print("The number is less than 0")
================= D:/ifstatement.py =================
Please enter a number:-4
The number is less than 0
```

(b) *if-else* Statements
If-else statements make it possible to execute a block of statements if a condition is true and a different block of statements if the condition is false. The following example is an extension of the previous example.

When there are multiple conditions, we can use *if-elif-else* statements. The program, after else, will be executed if and only if all conditions in *if* and *elif* are not satisfied. It is possible to have more than one *elif* statement.

```
a= int(input("Please enter a number: "))
if a<0:
    print("The number is less than 0")
elif a==0:
    print("The number is equal to 0")
else:
    print("The number is not less than 0")
================= D:/if-elsestatement.py =================
Please enter a number:4
The number is not less than 0
================= D:/if-elsestatement.py =================
Please enter a number: 0
The number is equal to 0
```

(c) *while* Loop Statements

While statements can be used to create a loop controlled by conditions. The statement block will be executed repeatedly until the condition is not met in a while loop. The following example illustrates how a *while* loop is used. It is crucial in Python syntax that there is a colon after the *while* condition and that the loop body is indented. In the following example, *while a<600*, the loop body will be repeatedly run — the value of *a* will be continuously updated by multiplying its previous value by three and be printed. This loop will only be broken when *a* is greater than or equal to 600.

```
>>> a=1
>>> while a<600:
...        a*=3 # Equivalent of a=a*3
...        print(a)
...
3
9
27
81
243
729
```

(d) *for* Loop Statements

Similar to *while* loop statements, *for* loop statements can be used to create a loop for elements in a sequence. The syntax of the colon after the condition and the indented loop body is required here. This sequence can be a string, a tuple, or a list. The following example shows a simple *for* loop.

```
>>> list1=[1,2,3]
>>> for element in list1:
        print(element)
1
2
3
```

In more complicated cases, *for* loops can be used together with conditional statements and operators. In the following example, a function called *a_prime()* is defined to return True if the number is a prime number. Defining functions will be explained further in the later sections. The *for* loop calculates the sum of the prime numbers between 2 to 100. Here, the *for* loop is used together with *if* statements and some assignment operators.

```
def a_prime(n):
    for i in range(2,n):
        if n%i==0:
            return False
    return True
sum=0
for i in range(2,100):
    if a_prime(i):
        sum+=i
print(sum)
================ D:/forloop.py ================
1060
```

(e) *break* and *continue* Statements

Also, Python provides two looping control keywords: *break* and *continue*. Like in C, the *break* statement breaks out the innermost enclosing *for* or *while* loop, and the *continue* statement continues with the next iteration of the loop. For example, we obtain entirely different results by changing *continue* to *break* in the following example.

```
>>> for c in "PYTHON":
...     if c=="T":
...             continue  # the following line is skipped when c=="T"
...     print(c)
...
P
Y
H
O
N

>>> for c in "PYTHON":
...     if c=="T":
...             break  # the entire loop breaks when c=="T"
...     print(c)
...
P
Y
```

(f) *pass* Statements

The *pass* statement does nothing. It can be used when a statement is required syntactically but the program requires no action. For example,

```
>>> while true:
        pass
```

This is commonly used for creating an empty class (and details can be filled in later) and test-run the code without the program raising any errors or warning messages.

```
>>>class MyEmptyClass:
        pass
```

Another place *pass* can be used as a placeholder for a function or conditional body when working on new code, allowing you to keep thinking at a more abstract level. The pass is silently ignored:

```
>>> def initlog(*args):
      pass # Remember to implement this!
```

1.2.3 *Modules and Functions*

Programmers may find the need to use certain functions repeatedly. It is tedious and inefficient to copy the definitions into each program. Thus, users should split the program into several files with some files used to define commonly used functions and the main file to execute the program. People can also define many open-source functions for others to use. In this case, it would be helpful to download these pre-defined functions and use them in the main code straightaway.

Learning Objectives
- Understand the meaning of modules and learn to import modules.
- Learn to define and call functions.

Main Takeaways

Main Points
- Users can put definitions in a file called a module and use them in a script or an interactive instance.
- Functions can be understood as subprograms to perform specific tasks.

Main Terms
- **Module:** A file in which users store definitions, and it can be used in a script or an interactive instance.
- **Function:** A function is a group of related statements that performs a specific task.
- **Function call:** This statement executes a function. A function call consists of the name of the function followed by a list of arguments enclosed in parentheses.

(a) Importing Modules
In Python, users can put definitions in a file called a **module** and use them in a script or an interactive instance. Python comes with a **library** of standard modules. You may have heard of *pandas*, a powerful library used

in data manipulation and analysis. There are three ways to import libraries or modules, as shown below.

```
>>> import pandas

>>> from pandas import*   # this imports all modules. To import
                            specific modules,
                          # the asterisk (*) is replaced by the
                            module name.
>>> import pandas as pd   # this allows the user to refer to the library
                            as pd when using
                          # functions in the library subsequently.
```

Also, users can define modules according to their own needs. For example, we can define a function or several functions and then import the corresponding module. This way, we can use the function in the module. The following shows an example of a module.

```
======================operations.py======================

# To define a function sum()
def sum(a, b):
    c=a+b
    print(c)
    return c

# To define another function product()
def product(x,y):
    z=x*y
    print(z)
    return z

================================================

>>> import operations
>>> operations.sum(10, 100)
110
>>> operations.product(10, 100)
1000
```

In this example, we need to create a file called *operations.py* in the current directory before entering the Python interpreter and importing this module.

(b) Defining and Calling Functions

A **function** is a stand-alone group of statements. It can be understood as a subprogram that performs a specific task. The syntax used to define a function in Python has been illustrated in the previous few examples. It starts with a *def* statement and the function's name with an optional parenthesis for its argument list and a colon. The definition of the function must be indented. It is common to provide a short description of what the function does. This description is called a documentation string (docstring) and is declared below the function declaration. They are encapsulated within triple single quotes or triple double-quotes. These help programmers understand what each other's functions do quickly. The following function calculates the factorial of n.

```
def fact(n):
"""This program calculates the factorial of n."""
    s=1
    for i in range(1, n+1):
        s*=i # Equivalent of s=s*i
    return s
```

We can also use this function by invoking it via a **function call**, as shown below.

```
y=fact(10)
```

More than one argument is passed to a function, depending on how it is defined and its purpose. When a function is called, the execution flow jumps to execute the instructions specified in the function and returns to the point where it is called.

(c) Open-Source Python Libraries

A library is a collection of useful functions that can be used iteratively to reduce the time required to code. Instead of writing codes from scratch each time, one can use them directly simply by importing them.

The following five libraries are frequently used in data analysis and data visualization.

Numpy: Numpy is a Python library used for working with arrays. It also has functions for working in domain of linear algebra, Fourier transform and random numbers.

```
import numpy as np
A=np.array([[1,3],
            [2,0]])
B=np.array([[1,0],
            [3,4]])
print(A.max())
print(B.sum())
print(A@B)  # matrix product
print(A.dot(B))  # another matrix product
==========================numpy_1.py==========================
3
8
[[10 12]
 [ 2 0]]
[[10 12]
 [ 2 0]]
```

Pandas: Pandas is a Python library mainly used for data analysis. Pandas allows importing data from various file formats such as comma-separated values, JSON, SQL, Microsoft Excel. Pandas allows various data manipulation operations such as merging, reshaping, selecting, as well as data cleaning, and data wrangling features.[5]

```
import pandas as pd
import numpy as np
dates=pd.date_range('20210301',periods=2)
print(dates)
df=pd.DataFrame(np.random.randn(2, 3), index=dates,
```

---

[5]Pandas Dataframes. Retrieved from https://en.wikipedia.org/wiki/Pandas_(software).

```
columns=list("ABC"))
print(df)
print(df.describe()) # a quick statistic summary of your data
print(df.sort_values(by="B")) # sorting by values


====================pandas_1.py====================
DatetimeIndex(['2021-03-01', '2021-03-02'], dtype='datetime64[ns]',
freq='D')
                A          B          C
2021-03-01 -1.150190   0.555267  0.441445
2021-03-02 -1.615756  -0.585824 -0.355301
                A          B          C
count  2.000000  2.000000  2.000000
mean  -1.382973 -0.015279  0.043072
std    0.329205  0.806873  0.563384
min   -1.615756 -0.585824 -0.355301
25%   -1.499364 -0.300552 -0.156114
50%   -1.382973 -0.015279  0.043072
75%   -1.266581  0.269994  0.242258
max   -1.150190  0.555267  0.441445
                A          B          C
2021-03-02 -1.615756 -0.585824 -0.355301
2021-03-01 -1.150190   0.555267  0.441445
```

Pandas_datareader: Pandas_datareader is a module extracted from the pandas codebase. It provides up-to-date remote data access for pandas.

```
import os
import pandas_datareader as web
AAPL = web.DataReader(name='AAPL', data_source='yahoo',st
art='2021-1-1', end='2021-3-12')
# Parameters of DataReader function
# (name=the ticker symbol,data_source=Data source,
# start=left boundary of range,end=right boundary of range(default
today))
print(AAPL.tail()) #The tail method provides us with the five last
rows of the data set
```

================pandas_datareader_1.py===================

	High	Low	Open	Close	Volume	Adj Close
Date						
2021-03-08	121.000000	116.209999	120.930000	116.360001	153918600.0	116.360001
2021-03-09	122.059998	118.790001	119.029999	121.089996	129159600.0	121.089996
2021-03-10	122.169998	119.449997	121.690002	119.980003	111760400.0	119.980003
2021-03-11	123.209999	121.260002	122.540001	121.959999	102753600.0	121.959999
2021-03-12	121.169998	119.160004	120.400002	121.029999	87963400.0	121.029999

Matplotlib: Matplotlib is a comprehensive library for creating static, animated, and interactive visualizations in Python, shown in Figure 1.1.

```
import os
import pandas_datareader as web
import matplotlib.pyplot as plt
GOOG = web.DataReader(name='GOOG',
data_source='yahoo',start='2017-1-1',end='2020-12-31')
GOOG['Close'].plot(figsize=(8,5))
# Retrieving data and visualizing it with the plot method
plt.show()
================matplotlib_1.py===================
```

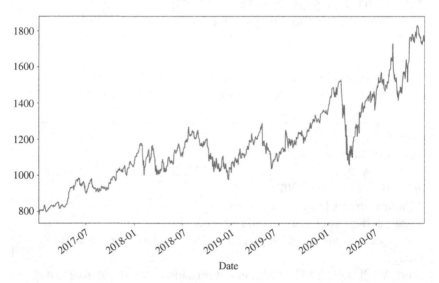

Figure 1.1:   Static, animated, and interactive visualizations matplotlib in Python.

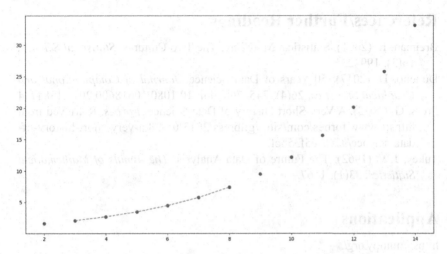

Figure 1.2: Solution of scientific and mathematical problems using SciPy in Python.

SciPy: SciPy is an open-source Python library which is used to solve scientific and mathematical problems (Figure 1.2).

```
import numpy as np
import matplotlib.pyplot as plt
from scipy import interpolate
x = np.arange(2, 15)
y = np.exp(x/4.0)
func = interpolate.interp1d(x, y)
#SciPy provides interp1d function to find the curve-fitting
# of a series of two-dimensional data points.
x_t = np.arange(3, 9)
y_t = func(x_t)
plt.plot(x, y, 'o', x_t, y_t, '--')
plt.show()
=================scipy_1.py=================
```

References/Further Readings

Breiman, L. (2001). Statistical Modeling: The Two Cultures. *Statistical Science*, **16**(3), 199–231.

Donoho, D. (2017). 50 Years of Data Science. *Journal of Computational and Graphical Statistics*, **26**(4), 745–766, doi: 10.1080/10618600.2017.1384734

Press, G. (2013). A Very Short History of Data Science. *Forbes*. Retrieved from https://www.forbes.com/sites/gilpress/2013/05/28/a-very-short-history-of-data-science/#7eace5f355cf.

Tukey, J.W. (1962). The Future of Data Analysis. *The Annals of Mathematical Statistics*, 33(1), 1–67.

Applications

https://numpy.org/.
https://pandas.pydata.org/.
https://pypi.org/project/pandas-datareader/.
https://matplotlib.org/.

1.3 Sample Questions

Question 1
Which of the following is the most accurate description of IDE?

(a) An application for a provider development environment typically includes code editors, compilers, debuggers, and graphical user interfaces.
(b) A program that reads and executes instructions written in the Python language.
(c) A built-in function in Python.

Question 2
Which of the following is the output for the following lines of code, and what is its type?

```
a = 23
b = '12'
c = str(a)+b
```

(a) 35, integer
(b) 2312, integer
(c) 2312, string

Question 3
Which of the following is the result of True + 32?

(a) 31
(b) 32
(c) 33

Question 4
Which of the following data type can **NOT** be a key of a dictionary?

(a) List
(b) Tuple
(c) String

Question 5
Which of the following shows an appropriate *if-elif* loop that returns A if the student got a score of 90 and above, B if the student scored 75 and above, C if the student scored 60 and above, and D if the student scored below 60?

(a)
```
if score >= 90:
    print("A" )
elif 75<=score<90:
    print("B")
elif 60<=score<75:
    print("C")
else:
    print("D")
```

(b)
```
if score >= 90
    print("A")
elif score >= 75
    print("B")
elif score >= 60
    print("C")
else
    print("D")
```

(c)

```
if score >= 90:
    print("A")
elif score >= 75:
    print("B")
    elif score >= 60:
        print("C")
        else:
            print("D")
```

Question 6

Which of the following is the output for the following chunk of code?

```
food = ["apple","banana","cucumber","donut","egg"]
for i in food:
    if i == "donut":
        break
    print(i)
```

(a) apple
    banana
    cucumber
    donut
(b) apple
    banana
    cucumber
(c) apple
    banana
    cucumber
    egg

Question 7

To ensure a has an integer value, which of the following operators is not possible?

```
>>> a = 20 ? 3
```

(a) a = 20/3
(b) a = 20%3
(c) a = int(20/3)

Question 8
Which is the output of the following code?

```
>>> 1 + 1 = 2
```

(a) True
(b) False
(c) SyntaxError

Question 9
What would be the output of the following code?

```
>>> 5+2%4
```

(a) 7
(b) 5
(c) 3

Solutions

Question 1

Solution: Option **a** is correct.

IDE is an application for a provider development environment that typically includes tools such as code editors, compilers, debuggers, and graphical user interfaces.

Question 2

Solution: Option **c** is correct.

The *str()* method changed the type of variable a from integer to string, and the math operator '+' adds both variables together as a string.

Question 3

Solution: Option **c** is correct.

True is 1, 1+32=33.

Question 4

Solution: Option **a** is correct.

Dictionary keys must be immutable, such as strings, numbers, or tuples. The only mutable data type amongst the options is List

Question 5

Solution: Option **a** is correct.

Option b does not make good use of the convenience of elif, and the indentation for option c is wrong.

Question 6

Solution: Option **b** is correct.

Option a is wrong as the loop has already been broken in its fourth iteration. Option c would be correct if the keyword were *continuing* instead of *break*.

Question 7

Solution: Option **a** is correct.

Question 8

Solution: Option **c** is correct.

Option a would be correct if a double equal sign is used (==). A single equal sign is used to assign values to variables.

Question 9

Solution: Option **a** is correct.

Chapter 2
Data Structure and Algorithms

2.1 Introduction to Data Structure and Algorithms

2.1.1 *Introduction*

This section introduces data structure and algorithms, followed by introducing basic terminologies and types of data structures and algorithms.

Learning Objectives
- Understand the need for data structure, related types, definitions, and functions.
- Understand the fundamentals of algorithms such as categories and characteristics.

Main Takeaways

Main Points
- Data structure is essential in the data centric world today. We need data structure to search and process large amounts of data more efficiently.
- Data should be atomic, traceable, accurate and concise.
- Algorithms are a set of programming instructions performed in a sequential order to solve a problem.
- Algorithms should fulfil the characteristics of being unambiguous, match desired output, finite, feasible, and independent of other programs.

Main Terms

- **Data structure:** a form of data organization, management, and storage format; data structure allows efficient access and utilization of the stored data.
- **Algorithm:** a finite sequence of well-defined instructions typically used to solve a class of problems.
- **Search:** The process of searching an item in a data structure.
- **Sort:** The process of sorting items in a specific order.

(a) Introduction of Data Structure

There are two components of Data Structure, namely, **interface** and **implementation**. **Interface** refers to operations such as insertion and deletion that a data structure supports. Most of the famous Data Structures, such as Array, List, etc., follow the same interface. The **implementation** of data structure is often carried out through its specific algorithm. Thus, in this way, we could tell how the Data Structure will organize the data and how the operations will perform on it.

There are two data types, **the built-in data type vs. the derived data type**. The built-in data type is the data type for which a language has built-in support. Examples include integers, Boolean, floating, characters, and strings. On the other hand, the derived data type is data types that are implementation-independent as they can be implemented in one or the other way: list, array, stack, and queue.

For each type of data to be desirable, they must have the following features: **atomic, traceable, accurate, clear, and concise**. Atomic means that the data definition should be defined as a single concept. Traceable means that the data's definition can be mapped to some data elements. Accurate refers to the unambiguity of data, while clear and concise definitions mean that definitions should be understandable.

Data structures are essential in carrying out the functions required by data scientists. Conceptually, the data structure functions like a well-arranged work desk. This arrangement can allow the operator to navigate the items with greater ease, thereby enhancing efficiency. For instance, the data structure includes organizing an extensive collection of data so that desired data can be **easily searched**. Also, the data structure should maintain a **high processing speed** even when the volume of data being processed is large. Lastly, data structures should accommodate **simultaneous searches** to be conducted on a server. All these functions add up to provide convenience for the data scientist when navigating through a large volume of data, which is commonplace today.

(b) Introduction of Algorithm

An essential aspect of data structures is algorithms. Data structures are implemented using algorithms. **Algorithms** are a set of programming instructions performed sequentially to solve a problem. When applied to a specific set of data, an algorithm can derive the desired output.

The efficiency of the algorithm is an essential indicator of program design. There are two common metrics, time complexity, and space complexity. Time complexity describes the amount of time an algorithm takes in terms of the amount of input to the algorithm. The less the time complexity, the better the program's efficiency. The space complexity defines the memory occupied by a particular data structure; the less memory it occupies, the best space complexity it has.

The algorithms have the following common categories based on their specific functions and associated operations. **Search** algorithms are typically used to search an item in a data structure. Some examples of the search algorithms that will be discussed later include binary search, linear search, and Fibonacci search. **Sort** algorithms are used to sort items in a certain order. The algorithms for inserting an item into a data structure are referred to as **Insert**. **Update** algorithms update an existing item in a data structure. **Delete** algorithms delete an existing item from a data structure.

Algorithms, apart from their functions, include their own set of characteristics. Firstly, algorithms should be clear and unambiguous. An algorithm should have well-defined inputs that match desired outputs. Being a step-by-step instruction, algorithms must be terminated after a finite number of steps. Subsequently, algorithms should be feasible with the given steps and constraints. Lastly, the step-by-step instructions should be independent of any programming codes.

Various mathematical problems can be solved using algorithms. For instance, the Fibonacci number series. Apart from solving mathematic problems, various functions pertaining to sorting and searching techniques rely on algorithms. We will explore linear search and binary search in later sections.

2.1.2 *Algorithm Complexity*

This section introduces different types of notations and classes of algorithms, including interpreting a matrix in algorithm analysis. As previously mentioned, algorithms are used to solve problems presented in a data set. What determines algorithms' efficiency in their problem-solving ability, which correlates with their complexity, and is defined by the relative time taken for the algorithm to solve the given problem.

Learning Objectives
- Understand the use of Big-O Notation in determining the complexity of algorithms.
- Understand the use of Omega Notation in determining the complexity of algorithms.
- Understand the use of Theta Notation in determining the complexity of algorithms.

Main Takeaways

Main Points
- Big-O notation expresses the worst-case time scenario.
- The Omega notation $\Omega(n)$ expresses the best-case scenario.
- The Theta notation $\theta(n)$ expresses the average-case scenario.
- Classes of algorithms include the following: constant, logarithmic, linear, log-linear, quadratic, cubic, and exponential. This list follows an increase in magnitude, the constant being the lowest and the exponential being the highest.

Main Terms
- **Big-O notation:** Expresses the worst-case time scenario.
- **Omega notation:** Expresses the best-case scenario.
- **Theta notation:** Expresses the average-case scenario.
- **For-loop:** An operation that iterates over the items within a sequence.

(a) Types of Notations
Big-O notation expresses the upper bound of the running time of an algorithm. Upper bound refers to the longest time taken for the algorithm to be executed, indicating the worst-case time scenario.

Let f(n) define the running time of an algorithm.

$O(g(n))$ = { f(n) : there exists positive constants c and n0 such that $0 <= f(n) <= c*g(n)$ for all n >= n0. }

The **Omega notation** $\Omega(n)$ is the formal way to express the lower bound of an algorithm's running time, indicating the best-case scenario.

$\Omega(g(n)) = \{ f(n) :$ *there exists positive constants c and n0 such that 0* $<=c*g(n)<=f(n)$ *for all* $n >= n0.$ *}*

The **Theta notation** $\theta(n)$ is the formal way to express both the lower bound and the upper bound of an algorithm's running time. It can be used to deduce the average time required, which is the average case scenario.

$\theta(g(n)) = \{ f(n) :$ *there exists positive constants c1, c2 and n0 such that 0* $<=c1*g(n)<=f(n)<=c2*g(n)$ *for all* $n >= n0.$ *}*

(b) Different Classes of Algorithms
Algorithms can be divided into the following classes:

- **Logarithmic algorithms** refer to an algorithm with a time complexity of $O(\log(a)n)$. These algorithms are generally very efficient since $\log(a)n$ will increase at a slower pace than n.
- **Polynomial algorithms** are efficiently expressed polynomials in the given form below:

$$a_m n^m + a_{m-1} n^{m-1} + \ldots + a_2 n^2 + a_1 n + a_{m0}$$

The equation is characterized by the time complexity of $O(n^m)$.

- **Linear algorithms** are common forms of polynomial algorithms with equation $O(n^m)$, $m = 1$.
- **Quadratic algorithms** are common forms of polynomial algorithms with equation $O(n^m)$, $m = 2$.
- **Cubic algorithms** are common forms of polynomial algorithms with equation $O(n^m)$, $m = 3$.
- **Exponential algorithms** are not the best form of algorithms in terms of time complexity. It is characterized by the exponential equation a^n.

(c) Inner and Outer For-loops in Algorithm Analysis of Matrix
The loop in the algorithm analysis of the matrix is divided into the inner and outer loop.

In this given example below we will consider the following algorithm for computing the sum of each row of an n × n matrix, *matrix*, and an overall *sum* of the entire matrix:

```
sum = 0
sum_row = [None]*n  # To generate an empty list to store the sum of
each row
for i in range(n):
    sum_row[i] = 0
    for j in range(n):
        sum_row[i] = sum_row[i] + matrix[i,j]
        sum = sum + matrix[i, j]
```

The algorithm contains two loops, one nested inside the other. The inner loop is executed twice, represented by equation $2n$. The outer loop is represented by n as it is executed once, j. hence, the combined equation is $2n^2$.

(d) New Version of the Algorithm

Consider a new version of the algorithm below which the second addition is removed from the inner loop. Instead of the matrix's elements, it is modified to sum the entries in the *sum_row* array.

```
sum=0
for i in range(n):
    sum_row[i] = 0
    for j in range(n):
        sum_row[i] = sum_row[i] + matrix[i,j]
    sum = sum + sum_row[i]
```

In the new version of this algorithm, the inner loop is executed "n" times. The only difference is that it only contains one additional operation. Note that *sum = sum + sum_row[i]* instead of the matrix indicated in version 1. This results in n additions for each iteration of the outer loop. However, the outer loop now contains an addition operator of its own, which gives us n*(n+1). The second version, version 2, will be executed faster than the first, albeit with an insignificant increase in execution time.

2.2 Abstract Data Types

2.2.1 *Introduction*

This section first describes abstract data types (ADTs), introduces the different kinds of operations, and defines the abstraction.

An ADT can be visualized as a form of an algorithmic black box. When the program interacts with ADT, it invokes several operations stored within the black box to provide the output. This simplifies the algorithm by showing users the end product instead of how to derive it.

Learning Objectives
- Understand what ADTs are.
- Understand how separation of ADT and their implementation is achieved.
- Comprehend how the four types of operations are implemented.

Main Takeaways

Main Points
- Procedural abstraction refers to applying a function or method, knowing what it does but not how it is accomplished.
- Data abstraction refers to the separation of a data type's property (including its values and operations) from the implementation of that data type.
- There are four types of operators, constructors, mutators, accessors, and iterators.

Main Terms
- **ADT:** A mathematical model for data types.
- **Information hiding:** The separation technique requires ADT to interact through an interface.
- **Interface:** A defined set of operation which interacts with ADT.
- **Abstraction:** The mechanism for the separation of an object's properties and restriction of the focus to those relevant in the current context.
- **Procedural abstraction:** The application of a function or method knowing what it does but not how it's accomplished.
- **Data abstraction:** The separating process of the properties of a data type (its values and operations) from implementing that data type.

(a) Abstract Data Type

ADTs can be interpreted as black boxes containing implementation details of different operations. User programs interact with the ADT instances by invoking one of the several operations defined by its **interface**, which is a defined set of operations with which ADT interacts. **Information hiding** is a separation technique that requires ADT to interact through an interface.

The black box contains the implementations of the various operations. We do not have to know the contents inside the black box to utilize the ADT. The advantages of working with ADTs and focusing on the "what" instead of the "how" will be introduced in later sections.

(b) Types of Operations

Operations are similar to types of functions that can be operated on the ADTs:

- **Constructors:** Creation and initialization of the new instances of the ADT.
- **Accessors:** Return data that are contained in an instance without any modification.
- **Mutators:** Modification of the contents of an ADT instance.
- **Iterators:** Sequential process of individual data components.

(c) Abstraction

An **abstraction** is a process for separating an object's properties and restricting the focus to the most important and relevant aspects while ignoring the unimportant aspects. The abstraction user does not have to be familiar with all the details to utilize the object. Instead, they only need to understand those relevant to the current task. Procedural abstraction and data abstraction are two common abstraction mechanisms.

Procedural abstraction refers to using a function or method knowing its objection or goal but without knowing its implementation. Think about the square root function, which one has probably used at some point. Procedural abstraction ignores the process from which the root function is computed but instead offers the square root computation answer.

On the other hand, **data abstraction** is the separating process of a data type's properties (its values and operations) from the implementation of that data type. It explains the data's internal structure and the implementation of various operations.

To use integer arithmetic in a computer program, programmers do not need to know the assembly language instructions required to evaluate a mathematical expression or understand the hardware implementation.

2.2.2 Data Types

This section introduces the different ADT types and gives specific examples of date ADT.

Learning Objectives

- Understand the types of ADTs, including simple ADT and complex ADT.
- Comprehend that complex ADTs are implemented using a particular data structure.

Main Takeaways

Main Points

- A simple ADT comprises a single or several individually named data fields.
- The complex ADTs are composed of a collection of data values.
- The complex ADTs are implemented with a particular data structure. It represents the organization and manipulation of data.

Main Terms

- **Simple ADTs:** Simple ADTs include individual data such as a date or a rational number.
- **Complex ADTs:** Complex ADTs include the collection of data values, including the Python list or dictionary.

(a) Types of ADTs

There are two main types of ADTs, simple ADTs, and complex ADTs. Simple ADTs include individual data such as a date or a rational number. Complex ADTs include a collection of data values such as the Python list or dictionary.

An **ADT** is first defined by specifying the domain of the data elements that make up the ADT and the set of operations performed on that domain subsequently. These two processes should be defined clearly to provide an unambiguous definition of the ADT. Within this sub-section, we provide the relevant operations of a simple ADT to represent a date in the proleptic (before the introduction of-) Gregorian calendar. Some of the codes below are important operators to be used in constructing ADTs.

- **Date (month, day, year):** Creates a new Date instance initialized to the given Gregorian date.
- **advanceBy(days):** Advances the date by the given number of days.
- **comparable(otherDate):** Compares this date to the otherDate to determine their logical ordering.
- **toString():** Returns a string representing the Gregorian date in the following format: mm/dd/yyyy.

(b) Examples of Date ADT

Pope Gregory XIII introduced the Gregorian calendar in 1582 to replace the Julian calendar. The new calendar solved the miscalculation of the lunar year and introduced the leap year. 15 October 1582 is the first date of the Gregorian calendar, officially. The example below shows the relevant codes representing a date ADT for Gregorian Calendar.

```
from datetime import date
gregorian_date = date.fromordinal(737500) # Returns the date corresponding to the expected Gregorian serial number, where January 1, AD 1 is numbered 1.
print(gregorian_date)
-------------
2020-03-16
```

2.3 Arrays and Lists

2.3.1 *Arrays*

This section will explore some of the operations and basics involved with the one-dimensional and two-dimensional array data structure.

Arrays are the most basic structure for storing and accessing a collection of data that can be used to solve a wide range of problems in computer science. Most programming languages provide the data type of an array as a primitive and allow for creating arrays with multiple dimensions.

Learning Objectives

- Understand what array is and relevant notations used in a one-dimensional array.
- Note the basic operations of an array.

Main Takeaways

Main Points

- An array can be defined conceptually as a container that holds a fixed number of items of the same type.
- An array can be one-dimensional or multi-dimensional.
- Indexes are used to represent the location of each item on the array.
- Array indexes start with "0"; the first index within an array of items is always "0".
- Arrays can be operated by a few simple operations.

Main Terms

- **Elements:** Most basic constituent items stored within an array or list, including integer, string, characters, etc.
- **Index:** Numerical list indicating the position of the element it represents within the array or list.
- **Traverse:** Operations access each record exactly once so that the desired operation can proceed.
- **Insertion:** Operations used to insert an element into a list or array.
- **Deletion:** Operations used to remove an element from a list or array.
- **Search and update:** A series of operations used to search up items within a list or an array or make the necessary changes.

(a) Basics of Array

The one-dimensional array is very similar to a **Python list**. Each item stored within an array is known as an **element**. Figure 2.1 is an example of a list that consists of seven elements.

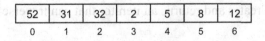

52	31	32	2	5	8	12
0	1	2	3	4	5	6

Figure 2.1: Example of Python list.

A numerical identification is given to an element in an array based on its location. Figure 2.1 illustrates how a one-dimensional array can store elements in a "list-like" manner. The subscript underneath the boxed elements indicates the numerical notation given to indicate the position of elements stored within the array. **Indexing** is important for **slicing** operations to be executed. This will be discussed in depth later.

Basic operations associated with one-dimensional arrays are summarized below:

- **Traverse** — Print out all the elements from the array in order.
- **Insertion** — Adds an element at the given index.
- **Deletion** — Deletes an element at the given index.
- **Search** — Searches an element using the given index or by the value.
- **Update** — Updates an element at the given index.

(b) Array ADT

Array ADT represents a one-dimensional array which is common in primitive programming language. A one-dimensional array contains a consecutive list of elements identified by their respective indexes, starting from zero for the first element, so on and so forth. It is important to note that an array's size cannot be changed once it is created. Below is a list of array operators commonly used:

- *array(size)*: Creates a one-dimensional array that consists of size elements with each element, initially set to None. *Size* must be greater than zero.
- *len()*: Returns the array's length or the number of elements in the array.
- *getitem(index)*: Returns the value stored in the array at element position index. The argument of the index must be within the valid range. It can be accessed using the subscript operator.
- *setitem(index, value)*: Modifies the element's contents from the array at position index to contain a value. The index must be within the valid range. It can be accessed using the subscript operator.
- *clearing(value)*: Clears the array by setting every element to value.
- *iterator()*: Creates and returns an iterator that can traverse the elements of the array.

(c) Two-Dimensional Arrays

Two-dimensional arrays are represented in rows and columns, much like a grid. **Array2D (nrows, ncols)** creates a two-dimensional array organized into rows and columns. There are several operations involved with a two-dimensional array which allows operators to return values and create the two-dimensional array. The **nrows** and **ncols** arguments indicate the table's size, determining the length of the columns and rows, respectively. On the other hand, **numRows()** returns the number of columns in the two-dimensional array.

2.3.2 *Lists*

Lists are one-dimensional arrays that have more operations compared to the conventional array. This section introduces the creation and components of a list in Python as an illustration. Different operations, including those to extend, remove items, insert items, slice a list, or implement list traversal, will be introduced.

Learning Objectives
- Understand how Python Lists are created and operated upon by different operators.
- Demonstrate ability to use iterations and traversal to evaluate the complexity of lists.

Main Takeaways

Main Points
- A sequence traversal accesses individual items one by one to perform some operation on every single item.
- **List creation** is an operation whose time complexity can be analyzed. This is done via filling an empty list or removing a list filled with n elements.

Main Terms
- **Slicing:** An operation to remove a certain specified segment from the list via indexing.
- **List traversal:** An operation that runs by iteration down a list.

(a) Python List
The Python list is a **one-dimensional array** that can be used to store constituent array elements. An example is offered in Figure 2.2, which indicates the list's length and capacity. The length of the array is only six (as it includes six elements), but the total capacity, including the empty boxes,

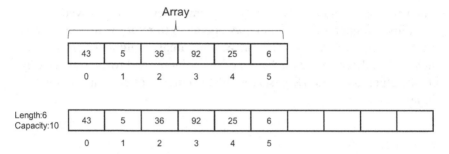

Figure 2.2:   Length and capacity of seven elements.

represents ten items. There is no method to access the capacity within Python, but the length can be accessed via the operator *len()*.

(b) Python List Related Operations
Constructor of the python list is created via the operator *list()*. A simple example of *list* creation is given below.

```
>>>list = [2, 3, 4, 5]
>>>list
[2, 3, 4, 5]
```

len() returns the number of elements stored within the *list*. Refer to the example below for a demonstration of the *len()* operator:

```
>>>list = [2, 3, 4, 5]
>>>len(list)
4
```

append() insert an element to the end of the list. Following the example, *append()* operations can be used to insert the element "10":

```
>>>list = [2, 3, 4, 5]
>>>list.append(10)
[2, 3, 4, 5, 10]
```

Subsequently, other items, such as words, can be appended, on top of the existing extended list. Following the example illustrated below, the key is to put words in " " quotation marks so that Python can read it as the string type.

```
>>>list = [2, 3, 4, 5]
>>>list.append("hello world")
>>>list
[2, 3, 4, 5, "hello world"]
```

extend(), in contrast, to *append()* can insert an entire list to an existing list. With reference to the example below, elements within list *list_b* are being added to list *list_a* via the operator, *extend()*.

```
>>>list_a = [2, 3, 4, 5]
>>>list_b = [5, 4, 3, 2]
>>>list_a.extend(list_b)
>>>list
[2, 3, 4, 5, 5, 4, 3, 2]
```

insert() operation follows the formula of *insert(n, m)*. Within the parenthesis, *n* refers to the index of insertion, whereas *m* refers to the item inserted at the index "*n*". The index starts from 0 in Python lists, so the *list.insert(2,100)* below will insert the number 100 at the 3rd element (with index 2, after the number 3).

```
>>>list = [2, 3, 4, 5]
>>>list.insert(2, 100)
>>>list
[2, 3, 100, 4, 5]
```

pop() removes *item(s)* from the given list. By default, *pop()* removes the last item. Position notation or slicing can be inserted within the *bracket ()* to indicate the *item(s)* to be removed. More on slicing will be introduced in the next section. The example below features a specific singular item being removed using *pop()*. To leave the number in the bracket blank will remove the last item in a list by default. Alternatively, we can include −1 in the bracket or use the command *list.pop(−1)*.

```
>>>list = [2, 3, 4, 5]
>>>list.pop(0) # remove the first item
1
>>>list
[3, 4, 5]
>>>list.pop() # remove the last item (default)
5
>>>list
[3, 4]
```

(c) Slicing

The example below gives an example of slicing a list. In this example, *list A* is created for the elements located between position "0" to position "2" to be sliced out using the operation *[0:2]*. Note that only two numbers, 2 and 3 are sliced out, as the element occupying position 2, in this case "4", is not included.

```
>>>list = [2,3,4,5]
>>>list_b = list[0:2]
>>>list_b
[2, 3]
```

(d) List Traversal

We must first examine the traversal's internal implementation to determine the order of complexity for this simple algorithm. Iteration over the contiguous elements of a one-dimensional array, which is used to store the elements of a list, requires a count-controlled loop with an index variable whose value ranges over the subarray indices. The list iteration below shows how a *for-loop* can be used.

```
list = [2,3,4,5]
sum = 0
for i in range(len(list))
    sum = sum + list[i]
```

```
print(sum)
-------------
14
```

Suppose the sequence runs n iteration, the time taken can be used to evaluate the performance of this particular python list.

2.4 Stacks and Queues

2.4.1 *Stacks*

A stack is a form of ADT. Conceptually, it represents a literal stack of items such as a stack of plates or a stack of paper. This section also introduces basic operations of stacks and the use of a singly list stack.

Learning Objectives
- Understand what stacks are, their characteristics, as well as their representation.
- Explore the various forms of basic operations and push operations for stacks.

Main Takeaways

Main Points
- A stack allows only operation at one end. This feature is known as LIFO.
- A stack can be implemented using **Array, Structure, Pointer**, and **Linked List**.
- Operators such as *peek()*, *pop()*, and *push()* are used in creating a stack from a list.

Main Terms
- **Last in first out (LIFO):** This is due to the unique feature of stacks so that an operation can only be performed at one end.
- **Push operation:** An operation that adds items into the stack on top.
- **Pop operation:** An operation that removes an item from the stack.

(a) Stack ADT
A **stack** is a data structure that gathers a linear collection of items with access to a **LIFO order**. The addition and removal of items are restricted

to one end, known as the top of the stack. An empty stack is one containing no items. The list below indicates some of the common codes used:

- *Stack()*: Creates a new empty stack.
- *isEmpty()*: Returns a Boolean value to indicate whether the stack is empty or not.
- *len()*: Returns the total number of items in the stack.
- *pop()*: Removes and returns the stack's top item if the stack is not empty.
- *peek()*: Returns a reference to the item on top of a non-empty stack without removing it.
- *push(item)*: Adds the given *item* to the top of the stack.

The code below illustrates how a stack is created:

```
class Stack:
    ...(See the next code block for details)
stack_a = Stack()
value = int(input("Please enter an integer"))
while value >= 0:
    stack_a.push(value)
    value = int(input("Please enter an integer"))

while not stack_a.isEmpty():
    value = stack_a.pop()
    print(value)
```

(b) Basic Operations
Stacks and queues have a series of operations. The list below summarizes some of the key operations associated with stacks and queues.

- *push()* — Pushing (storing) an element on the stack.
- *pop()* — Removing (accessing) an element from the stack.
- *peek()* — Get the top data element of the stack, without removing it.
- *isFull()* — Check if stack is full.
- *isEmpty()* — Check if stack is empty.

Within the list, two operations, namely *push ()* and *pop()* are characteristic of stacks and queues. They represent insertion and removal operations conducted on stacks and queues. Here, we will discuss their mechanisms in step. Firstly, **push operations** can also be known as insertion operations for stacks.

On the other hand, **pop operations** are removal operations for stacks. The summary of the steps taken to conduct this operation is summarized below:

- **Step 1** — Checks if the stack is empty.
- **Step 2** — If the stack is empty, it produces an error and exit.
- **Step 3** — If the stack is not empty, accesses the data element at which **top** is pointing.
- **Step 4** — Decreases the value of top by 1.
- **Step 5** — Returns success.

(c) Python List Stack

A list in Python can be used to build up the Stack ADT. Regarding the illustrating codes below, the *peek()* and *pop()* operations can be applied with a non-empty stack only because it is impossible to remove or peek at something that is not there. To enforce this requirement, we must ensure that the stack is not empty before applying the given operation. The *peek()* method returns a reference to the last item in the list. To implement the *pop()* method, we call the *pop()* method of the list structure, which performs the same operation that we are trying to implement.

```python
# Using a Python list to construct the Stack ADT
class Stack:
    # Create stack
    def __init__(self):
        self._items = list()

    # If the stack is empty, return True
    def isEmpty(self):
        return len(self) == 0

    # Return the number of items
    def __len__(self):
        return len(self._items)
```

```
    # Return the top item
    def peek(self):
        assert not self.isEmpty(), "Cannot peek because of the stack is
empty"
        return self._items[-1]

    # Return the top item and remove the top item
    def pop(self):
        assert not self.isEmpty(), "Cannot pop because of the stack is
empty"
        return self._items.pop()

    # Push an item
    def push(self, item):
        self._items.append(item)

a=Stack()
a.push(1)
print(a.peek())
a.push(2)
print(a.pop())
print(a.isEmpty())
========================= stack1.py =========================
1
2
False
```

(d) Singly List Stack

For stacks with a large number of push and pop operations, the Python list-based implementation may not be the best option. A singly linked list can be used to implement the Stack ADT, which moderates the concern over array reallocations. Refer to below for the relevant codes in creating a singly linked list.

```
class Stack(object):
    # Create a stack
    def __init__(self):
        self._top = None
```

```
      self._nsize = 0
      self.inner=self._stack_node()

  def isEmpty(self):
      return self._top is None

      # Return the number of items
  def __len__(self):
      return self.nsize

      # Return the top item
  def peek(self):
      assert not self.isEmpty(), "Cannot peek because of the stack is
empty"
      return self._top

  # Return the top item and remove the top item
  def pop(self):
      assert not self.isEmpty(), "Cannot pop because of the stack is
empty"
      node = self._top
      self._top = self.inner.next
      self._nsize -= 1
      return node


  # Push an item
  def push(self, item):
      self._top = self.inner.create (item, self._top)
      self._nsize += 1

  class _stack_node:
      def create(self, item, link):
          self.item = item
          self.next = link
          return self.item
a=Stack()
a.push(1)
a.push(3)
```

```
print(a.isEmpty())
print(a.peek())
print(a.pop())
print(a.peek())
a.push(2)
print(a.pop())
print(a.peek())
================================ stack2.py ================================
False
3
3
1
2
1
```

2.4.2 *Queues*

Queues, as previously introduced, represent a physical queue as a form of data storage. It follows a first-in-first-out (FIFO) principle. However, unlike stack, a queue is opened at both ends. This section introduces relevant queue ADTs and how to use the Python list, the **circular array**, and the **linked list** to construct the queue ADT.

Learning Objectives
- Understand what a queue is and comprehend the FIFO concept related.
- Note the basic operations involving queue.

Main Takeaways

Main Points
- A queue is open at both sides of its ends. One end is often used to insert data (enqueue) and the other is used to remove data (dequeue).
- Queue follows FIFO methodology, which indicates that the data item stored first will be the first one to be accessed.

Main Terms
- **Enqueue:** Adding an item to the queue from the rear pointer end.
- **Dequeue:** Removing an item from the queue from the rear pointer end.

- **Front pointer:** Contains the starting element of the queue.
- **Rear pointer:** Contains the ending element of the queue.
- **FIFO:** First-in-first-out concept, whatever is added to the queue first will be first to be removed.
- **Linked list:** Lists with the front and end element being linked together.
- **Circular array:** A circular-shaped list with an end element linked to the start element.

(a) Queue ADT

A *queue* is a data structure that is a linear collection of items, which follows the first-in-first-out methodology. New items are appended at one end of the queue, and existing items are removed from the other end. The items always stay in the same order in which they are added to the structure.

The list below contains relevant operations associated with queue ADT:

- *Queue()*: Creates a new empty queue, which contains no items.
- *isEmpty()*: Returns a Boolean value to indicate the queue is empty or not.
- *len()*: Returns the number of items in the queue.
- *enqueue(item)*: Adds the given *item* to the end of the queue.
- *dequeue()*: Removes and returns the first item from the queue. Nothing can be dequeued from an empty queue.

(b) Python List

The **python list** is the simplest form of a queue. Its python code is illustrated below:

```
# Using a python list to construct the Queue ADT
class Queue:
    # Create a queue
    def __init__(self):
        self._q_list = list()

    def isEmpty(self):
        return len(self) == 0
```

```
# Return the number of items
def __len__(self):
    return len(self._q_list)

# Insert a item to the queue
def enqueue(self, item):
    self._q_list.append(item)

# Return the first item and remove it from the queue
def dequeue(self):
    assert not self.isEmpty(), "Cannot dequeue because the queue is
empty."
    return self._q_list.pop(0)

a=Queue()
a.enqueue(1)
a.enqueue(9)
print(a.dequeue())
print(a.dequeue())
print(a.isEmpty())
================= queue1.py =================
1
9
True
```

(c) Circular Array

The **circular array** is a more efficient form of the queue than the Python list. As its name suggests, it is a form of a queue that is circular. Its code is illustrated below:

```
class Array:
    def __init__(self):
        pass
    def create(self,size):
        return [None]*size
# Using a circular list to construct the Queue ADT
class Queue:
    # Create a queue
```

```python
def __init__(self, max_size):
    self._count = 0
    self._front = 0
    self._back = 0
    self._back = max_size -1
    self._array = Array.create(self, max_size)

def isEmpty(self):
    return self._count == 0

def isFull(self):
    return self._count == len(self._array)

# Return the number of items
def __len__(self):
    return len(self._q_list)

# Insert a item to the queue
def enqueue(self, item):
    assert not self.isFull(), "Cannot enqueue because the queue is full."
    max_size = len(self._array)
    self._back = (self._back + 1) % max_size
    self._array[self._back] = item
    self._count += 1

# Return the first item and remove it from the queue
def dequeue(self):
    assert not self.isEmpty(), "Cannot dequeue because the queue is empty."
    item = self._array[self._front]
    max_size = len(self._array)
    self._front = (self._front + 1) % max_size
    self._count -= 1
    return item

a=Queue(2)
a.enqueue(1)
```

```
a.enqueue(2)
print(a.isFull())
print(a.dequeue())
print(a.dequeue())
print(a.isEmpty())
================== queue2.py ==================
True
1
2
True
```

(d) Linked List

The **linked list** is the most efficient form of a queue. Its list is illustrated in the following codes.

```python
class Node(object):
    def __init__(self, item):
        self.item = item
        self.next = None
# Using a linked list to construct the Queue ADT
class linked_list:
    def __init__(self):
        self.__head = None

    def is_empty(self):
        return self.__head is None

# Insert an item to the queue
    def enqueue(self, item):
        new = Node(item)
        if self.__head is not None:
            new.next = self.__head
        self.__head = new

# Return the first item and remove it from the queue
    def dequeue(self):
        t = self.__head
```

```
        if self.__head is not None:
         if self.__head.next is None:
          self.__head = None
         else:
            while t.next.next is not None:
             t = cur.next
             t.next,t = (None, t.next)
         return t.item

a=linked_list()
a.enqueue(1)
a.enqueue(3)
print(a.dequeue())
print(a.dequeue())
print(a.is_empty())
================== queue3.py ==================
1
3
True
```

2.5 Searching and Sorting

Searching and sorting are two of the most common computer science applications. It involves searching for specific items within a collection and, similarly, sorting items to be searched easily. Principles included in this section have been explored in the previous chapter.

2.5.1 *Searching*

This section introduces two different search techniques, the **linear search** and the **binary search**, including related arguments.

Learning Objectives
- Understand the basic definitions of searching and sorting.
- Understand the functions of a linear search.
- Comprehend basic operations "if" – "else" in performing a linear search.

- Understand what binary search does and how the mechanism is carried out.
- Aware of the divide and conquer principle and note its mechanism.

Main Takeaways

Main Points
- Searching is the process of selecting any specific information from a collection of data based on a particular criterion.
- A linear search is a form of a search technique that iterates down the sequence of a list.
- A binary search is a form of a search technique that searches half the list at one time.
- Sorting is the process of ordering or arranges a set of items such that each item and its successor satisfies a prescribed relationship.

Main Terms
- **Sequences search:** Sequences search refers to the process of finding an item within a sequence using a search key.
- **Search key:** A unique value used to identify the data elements from a collection. This helps the process of sequence search to identify a specific item.
- **Sort key:** Sort key refers to a specific value from which the ordering of items is based during sorting.
- **If-else:** A conditional argument specifies two alternating conditions.
- **Binary search algorithm:** A search algorithm that searches half the list at one time.
- **While-loop:** A loop that repeats an iteration based on a Boolean statement.
- **If-else-elif:** An argument that specifies three or more types of conditions.

(a) The Linear Search

A **linear search** is a form of a search technique that iterates down the sequence of a list, one item at a time until the specific item had been found. Loop and if-else statements can be used to perform iterative linear searches. The **if-else statement** works in the following manner. The "*If*" sets the condition, and the respective statement will be printed when the element can be located "in" the array. "*Else*" sets the condition for when the if-statement is not fulfilled. It can be treated as if-not. So, if the element is not in the array, the other statement will be printed. Refer to the code below for a reference.

```
if element in arrayA:
    print("The element is in arrayA.")
else:
    print("The element is not in the arrayA.")
```

To run the search through a given array, a for-loop can be used, just like the following example below. The **for-loop** runs the **if-else argument** down the elements on the list.

```
def linearSearch(values, target ):
    n = len(values)
    for i in range(n):
        # If the target is in the values, return True
        if values[i] == target
            return True
    return False #If not found, return False
```

(b) The Binary Search

The **binary search** is a more complex form of searching algorithms. This search uses a sorted sequence of items and begins by comparing the target value against the item in the middle. If the middle item is greater, then the search will continue on the left half and vice versa. The new round of search begins once again by identifying the middle item and compares it against the value of the item we are searching for. Each time, the search is done on the targeted 50% length of the remaining sequence until- the index is eventually located. Relevant code usually includes a while-loop followed by if-elif-else argument.

Regarding the flow chart below, the **while-loop** is an infinite argument. The while-loop will first test the condition, in this case, in Figure 2.3, condition 1. If condition 1 is true, then the statement will be repeated repeatedly until other operators break it.

To set the condition to perform a loop, the **if-else-elif statement** is adopted. A simple analogy of the if-else-elif argument follows the if-statement first. If the conditions of the if-statement are not fulfilled, we proceed to the else-statement. If the condition in both the if- and

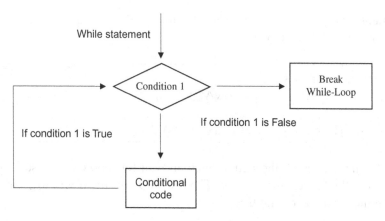

Figure 2.3: While-loop.

else-statements are then found to be unfulfilled, we move to the elif-statement.

The binary search works by identifying mid-points. As each mid-point is identified, half of the segment will be searched. If the target sequence is not found, the remaining segment will be halved, followed by a similar search in half of the segment. This search continues until the target segment has been found. Hence, the terminology is defined as a divide and conquer strategy as the list is divided into half, with each half being searched till the target is found. The following code illustrates how the search can be performed.

```python
def binarySearch(values, target):
    low = 0
    high = len(values) - 1

    while low <= high :
        mid = (high + low) // 2
        if values[mid] == target:
            return True
        elif target < values[mid]:
            high = mid - 1
        else:
            low = mid + 1
    return False
```

2.5.2 *Sorting*

This section introduces appropriate sorting methods, including bubble sort, selection sort, and insertion sort. Sorting involves arranging a list of elements in a more organized manner.

Learning Objectives
- Understand what bubble sort does and how bubble sort works.
- Explore the algorithmic code involved with performing a bubble sort.
- Understand how selection sort is performed and the relevant Python codes.
- Understand how the insertion sort is performed.

Main Takeaways

Main Points
- Bubble sort is a comparison-based sorting algorithm that compares adjacent elements and swaps elements that are not in order.
- Bubble sort is not suitable for large data sets.
- Selection sort works by scanning all the elements, picking the desired ones, and re-arranging them in a separate list.
- Insertion sort is done by going down the list sequentially, and any element that does not fall in order is swapped with the other element, which should have been in its position.

Main Terms
- **Bubble sort:** A form of sorting that re-arranges adjacent pairs, one at a time.
- **Selection sort:** Sorting that sorts the list from the smallest to the largest.
- **Insertion sort:** Sorting that swaps wrongly positioned elements with the correct one.

(a) Bubble Sort

Bubble sort works by switching the order of adjacent elements. For example, suppose the sorting requirement is to ensure that a list of numbers proceeds in increasing order. In that case, bubble sort will compare each pair of adjacent numbers, shifting the smaller number constantly to the left and the larger ones to the right. The sorting is done so that the list is re-arranged into ascending or descending order. Figure 2.4 illustrates

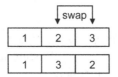

Figure 2.4:   Swapping because of bubble sort.

this principle, as 2 and 3 are swapped adjacently to ensure the desired order obtains.

The diagram below contains the Python codes to perform the bubble sort. Note that the *len ()* **operator** is first used to define the list's total capacity to be sorted. A *for-loop* is then used to set the conditions for sorting the entire list together with the if statement.

```
def bubble_sort(arr):
    n = len(arr)
    for i in range(n-1):
        for j in range(n-i-1):
            if arr[j] > arr[j+1]:
                a[j],a[j+1]=a[j+1],a[j]
a=[67,90,5,6,76,34,2]
bubble_sort(a)
print(a)
================= bubblesort.py =================
[2, 5, 6, 34, 67, 76, 90]
```

(b) Selection Sort
Selection sort works as the terminology describes. It selects elements and arranges them into the order which we desire. It works by identifying the smallest element within the range of the list. Each smallest element is picked from the main list and inserted into the blank list until all original list elements have been sorted into a new list.

```
def selection_sort(arr):
    n = len(arr)
    for i in range(n):
        low_index = i
```

```
    for j in range(i+1, n):
        if arr[j] < arr[low_index]:
            low_index = j
        arr[i],arr[low_index]=a[low_index],arr[i]
a=[67,90,5,6,76,34,2]
selection_sort(a)
print(a)
================ selectionsort.py ================
[2, 5, 6, 34, 67, 76, 90]
```

A summary of the steps is shown below:

- **Step 1** — Set *low_index* to location 0.
- **Step 2** — Search the minimum element in the list.
- **Step 3** — Swap with value at location MIN.
- **Step 4** — Increment *low_index* to point to the next element.
- **Step 5** — Repeat steps 1 to 4 until the list is sorted.

(c) Insertion Sort

The final form of sorting is the **insertion sort**, which picks up items sequentially down the list and inserts them into the order of desire. The **insertion sort** operation moves down the list while swapping the wrongly positioned element with the correct element. The elements swapped need not be adjacent like what we witnessed in the binary sort. The key behind the Python code includes a while-loop with the argument, and the operator refers to the fact that both arguments must be fulfilled for the while condition to be true. Below is the illustration of how the insertion sort is coded. Like other list sorting, a *len()* operator is first used to define the total capacity, followed by a **for-loop** to operate down the list.

A summary of the steps is offered below:

- **Step 1** — If it is the first element, it is already sorted. Return 1.
- **Step 2** — Pick the next element.
- **Step 3** — Compare with all elements in the sorted sub-list.
- **Step 4** — Shift all the elements in the sorted sub-list that is greater than the value to be sorted.
- **Step 5** — Insert the value.
- **Step 6** — Repeat until list is sorted.

```
def insertion_sort(arr):
  n = len(arr)
  for i in range(1, n):
    value = arr[i]
    index = i
    while index > 0 and value < arr[index - 1]:
      arr[index] = arr[index - 1]
      index -= 1
    arr[index] = value
a=[67,90,5,6,76,34,2]
insertion_sort(a)
print(a)
================== insertionsort.py ==================
[2, 5, 6, 34, 67, 76, 90]
```

(d) Built-in Sort in Python

Python lists have a built-in sort() method that modifies the list in-place and a sorted() built-in function that builds a new sorted list from an iterable.[1] In Python programming, we recommend using python's sort directly. Python's built-in sorting algorithm uses a particular version of merge sort, called Timsort, which runs in O(nlog(n)). However, the worst-case and average complexity of bubbling, insertion, and selection sorting are all O(n^2). So, using Python built-in sorting is a more efficient and optimized choice.

```
>>> sorted([4, 5, 3, 1, 2])
[1, 2, 3, 4, 5]
>>>a=[4, 5, 3, 1, 2]
>>>a.sort()
>>>a
[1, 2, 3, 4, 5]
```

(e) Examples of Applications in Finance

After understanding the data structure and algorithm, we can apply them to practical finance examples. There are two main steps to solve problems

---

[1] Sorting Mini-HOW, TO. Retrieved from https://wiki.python.org/moin/HowTo/Sorting (accessed March 3, 2021).

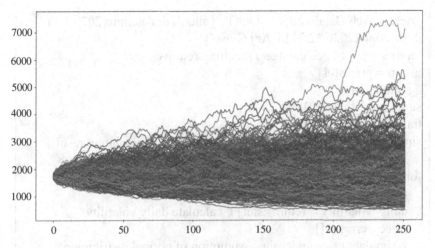

Figure 2.5: Monte Carlo simulation.

with python programming. The first thing we need to do is clarify its data structure and the algorithm that needs to be used.

The following introduces the Monte Carlo simulation of stock prices and binary search for implied volatility.

Monte Carlo simulation of stock prices: Monte Carlo is a standard method for predicting uncertain events in finance. The raw data is a price series, which should be stored in a list. The core algorithm of Monte Carlo is to repeat random samples to obtain results. We use loop statements for the repeated process. Results are shown in Figure 2.5.

```
import pandas as pd
from matplotlib import style
import numpy as np
import datetime as dt
import pandas_datareader.data as web
import matplotlib.pyplot as plt

style.use('fast')

# get GOOGLE stock prices from yahoo
```

```
prices = web.DataReader('GOOG','yahoo', dt.datetime(2020,1,1),
dt.datetime(2020,12,31))['Adj Close']
returns = prices.pct_change() # getting returns
last_p = prices[-1]
# simulation
simulation_times = 1000
trading_days = 252
simulate_data = pd.DataFrame() #dataframe for simulation results

for k in range(simulation_times):
    count=0
    daily_volatility = returns.std() # calculate daily volatility
    price_series = []
    # simulate price under the assumption of normal distribution
    price = (1+np.random.normal(0,daily_volatility))*last_p
    price_series.append(price)

    for i in range(trading_days-1):
        price = (1+np.random.normal(0,daily_volatility))*price_series
[count]
        count+=1
        price_series.append(price)

    simulate_data[k] = price_series

fig = plt.figure()
fig.suptitle('Monte Carlo Simulation')
plt.plot(simulate_data)
plt.show()
```

Binary search for implied volatility: The data to obtain implied volatility comprises five variables: the market price of the option, the underlying stock price, the strike price, the time to expiration, and the risk-free interest rate. The methods of calculating implied volatility are mainly iteration and trial and error. We learned the binary search before combining these two methods to check the implied volatility within a specific range. When the accuracy reaches 0.0001, we have found the implied volatility's approximate value.

```python
from scipy import log,exp,sqrt,stats

# Black–Scholes–Merton model
def BSM_Call(S,X,T,r,sigma):
    d1 = (log(S/X)+(r+sigma*sigma/2)*T)/(sigma*sqrt(T))
    d2 = d1-sigma*sqrt(T)
    return S*stats.norm.cdf(d1)-X*exp(-r*T)*stats.norm.cdf(d2)

# binary search for implied volatility
def implied_vol_bi_search(S,X,T,r,c):
    vol_l=0.001
    vol_h=1.0
    c_low=BSM_Call(S,X,T,r,vol_l)
    c_high=BSM_Call(S,X,T,r,vol_h)
    # if the given call price is unreasonable,
    # we would jump out of the function.
    if c_low>c or c_high<c:
        print("wrong option price")
        return 0,0,0
    while abs(c_high-c_low)>0.0001:
        c_high=BSM_Call(S,X,T,r,vol_h)
        c_low=BSM_Call(S,X,T,r,vol_l)
        vol_mid=(vol_l+vol_h)/2
        c_mid=BSM_Call(S,X,T,r,vol_mid)
        if c_mid>c:
        # if the price being checked is greater than the actual price,
        # the implied volatility should fall in the lower range.
            vol_h=vol_mid
        else:
        # if the price being checked is smaller than the actual price,
        # the implied volatility should fall in the higher range.
            vol_l=vol_mid
    return vol_mid, c_low, c_high

S=65;X=60;T=0.5;r=0.03;c=7.0
volatility,c_Low,c_High=implied_vol_bi_search(S,X,T,r,c)
print("Volatility{:.6f}, cLow:{:.6f}, cHigh:{:.6f}".format(volatility,c_Low,c_High))
```

```
================implied_volatility.py================
Volatility0.185056, cLow:6.999979, cHigh:7.000030
```

References/Further Readings

Breiman, L. (2001). Statistical Modeling: The two cultures. *Statistical Science*, **16**(3), 199–231.

Data Structure and Algorithms Tutorial. Retrieved from https://www.tutorialspoint. com/data_structures_algorithms/index.htm; http://examradar.com/data-structure-mcq-set-9/; https://wiki.python.org/moin/HowTo/Sorting.

Ma, W. (2015). *Mastering Python for Finance*. Packt Publishing.

Necaise, R. D. (2010). *Data Structures and Algorithms Using Python*. Wiley Publishing.

NUS Course CS2040c. Data Structures and Algorithms. Retrieved from https:// www.comp.nus.edu.sg/~stevenha/cs2040c-sem1.html#intro.

Yan, Y. (2014). *Python for Finance*. Packt Publishing.

2.6 Sample Questions

Question 1

A PDF file of an essay includes some information about the time it was created and the author's name. It is an example of:

(a) Structured data
(b) Unstructured data
(c) Semi-structured data

Question 2

The following formula below will produce:

$$F_n = F_{n-1} + F_{n-2}$$

(a) Armstrong number
(b) Fibonacci series
(c) Euler number

Question 3
Which is a set of data values and associated operations that involves the separation of the properties of a data type (its values and operations) from the implementation of that data type?

(a) Stack & Queues
(b) Hash tables
(c) ADT

Question 4
Which of the following is not a form of primitive data structure?

(a) Boolean
(b) Integer
(c) Arrays

Question 5
Which of the following case does not exist in complexity theory?

(a) Best case
(b) Null case
(c) Worst case

Question 6
The average case scenario occurs when:

(a) Item is the first element within the array
(b) Item is in the middle of the linked list
(c) Item is in the middle of the array

Question 7
The Θ notation in asymptotic evaluation represents

(a) Best case
(b) Average case
(c) Worst case

Question 8
Which of the following operations access each record exactly once so that
the desired operation can proceed?

(a) Inserting
(b) Deleting
(c) Traversing

Question 9
Which of the following answers demonstrates the correct result from the
slicing operation in the following codes?

```
listA = [4, 12, 2, 34, 17]
listB = listA[0:2]
print(listB)
```

(a) –4, 12
(b) –4, 12, 2
(c) –34, 17

Question 10
What is the main difference between a list and an array?

(a) Python's list structure is a mutable sequence container that can change
size as items are added or removed. Array, however, holds a fixed
number of items of the same type
(b) Array is a mutable sequence container that can change size as items
are added or removed. Python's list, however, holds a fixed number
of items of the same type
(c) They have no difference

Question 11
What is the worst-case time complexity of a linear search algorithm?

(a) O(1)
(b) O(log(n))
(c) O(n)

Question 12
For a binary search algorithm to work, the array (list) must be:

(a) Sorted
(b) Unsorted
(c) In a heap

Question 13
Which of the following searching techniques can work with data, not in sorted form?

(a) Binary search
(b) Interpolation search
(c) Linear search

Question 14
The binary search tree has the best case run-time complexity of $O(\log n)$. What could the worst case?

(a) $O(n)$
(b) $O(n^2)$
(c) $O(n^3)$

Question 15
Which of the following has a search efficiency of $O(1)$

(a) Tree
(b) Linked-list
(c) Hash table

Question 16
After each iteration in bubble sort:

(a) At least one element is at its sorted position.
(b) One less comparison is made in the next iteration.
(c) Both (a) & (b) are true.

Question 17
Which of the following sorting algorithms maintains two sub-lists, one sorted and another to be sorted?

(a) Selection sort
(b) Insertion sort
(c) Both (a) & (b)

Question 18
push() and pop() functions are found in:

(a) Queues
(b) Lists
(c) Stacks

Question 19
A circular linked list can be used for

(a) Stack
(b) Queue
(c) Both (a) & (b)

Question 20
The statement "A linked-list is a dynamic structure" is

(a) True
(b) False
(c) Unable to tell

Solutions

Question 1

Solution: Option **c** is correct.

A PDF file by itself is an example of unstructured data. With the metadata, it becomes a semi-structured data file.

Question 2

Solution: Option **b** is correct.

Pluck in n, and you will get the Fibonacci sequence

Question 3

Solution: Option **c** is correct.

ADT is about figuring out the "how" by separating the operations from the implementation.

Question 4

Solution: Option **c** is correct.

An Array represents a collection of elements and is not primitive.

Question 5

Solution: Option **b** is correct.

Best case, worst case, and average case are the 3 cases available.

Question 6

Solution: Option **c** is correct.

The middle of the array determines the average case, not the linked list.

Question 7

Solution: Option **a** is correct.

Best case, by definition.

Question 8

Solution: Option **c** is correct.

The Insert function inserts an item while the delete function removes an item. Only traversing fulfills the definition.

Question 9

Solution: Option **a** is correct.

[0:2] extracts items 4 & 12, located at position 0 and 1, respectively. Item located at position 2 is not inclusive.

Question 10

Solution: Option **a** is correct.

The Python list can change its size. However, an array has a fixed capacity.

Question 11

Solution: Option **c** is correct.

The worst-case performance for linear search falls under the class of $O(n)$. $O(1)$ is the best-case performance. $O(\log n)$ represents the best-case complexity for binary search instead of linear.

Question 12

Solution: Option **a** is correct.

Sorting must be done first. Recall the divide and conquer concept in finding the mid-point first.

Question 13

Solution: Option **c** is correct.

Binary search requires sorting. Interpolation search is not introduced in this topic. Linear requires sorting.

Question 14

Solution: Option **a** is correct.

$O(n)$ refers to the worst-case complexity.

Question 15

Solution: Option **c** is correct.

Best case efficiency is reserved for the hash table from within the given options.

Question 16

Solution: Option **a** is correct.

The Bubble sorts technique sorts pair by pair, arranging one into a sorted position while leaving the other to be sorted next.

Question 17

Solution: Option **c** is correct.

Both selection sort and insertion sort maintain the two sub-lists. One list contains the sorted items, while the other list of items undergoes sorting. Sorted elements will be transferred to the sorted list.

Question 18

Solution: Option **c** is correct.

Stacks contains both functions, with push() being unique.

Question 19

Solution: Option **c** is correct.

Both can be used due to the structure.

Question 20

Solution: Option **a** is correct.

Part II

Big Data and Data Science

Chapter 3
Big Data

3.1 Introduction

3.1.1 *Brief History*

Big Data has only come into prominence recently, but data has always been present in human history. Outlined below is an introduction of Big Data and a brief timeline of key events.

Learning Objectives
- Understand the important milestones of Big Data.

Main Takeaways

Main Points
- Big Data is a term for the massive data sets that are larger, more varied, and more complex than regular data.
- Technology has now evolved to read and interpret such large data sets.

Main Terms
- **Big Data:** This is a term for massive data sets having large, more varied, and complex structures.
- **Online analytical processing (OLAP):** OLAP is a database management process that applies complex queries to historical data for data analytics purposes.

- **Edge computing:** It is a distributed computing on the cloud allows computation and data storage closer to the location where it is needed, which improves the response times and saves bandwidth for data centers.

(a) What is Big Data?

Big Data is a term for massive data sets having large, more varied, and complex structures with the difficulties of storing, analyzing, and visualizing when compared to using traditional data. Roger Mougalas coined the term Big Data in 2005.

(b) A History of Big Data

Big Data Phase 1.0: Big Data originates from the longstanding domain of databases and database management. **Database management and data warehousing** are considered the key aspects of Big Data Phase 1. They provide the foundation on which Big Data is formed, with queries, OLAP, and standard reporting tools.

Pre-2000s: Data has always been present throughout history, whether memorized, written on paper, or stored on a memory chip. Humanity has always needed to keep its information somewhere; it has only been the method that differed. Also, while the storage method has continually improved to store more and more data, ways to collate and draw meaning from the data are needed to evolve in efficiency and efficacy. The 20th century introduced computers and the internet to users, bringing an onslaught of information to everybody.

Big Data Phase 2.0: Big Data Phase 2.0 begins in the early 2000s, with the advent of the internet and web offering new data sources. Web 2.0, as explained below, introduced a massive increase in semi-structured and unstructured data (described in a later chapter), which posed the challenge of finding an appropriate method to store and analyze them.

2005, commentators claimed a paradigm shift had occurred in creating content and data. Web 2.0 introduced the idea of a user-generated web where users of services rather than the providers of said services created the majority of content. YouTube and Facebook are premier examples of Web 2.0. These volumes of data generated were then termed Big Data, and the entities that could first interpret and take advantage of such data would reap immense benefits. Hadoop was also created this year as a framework for managing such unstructured data.[1]

In 2008, the number of internet-connected devices exceeded the world's population.[2] Global servers processed approximately 12 gigabytes of information per person per day that year as well.[3] At the same time, companies also started to store data; data was viewed as an asset. According to a McKinsey report, in 2009, US companies with over 1,000 employees kept an average of 200 terabytes of data (200,000 gigabytes).[4]

Big Data Phase 3.0: Big Data Phase 3.0 began around 2010 and continues today. Instead of the web providing new data sources, the devices connected to the internet, coined as the Internet of Things (IoT), especially mobile devices that are driving data collection. This introduces a slew of new opportunities for data analysis.

From 2011, many industries, especially the tech industry, started to embrace Big Data. Below are some capstone events of Big Data during this phase:

- In 2011, IBM's Watson analyzed four terabytes of data in seconds to win two human players on the game show "Jeopardy!".[5]
- Facebook launched its Open Compute Project to share specifications for energy-efficient data centers in the same year.
- In 2015, Google and Microsoft led a massive build-out of data centers, and Huawei and Tencent joined Alibaba in significant data center buildouts in China. All these leading data center operators started the migration to 400G data speeds in 2018.

---

[1] GCN (2013). Tracking the Evolution of Big Data: A Timeline. Retrieved from https://gcn.com/articles/2013/05/30/gcn30-timeline-big-data.aspx.

[2] Same as Footnote 1.

[3] Short, J., Bohn, R., & Baru, C. (2010). Enterprise Server Information. How Much Information? Retrieved from https://www.clds.info/uploads/1/2/0/5/120516768/hmi_2010_enterprisereport_jan_2011.pdf.

[4] Manyika, J., Chui, M., Brown, B., Bughin, J., Dobbs, R., Roxburgh, C., & Byers, H. (2011). Big Data: The Next Frontier for Innovation, Competition, and Productivity. McKinsey Global Institute. Retrieved from https://www.mckinsey.com/business-functions/mckinsey-digital/our-insights/big-data-the-next-frontier-for-innovation.

[5] Same as Footnote 1.

- More recently, distributed computing on the cloud realizes computation and data storage closer to the location needed, improving response times and saving bandwidth for data centers. This technique is named edge computing. Edge computing is changing the cloud's role in the economy's key sectors. A Big Data center's speed is expected to exceed 1,000G in 2021.

3.1.2 Types of Big Data

Data comes in many forms, and Big Data is no exception. Big Data can be organized into three groups.

Learning Objectives
- Understand the three types of Big Data.

Main Takeaways

Main Points
- There are three types of Big Data: structured, unstructured, and semi-structured.

Main Terms
- **Structured data:** Data that is in a fixed form and field.
- **Unstructured data:** Data that does not conform to a fixed format.
- **Semi-structured data:** Data that has traits of both structured and unstructured data.

(a) Structured Data
Structured data refers to data in a fixed field and has a well-defined structure. It follows a consistent order and design in a way that makes it easy to enter, store, be queried, and analyzed. The disadvantage of structured data is also where it draws its strength. As Structured data is fixed, it has no room to manage and evaluate responses that were not pre-defined beforehand. Life, after all, does not always fit into neat little boxes.

Examples of structured data include:

- Meta-data (time, date of creation, file size, author, etc.)
- Library catalogue
- Census records

- Economic data
- Phone numbers

(b) Unstructured Data

Unstructured data is a data that is not structured, i.e., information that does not have a fixed format or response or cannot be easily and readily classified. The advantage of such data is that there tend to be huge volumes of such data which have not been analyzed yet, leading to a potentially untapped asset class. Given how Web 2.0 churns out vast amounts of such data daily, it could be a huge revenue driver for companies. The disadvantage is that its unstructured nature makes it hard for traditional database management systems to analyze and sort into anything meaningful.

Examples of unstructured data include:

- Text files (presentations, research papers, reports, etc.)
- Social media
- Photos
- Text messages
- Media
- Websites
- E-mail body

(c) Semi-Structured Data

Semi-structured data is a combination of the two. It is a form of structured data without a strict data model structure. Unstructured data like photos and videos could have metadata attached to them to tag them with structure data such as author name, date created, and GPS location to make them semi-structured data. This makes organizing such data a more straightforward process as they can be organized based on their structured data.

(d) Characteristics of Structured and Unstructured Data

Table 3.1 summarizes the similarities and differences between structured and unstructured data.

(e) Machine- and Human-Generated Data Examples

A few machine-generated and human-generated data examples are presented in Table 3.2.

Table 3.1: Differences between structured and unstructured data.

	Structured Data	Unstructured Data
Flexibility	Schema dependent rigorous	Absence of schema, very flexible
Scalability	Scaling DB schema is difficult	Highly scalable
Robustness	Robust	—
Query Performance	Structured query allows complex joins	Only textual query possible
Accessibility	Easy to access	Hard to access
Availability	Percentage-wise lower	Percentage-wise higher
Association	Organized	Scattered and dispersed
Analysis	Efficient to analysis	Additional pre-processing is needed
Appearance	Formally defined	Free-form

Table 3.2: Machine- and human-generated data.

Machine Generated	
Structured Data Sources	Unstructured Data Sources
Sensor data: ID tags, GPS data, and other structured data from devices fall in this category. Data from such sources can be used for supply chain management and inventory control, amongst others.	**Satellite images:** While unstructured, satellite images can be used in many situations, such as weather prediction or mapping tech like Google maps.
Weblog data: Servers, applications, and networks receive and produce a lot of structured data as well, which can be utilized for server management and data security checks.	**Scientific data:** Many unstructured data such as seismic imagery and high energy physics are used in scientific studies, drawing impressive new conclusions with Big Data analysis.
Point-of-sale data: A lot of data is produced when making sales, including the products' barcodes and details on the payment method.	**Media:** Surveillance equipment generate a ton of unstructured data for diverse purposes.
Financial data: Information on stocks listed and traded, such as ticker name and stock price, are all structured data used in the financial industry.	

Table 3.2: (*Continued*)

Human Generated	
Structured Data Sources	Unstructured Data Sources
Input data: Survey responses such as age, income, gender, and name are examples of structured data generated by humans.	**Company text:** E-mails and reports are examples of data sources that produce unstructured data for analysis.
Clickstream data: Refers to data generated when human users click on a website link.	**Social media:** This data is generated when human users interact with these platforms such as YouTube, Instagram, and Facebook.
Gaming-related data: How users navigate a game via inputs are recorded as structured data for analysis.	**Mobile data:** Text messages and location information are unstructured data collected through mobile devices.

3.2 Characteristics of Big Data

The characteristics of Big Data can be summarized from multiple perspectives.

3.2.1 *The 5Vs and 8Vs*

Learning Objectives
- Understand the importance of the 5Vs and 8Vs of Big Data.

Main Takeaways

Main Points
- **Big Data has 5V characteristics:** Volume, Variety, Velocity, Value, Veracity.
- **In a broader sense, Big Data has additional 3V characteristics:** Visualization, Viscosity, Virality.

Main Terms
- **Volume:** The total amount of data collected by an entity for analysis.
- **Velocity:** Data processing rate and data collection rate.
- **Variety:** How many types of data are being collected and how many sources.

- **Value:** How much value the data adds to the company.
- **Veracity:** How reliable is the data.
- **Visualization:** Represent or visualize data in a meaningful way.
- **Viscosity:** The resistance to flow in the volume of data.
- **Virality:** How quickly data is spread and shared.

In 2001, MetaGroup (now Gartner) introduced data scientists and analysts to the 3 Vs of 3D Data, Volume, Velocity, and Variety.

Data analytics as a field saw a rampant change in how data is captured and processed over the past decade. As part of this evolution, data was increasing in size that it came to be known as Big Data. With the astronomical growth of data, two new Vs — Value and Veracity — have been added by Gartner to the data processing concepts, which is named 5 Vs of Big Data.

In an age where shifting from transactions to engagement and then to experience, the forces of social media, mobile, cloud, and IoT add three more Big Data characteristics that should be considered when seeking insights[6] — Visualization, Viscosity, and Virality. Together with the 5 Vs, we usually call it 8 Vs of Big Data (shown in Figure 3.1).

(a) Volume

Volume refers to the amount of data churned out or available for analysis. As the name implies, good Big Data have vast data volumes to analyze. This data must then be used to gain vital information; if not, it should not be considered part of the data.

For example, the cat pictures data set's volume would be larger than the volume of the data set of orange cats as orange cats are a subset of cats.

(b) Velocity

Velocity refers to the speed at which data is being created over time and its processing rate. Rate of change, activity bursts, and linking data sets of varying speeds are aspects of velocity.

For example, commuting data records the journey to work. It includes where people work, when their trip starts (such as from home to workplace),

---

[6]"Ray" Wang, R. (2012). Beyond the Three V's of Big Data — Viscosity and Virality. Retrieved from https://www.enterpriseirregulars.com/46120/beyond-the-three-vs-of-big-data-viscosity-and-virality/.

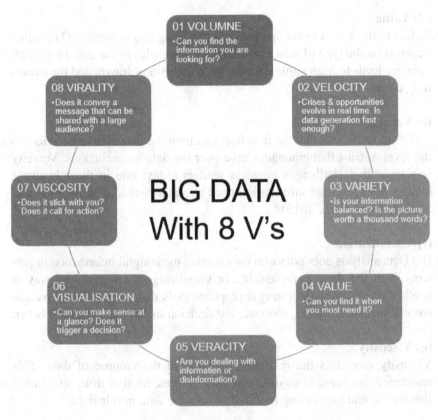

Figure 3.1: Big Data with 8V's.

which transportation they use to get there, and how long it takes. The velocity of commuting data features activity bursts during the day's peak hours.

(c) Variety
Variety refers to the type of data collected: structured, unstructured, and semi-structured. In the past, data was generated from more fixed points such as company surveys or monthly reports. Nowadays, with Web 2.0, users create data themselves and can be from various sources such as e-mail and social media.[7]

---

[7]upGrad (2020). What is Big Data. Retrieved from https://www.upgrad.com/blog/what-is-big-data-types-characteristics-benefits-and-examples/#Velocity.

(d) Value
Refers to the added value that the data can bring to a company. Data value depends on the type of data, the other characteristics of the data (e.g., high veracity leads to high value-added), the conclusions drawn, and the events they cover.

(e) Veracity
Refers to the extent that the data user can trust the data. This also refers to the level of trust that managers have over the data's conclusions. Veracity is a topic that challenges business leaders today; one in three business leaders does not trust information used to reach decisions in their organizations (Hiba *et al.*, 2015).[8]

(f) Visualization
Big Data analysis does not mean only mining meaningful information or patterns from the data. Representable or visualizing in a meaningful way is another way of analysis. Using appropriate tools that serve different parameters helps data scientists, analysts, and decision-makers understand it better.

(g) Viscosity
Viscosity measures the resistance to flow in the volume of data. This resistance can come from different data sources, friction from integration flow rates, and processing required to turn the data into insight.

(h) Virality
Virality describes how quickly information gets dispersed across people-to-people networks. It measures how fast data is spread and shared to each network's unique node.[9] For example, nearly 70% of people living in the United States use at least one social media network. Think of virality as an exponential curve. If two people connected share a piece of information and suppose that number doubles 30 times, over a billion people will have shared the content.[10]

---

[8]Shnain (2015). Big Data and Five V's Characteristics. Retrieved from https://www. researchgate.net/publication/332230305.

[9]Rafael (2019). How to Measure Virality. Retrieved from https://www.search-digital.com/ social-virality.

[10]Deep Patel (2017). 10 Secrets to Going Viral on Social Media. Retrieved from https:// www.entrepreneur.com/article/302286#:~:text=Think%20of%20virality%20as%20 an,a%20powerful%20tool%20for%20businesses.

3.3 Big Data Architecture

3.3.1 *Architecture*

Big Data's architecture consists of the mechanisms and methods to collect, store, secure, process, and convert the data into a structure stored in databases and file systems. The Big Data architecture also requires tools to analyze the data, make sense of it, and finally make intelligent decisions based on analyzing this collected data.

Learning Objectives
- Understand the architecture of Big Data analysis and its components.
- Understand the three types of Big Database management.

Main Takeaways

Main Points
- **Big Data architecture has four layers:** Data Sourcing, Data Storage, Processing, and Analytics.
- **Big Database management has three types:** Centralized, Decentralized, and Distributed.

Main Terms
- **Batch processing**: A way to aggregate data sets together to make handling the data more manageable for the analytical tools.

(a) Big Data Architecture
The architecture of Big Data is summarized in Figure 3.2.

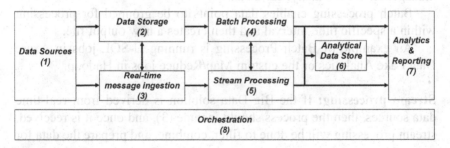

Figure 3.2: Data architecture.

Source: Yaseen (2020).

Data sources: Big Data analysis always begins with the data. Data sources refer to the channels that the company receives its data from and the type of data received. The data is then identified as regular data (and channeled elsewhere) or Big Data based on whether they have the 5Vs or 8Vs characteristics.

Examples of data sources can be third-party data providers, company servers, satellite images, etc.

Data storage: Data received from the various sources are received in this layer. If the data received is unstructured and not in a format that the analytics tool can handle, this is the component that converts the data into a format that can be analyzed.

For example, unstructured data (e.g., image, audio, video, social media data, and sensor data) can be stored in specialized file systems such as in a NoSQL database or Hadoop Distributed File System (HDFS).

Real-time message ingestion: If the Big Data comes from real-time data sources, then the Data Storage architecture component may not adequately collect and process it. In this case, the architecture should include a real-time message ingestion system to manage real-time messages for stream processing.

Many vendors provide real-time ingestion tools. One example is Apache Kafka. Apache Kafka is an event streaming platform that combines messages, storage, and data processing.

Batch processing: In some cases, the data source data sets are huge and cannot be adequately prepared in the Data Storage section (2). Batch processing is then done to aggregate data sets to make handling the data more manageable for the analytical tools.

Batch processing enables data points to be grouped for processing within a specific time interval and then creates a new output file.

An example of Batch Processing is running U-SQL jobs in Azure Data Lake Analytics or the custom Map/Reduce jobs in Hadoop.

Stream processing: If the Big Data solution is derived from real-time data sources, then the process should include (3), and once it is received, stream processing will be done to filter, combine, and prepare the data for analysis. Like Batch Processing, an output sink will generate the final output for analysis.

Analytical data store: Unlike traditional databases, analytical databases store and manage big data in a structured format for further business intelligence analysis. They are specially optimized for faster queries and scalability.

Analytics and reporting: Finally, once the data is received and processed, this section analyzes and presents the data, giving meaning to the information received. Data modeling and analytic services are done in this section, and it is this section where Data scientists and analysts can interact with the data to explore it.

Orchestration: Data orchestration is the automation of data-driven processes. It includes procedures that span both ends of the architecture, including preparing data, making decisions based on the data, and taking actions based on that data.

(b) Centralized, Decentralized, and Distributed
As the volume of data increases dramatically, an obvious challenge is how to manage the Big Database so that users can easily access and use it whenever needed. The Big Databases can be divided into three types: centralized, decentralized, and distributed, as shown in Figure 3.3.[11]

Centralized: Maintain all the data in a single computer, and to access the information, users must access the main computer of the system, known as "server."[12] It is easy to maintain.

Decentralized: There is no central storage. Some servers provide information to the clients. There is no direct connection between the two clients, and only the servers are connected.

---

[11] Andrew Tar (2017). Decentralized and Distributed Databases, Explained. Retrieved from https://cointelegraph.com/explained/decentralized-and-distributed-databases-explained.

[12] icommunity (2021). Distributed VS Centralized Networks. Retrieved from https://icommunity.io/en/redes-centralizadas-vs-distribuidas/.

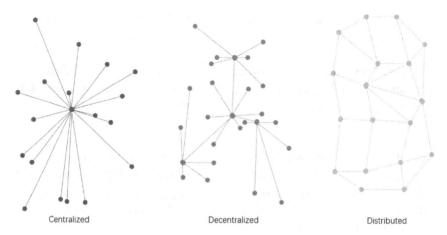

Centralized   Decentralized   Distributed

Figure 3.3: Distributed databases.

Distributed: There is no data storage. A distributed database works as a single logical data network, installed in a series of computers (nodes) located in different geographic locations and not connected to a single processing unit, but are fully connected to provide integrity and accessibility to information from any point.

In a distributed database, all the nodes contain information, and all the clients of the system are in equal condition. In this way, distributed data networks can perform autonomous processing. A clear example is a blockchain, but there are others, such as Spanner, a distributed database created by Google.

Distributed databases, in theory, are more challenging to maintain.

3.4 Big Data Technologies

3.4.1 *Tools/Software*

Big Data's development has progressed significantly from its conceptual roots in the early 2000s. There are now multiple tools or software that can process and analyze Big Data.

Learning Objectives
- Introduce the popular Big Data tools and software.

Main Takeaways

Main Points
• **Big Data technologies generally have four domains:** Data storage, Data analytics, Data mining, and Data visualization.

Main Terms
• **Domain:** A category for Big Data technologies.

(a) Types of Big Data Technology
These technologies can be grouped into four main categories, also known as domains, such as Data Storage, Analytics, Data Mining, and Visualization.

Data storage: Data Storage technologies help the company store data from the data sources.

Data analytics: Data Analytics technologies give insights or test hypothesis or models from a data set.[13] The idea is to create business decisions from the data available.
Analytics can be used on both structured and unstructured data.

Data mining: Data mining is the process of posing various queries and achieving actionable information, patterns, and trends from Big Data, which are possibly stored in databases (Thuraisingham, 1998). Unlike Analytics, data mining aims to find hidden patterns or correlations rather than test models.
Data mining is also mostly done on structured data.

Data visualization: Data Visualization tools aim to provide a simple overview of complex data. It is the preferred method for data predictions and forecasting.

(b) Popular Tools/Software Available
Table 3.3 summarizes the popular tools or software in Big Data technology.

---

[13]Educba (2020). Difference Between Data Mining vs Data Analysis. Retrieved from https://www.educba.com/data-mining-vs-data-analysis/.

Table 3.3:   Popular tools/software available.

Tools/Software	Domain	Main Functions
Hadoop	Storage	Hadoop is a collection of open-source software that aims to solve Big Data problems using a network of many computers using the MapReduce programming model. It is one of the more prominent tools in Big Data. The core of Hadoop lies in its storage domain, known as the HDFS.
MongoDB	Storage	MongoDB is a NoSQL database program that supports field, range, and regular-expression queries. At its core, it is a database that allows data scientists to run their applications across the platform. MongoDB is developed and maintained by MongoDB Inc.
Hunk	Storage	Hunk's specialty is accessing data through remote Hadoop clusters through virtual indexes and other search processing languages like Splunk. Such "hunks" of data can then be reported or analyzed based on their needs.
Cassandra	Storage	Cassandra is a free, open-source, NoSQL distributed database management system. Its distributed nature has built-in fault tolerance as it follows no single point of failure mechanism.
Presto	Data mining	Presto can be used to query data from Storage domains using its popular open-source and SQL-based distributed query engine. Netflix and Facebook are companies that make use of the Presto data mining domain.
ElasticSearch	Data mining	ElasticSearch is an essential part of the ELK stack (ElasticSearch, Logstash, Kibana) to allow users to take data from any source to search, analyze and visualize in real-time. LinkedIn and Google are companies that use the ElasticSearch data mining domain.
Apache Kafka	Analytics	Apache Kafka is an asynchronous messaging broker system used for data processing or real-time streaming data. It is one of the most popular streaming platforms and boasts Spotify and Twitter users.

Table 3.3: (*Continued*)

Tools/Software	Domain	Main Functions
Splunk	Analytics	Splunk is an analytics domain used to capture, correlate, and index real-time streaming data and generate reports, graphs, and other visualization outputs.
Apache Spark	Analytics	Now considered one of the more prominent technologies, Apache Spark uses Spark Streaming, which batches and windows operations to process and handle real-time streaming data and create data frames. This allows for flexibility in the output. It also features in-memory computing techniques, distinguishing it from other analytics domains.
R	Analytics	R is a programming language catering to data analytics, making it extremely popular amongst data scientists and miners.
Tableau	Visualization	Tableau is a data visualization tool that makes data analysis more efficient, and visualizations are created in the form of worksheets and dashboards.
Plotly	Visualization	Plotly is mainly used for creating graphs. Interactive graphs are also possible to be made with this domain.

3.5 Big Data Applications

3.5.1 *Big Data in Finance*

Big Data has become a core part of the financial services sector and continues to drive innovation. From peer-to-peer lending to digital currencies, all these services produce a vast amount of data for Big Data to thrive. In some finance areas, Big Data shows that the industry has seen accelerated growth with innovative solutions and can survive on smaller margins.

Learning Objectives
• Understand how Big Data is affecting financial service industries.

Main Takeaways

Main Points
• Big Data has implications in the financial industry across three main areas such as financial markets and company growth, internet finance and related value creation, and financial and risk management.

Main Terms
- **Big Data:** A term for massive data sets having large, more varied, and complex structures.

(a) Big Data in Finance

Big Data had implications on the financial industry in three main areas such as financial markets and company growth, internet finance and related value creation, and financial and risk management (Hasan *et al.*, 2020).

Financial markets and company growth: Market efficiency results from the amount of information in circulation and its spread (Chen and Yu, 2018). Web 2.0 has undoubtedly contributed to the information side, with millions of pieces of information regarding financial markets being generated every day (Bollen *et al.*, 2011). Big Data helps aggregate and explain these data entries as it is not feasible for humans to interpret such large amounts of data. Return predictions, volume analysis, option pricing, and other financial indicators are all handled and influenced by Big Data now.

Surprisingly, Big Data offers positive impacts on big companies' growth because of their extensive history and economic activity generating exponentially more data than their smaller peers (Begenau *et al.*, 2018). Such companies also attract more analyst attention and reduce uncertainties (from their long history) and the unexpected consequences of an increasingly connected world.

Internet finance and its value creation: Hasan *et al.* (2020) also discuss how Big Data has revolutionized financial services, especially how they provide relevant financial services. As an example, technology has modernized financial access by providing internet applications and e-wallets to make cashless payments the norm rather than the exception. These applications and internet banking fuel the information explosion by producing massive data every day.

Credit service departments have also been impacted. With an increasing number of digital transactions, credit-scoring companies now benefit from an increased amount of data to create a more accurate credit score for their customers. For example, Zhima Credit (also known as Sesame Credit) is a private credit-scoring program that uses data from Alibaba's services to compile user's credit profiles. Such innovation cannot be possible without the advent of Web 2.0 and Big Data analytics.

Financial and risk management: Finally, Big Data also helps companies to analyze risk better. Again, theoretically, the model's quality improves with more information, allowing more refined tuning of risk mechanisms (Choi and Lambert, 2017). Big Data analysis can also interpret the data and provide solutions faster than traditional methods.

3.5.2 *Big Data for Big Problems — Others*

The global Big Data market size revenue is forecasted to grow from US$35 billion in 2017 to US$103 billion in 2027,[14] with a compound annual growth rate of 11% over 10 years. As more and more Big Data analysis applications are found, the technology demand will only continue to rise from here.

Learning Objectives
- Understand a few of the Big Data applications across various industries.

Main Takeaways

Main Points
- **Big Data can be applied in many ways, including but not limited to the following industries:** Banking and finance, media and entertainment, and healthcare and insurance.

Main Terms
- **Recommendation engines:** Information filtering systems that aim to categorize users and predict their preference and rating towards its products and services.

(a) Banking and Finance Industry
Fraud detection: In the United States, the Securities Exchange Commission (SEC) utilizes Big Data to monitor financial market activities for unusual trading activities or potential fraud incidents. Big Data's ability to analyze vast volumes of data allows the SEC to spread the net wider instead of using smaller samples for their investigations. Additionally, the variety of data sources is also a boon to identify trends

---

[14]Statista (2018). Big Data Market Size Revenue Forecast Worldwide from 2011 to 2027. Retrieved from https://www.statista.com/statistics/254266/global-big-data-market-forecast/.

and correlations that were not previously present in more traditional data sets.

Algorithm trading: Big Data processing is a core tool that traders in the finance industry use to include more factors and inputs into their multifactor models. Such Big Data analysis is another way for such companies to chase the elusive alpha of potential investments and stay one step ahead.

(b) Media and Entertainment Industry
Recommendation engines: Media and entertainment companies such as YouTube and Netflix use recommendation engines to suggest videos or songs that the user might like. Recommendation engines are analytical tools that parse through tons of user history (a vast data source) to find keywords or important tags. Using their algorithms, identify their products that you might like.

(c) Healthcare and Insurance Industry
Healthcare providers: As evidenced in other industries, Big Data analytics can provide efficient solutions and answers to any problem when there is sufficient data. Healthcare providers can use Big Data analytics to provide a more targeted and customized user experience and conduct better stock preparations for seasonal infections from the trend analysis that Big Data can provide.

Insurance: The insurance industry, at its core, is about understanding and managing risk. Suppose the company can understand each customer better. In that case, it might assess the individual's risk with more precision and thus offer products more suited to the customer's needs. Insurers have always used data to predict outcomes and suggest a price for their policies. With data from both public and private sources, the companies can calculate risk more accurately and offer more competitively priced and appropriate insurance for their customer base.

3.6 Advantages and Disadvantages of Big Data

3.6.1 *The Advantages*

Many companies are now using Big Data to improve their core competencies further. Outlined below are a few advantages that a company may have when using this new asset class.

Learning Objectives
- Understand various key advantages that Big Data provides to companies.

Main Takeaways

Main Points
- Some of the critical advantages that Big Data provides include: better decision-making, increased productivity, improved customer service, fraud detection, and more significant innovation.

Main Terms
- **Fraud detection:** A set of processes and analyses that allow businesses to identify and prevent unauthorized activity.

(a) Advantages of Big Data
Below are some advantages that Big Data brings to companies.

Better decision-making: According to a survey by NewVantage[15] partners in 2018, developing advanced Big Data analysis tools to support business decision-making was the most common reason why companies invest in Big Data. It was also the reason for the highest success rate objectively. 36% of the respondents listed improving business decisions as their "top objective of Big Data and AI investments", with 84% surveyed investing in this objective with a 69% success rate.

For example, data analytics regarding consumer's Google searches for a specific product or service can help business owners understand their customer demographic better, potentially improving marketing efforts (Jeble *et al.*, 2018).

Increased productivity: A survey by Syncsort[16] found that 60% of respondents used Big Data analytics tools like Spark and Hadoop to increase their workforce productivity. Such tools allow analysts to analyze more data at a more efficient rate, improving their workflow. The insights

---

[15]NewVantage Partners (2018). Big Data Executive Survey 2018. Retrieved from http://newvantage.com/wp-content/uploads/2018/01/Big-Data-Executive-Survey-2018-Findings.pdf.
[16]Datamation (2018). Big Data Pros and Cons. Retrieved from https://www.datamation.com/big-data/big-data-pros-and-cons.html.

they gather can also translate into decisions quicker. As a result, they are bringing positive impacts to other associated departments.

Improved customer service: The NewVantage survey found that improving customer service was the second most common top objective for using Big Data and their associated analytics tools, with 23% of respondents listing it as their principal objective. Out of the 65% of respondents whose companies invested in the objective, 53% found success in their ventures.

An example of how Big Data can improve customer service would be to churn and analyze customer feedback throughout the product or service life cycle. Given the volumes of complaints, queries, or opinions that the customers raise, it would not be feasible for a human workforce to resolve all the feedback meanings. However, with Big Data analytics, trends can be quickly found, and pain points can be readily identified, improving the customer's experiences significantly.

Fraud detection: Big Data analytics can help companies conduct fraud detection by analyzing customer and staff behavior on a grand scale, thereby further preventing potential leakages of information or criminal activities. Big Data analytics's ability to draw from its voluminous data and provide fraudulent behavior patterns can help companies detect fraud in real-time.

Fraud detection has significant ramifications across industries, but it is especially pertinent to companies with chronic issues involving fraudulent statements. Two examples are the issue with fake medical claims for insurance companies and the company's internal audit department that needs to monitor fraudulent behavior across many departments.

Greater innovation: Finally, Big Data analysis contributes to the innovation of companies. Companies that have been making attempts to integrate various types of data, especially the unstructured data, into their operations is a sign of innovation. The insights that such analysis uncovers are another motivation for companies to innovate.

Knowledge is worthless without action taken based on the learnings. Thus, Big Data analysis cannot be considered to be completed unless measures are taken based on learnings from the knowledge gained by the data sets and interpretation.

3.6.2 *The Disadvantages*

Nevertheless, Big Data analytics also has some cons to its usage. This section will briefly outline a few of the key areas.

Learning Objectives
• Understand various disadvantages that companies face when using Big Data

Main Takeaways

Main Points
• Some primary challenges for Big Data include the following: need for new talent, data quality, compliance, cybersecurity risk, hardware needs, and costs.

Main Terms
• **Data quality:** "Garbage in, garbage out." Data is of high quality means the data is fit for the intended purpose of use, or the data correctly represent the real-world construct that the data describes.
• **Cyber attack:** It is an assault launched by cybercriminals using one or more computers against computers or networks.

(a) Need for New Talent
Data scientists and experts are a new talent area becoming more sought after. Currently, there is a shortage of competent data scientists, which makes hiring them a more challenging and more costly process for companies. While this is good news for the data scientists, it is a bad situation for the companies competing for scarce human resources. Hiring and paying competitive wages for quality data scientists and experts will be costly.

(b) Data Quality
In the Syncsort survey, a significant disadvantage of working with Big Data was addressing data quality issues. As the saying goes: "garbage in, garbage out." Data is of high quality, which means the data is fit for the intended purpose of use, or the data correctly represent the real-world construct that the data describes.[17] Data scientists need to ensure that the

---

[17] Profisee (2020). Data Quality — What, Why, How, 10 Best Practices & More! Retrieved from https://profisee.com/data-quality-what-why-how-who/.

source data has a reasonable rating for Veracity and Value. The 5Vs of Big Data need to be present for the source data to be usable.

(c) Compliance

Government regulation is also increasing in strictness as privacy concerns increase. Personal data from clients need to be authorized by each client before usage as the government recognizes that unauthorized use goes against its citizens' rights. Companies need to ensure that their data usage is both legal and ethical.

(d) Cybersecurity Risk

Storing Big Data can make a system more susceptible to cyberattacks. This is especially true when the data pertains to sensitive information, such as client details. A survey by AtScale (2018)[18] suggests that the top concern for companies regarding Big Data is the security risk it might entail.

(e) Hardware Needs

Big Data analytics requires a significant IT infrastructure to support the gathering, processing and analyzing the data. The sizeable computing power required will naturally scale with the amount of computing and processing power the company needs, which is also proportional to its size. Better analysis needs more data and, thus, more robust infrastructure. The computers also need to be maintained; therefore, a higher upkeep cost will be expected.[19]

Legacy systems are also complicated to integrate with Big Data systems. The cost to change such systems to be Big Data compatible could prove troublesome to companies not prepared to conduct an IT system overhaul.

(f) Costs

As listed above, the extra staffing and hardware requirements are just some of the additional costs that a company needs to bear to use Big Data analysis technologies. This is a case of "the rich getting richer" as larger

---

[18]AtScale (2018). Big Data Maturity Survey. Retrieved from https://www.atscale.com/resource/survey_2018_big_data_maturity_survey/.

[19]SMBCEO (2019). What are the Costs of Big Data? Retrieved from http://www.smbceo.com/2019/09/04/what-are-the-costs-of-big-data/.

companies have more capital to invest in such analytic tools and people, thus gaining a more significant lead on smaller companies who do not have the financial means to invest in such tech.

3.7 Trends and Challenges of Big Data

3.7.1 *Trends and Challenges*

Outlined below are a few trends and challenges of Big Data.

Learning Objectives
- Understand the trends and challenges of Big Data.

Main Takeaways

Main Points
- The transparency trend describes how data privacy and company hoarding are limitations that companies need to address to achieve more accessible and timely data.
- The decision-making trend describes how companies need a structure to execute and apply Big Data solutions properly.
- Information development describes how companies should be more creative in using data received, even if it is not relevant to their usage, and how data quality needs to be continually improving.

Main Terms
- **Data-driven:** It means making strategic decisions based on data analysis and interpretation.

As mentioned above, data is instrumental in many industries, ranging from manufacturing to entertainment. With data becoming more abundant and various in scope, source, and variety, the insights that can be garnered from analyzing them can prove beneficial to the companies that invest in such Big Data technologies. Outlined below are some trends and challenges in the Big Data world.

(a) Transparency
Both the governments and company greed are contesting the easy availability of data. Governments are pushing for further privacy requirements

for their citizens, making data harder to acquire. Furthermore, companies are notoriously guilty of hoarding data. Big Data analytics cannot churn out solutions as quickly or as efficiently without a sufficient volume of data. Thus, this is a challenge that companies will have to face in the short and long-term moving forward.

(b) Decision-Making — Efficient Management

As the world economy continues to increase in pace and transformation speed, it becomes increasingly important to rely on data-driven strategies to stay ahead of the pack in competitiveness. Companies need to develop proper procedures in place to be able to efficiently make use of the solutions provided by Big Data analytics in a timely fashion.

(c) Information Development

As the technology for processing Big Data continues to improve, the data sources are also set to experience an increase in both cross-industry and inter-industry. For example, a transportation company might receive a lot of information about global shipments primarily based on local deliveries. Such data can be sold to global shipping companies that would gladly use it for their analytics. This feeds into the transparency trend, and as more data is shared, the insights would improve.

Data quality is also essential. The 5Vs will continue to be the hallmark of good Big Data, and thus improving these characteristics will make the solutions more actionable, agile, and accurate.

References/Further Readings

AtScale (2018). Big Data Maturity Survey. Retrieved from https://www.atscale.com/resource/survey_2018_big_data_maturity_survey/.

Begenau, J., Farboodi, M., & Veldkamp, L. (2018). Big Data in Finance and the Growth of Large Firms. *Journal of Monetary Economics*, **97**, 71–87.

Bollen, J., Mao, H., & Zeng, X. (2011). Twitter Mood Predicts the Stock Market. *Journal of Computational Science*, **2**(1), 1–8.

Chen, S.H. & Yu, T. (2018). Big Data in Computational Social Sciences and Humanities: An Introduction. In *Big Data in Computational Social Science and Humanities* (pp. 1–25). Springer, Cham.

Choi, T. & Lambert, J.H. (2017). Advances in Risk Analysis with Big Data, doi:10.1111/risa.12859.

Hasan, M.M., Popp, J., & Oláh, J. (2020). Current Landscape and Influence of Big Data on Finance. *Journal of Big Data*, 7(1), 1–17.

Hiba *et al.* (2015). Big Data and Five V's Characteristics. Working paper. Retrieved from https://www.researchgate.net/publication/332230305_BIG_DATA_AND_FIVE_V'S_CHARACTERISTICS.

Jeble, S., Kumari, S., & Patil, Y. (2018). Role of Big Data in Decision Making, doi:10.31387/oscm0300198.

Short, J., Bohn, R., & C. Chaitanya Baru (2010). Enterprise Server Information How Much Information? Retrieved from https://www.clds.info/uploads/1/2/0/5/120516768/hmi_2010_enterprisereport_jan_2011.pdf.

Thuraisingham, B. (1998). *Data Mining: Technologies, Techniques, Tools, and Trends*. CRC Press.

Yaseen, O. (2020). Big Data: Definition, Architecture & Applications, doi:10.30630/joiv.4.1.292.

3.8 Sample Questions

Question 1
Which of the following statements are true?

 (i) Big Data is costly and should not be invested in
 (ii) Big Data has high costs, but the pros generally outweigh the cons
(iii) Big Data is entirely different from traditional data
(iv) Big Data is a subset of traditional data

(a) i and iii
(b) ii and iv
(c) i and iv

Question 2
A PDF file of an essay includes some information about the time it was created and the author's name. It is an example of:

(a) Structured data
(b) Unstructured data
(c) Semi-structured data

Question 3
A company that has stored 10 terabytes of data is said to have a higher
_____ than a company that only has 1 terabyte of data.

(a) Veracity
(b) Volume
(c) Value

Question 4
What is true about the Velocity of Big Data?

(a) Simple data has a higher velocity than more complex data
(b) Velocity refers to the amount of data available for the company to use
(c) A lower velocity is better as it is easier to manage

Question 5
Which of the following statements are true?

(a) Big Data does not require significant IT upgrades for typical
    companies.
(b) IT infrastructure is a costly upfront expenditure only.
(c) Big Data infrastructure can be costly to implement and maintain if its
    current infrastructure is not ready or compatible.

Question 6
Which of the following is NOT how data goes through the Big Data
architecture?

(a) Data source > Data storage > Batch processing > Analytical data
    store > Analytics & Reporting
(b) Data source > Data storage > Batch processing > Analytics &
    Reporting
(c) Data source > Real-time messaging ingestion > Batch processing >
    Analytical data store > Analytics & Reporting

Question 7
Which of the following can be a potential data source?

(i) Third party providers
(ii) Raw material suppliers
(iii) Customer sales
(iv) Staff servers

(a) i, ii. iii
(b) i, iii, iv
(c) All of the above

Question 8

What were the original 3Vs in the characteristics of Big Data?

(a) Volume, Velocity, Variety
(b) Veracity, Velocity, Volume
(c) Veracity, Volume, Variety

Question 9

Which of the following is NOT a domain of Big Data tools/software?

(a) Data storage
(b) Analytics
(c) Virtualization

Question 10

What is true about Big Data applications?

(a) Only technology companies can use Big Data as only they have the technology to use it.
(b) Fraud Detection is not a useful application of Big Data.
(c) Big Data is used to provide more precise and tailored products for customers.

Solutions

Question 1

Solution: Option **b** is correct.

Big Data generally has more pros than cons, and is a subset of traditional data.

Question 2

Solution: Option **c** is correct.

A PDF file by itself is an example of unstructured data. With the metadata, it becomes a semi-structured data file.

Question 3

Solution: Option **b** is correct.

Volume refers to the size of data available for the company to use.

Question 4

Solution: Option **a** is correct.

B refers to volume. C is not true as a higher velocity is preferable.

Question 5

Solution: Option **c** is correct.

Big Data requires significant IT infrastructure, which also has significant upkeep.

Question 6

Solution: Option **c** is correct.

Real-time data sources are processed through Stream Processing instead of batch processing.

Question 7

Solution: Option **c** is correct.

Almost all aspects of a company's operations can be a data source, so Big Data is so ubiquitous to all companies.

Question 8

Solution: Option **a** is correct.

Volume, Velocity, Variety were the original Vs of big data.

Question 9

Solution: Option **c** is correct.

Visualization is a domain, not virtualization.

Question 10

Solution: Option **c** is correct.

Big Data is applicable to multiple industries, of which fraud detection features prominently in the finance industry.

Chapter 4

Data Science

4.1 Introduction

4.1.1 *Definition and History of Data Science*

Learning Objectives
- Understand the definition and brief history of Data Science.

Main Takeaways

Main Points
- Data Science unifies the power of multiple areas, including mathematics, statistics, computer science, data analysis, machine learning, Big Data, domain knowledge, and information science to extract knowledge and insights.

Main Terms
- **Data Science:** This is a multidisciplinary field that uses scientific methods, processes, algorithms, and systems to extract knowledge and insights from various data types.

(a) Definition
Data Science is defined as a multidisciplinary field that uses scientific methods, processes, algorithms, and systems to extract knowledge and insights from various data types. Data Science unifies the power of multiple areas, including mathematics, statistics, computer science, data analysis, machine learning, Big Data, domain knowledge, and information science to extract knowledge and insights.

(b) History

The term "Data Science" has only recently been introduced to denote a profession (Press, 2013) relating to Big Data analytics' growing field.

However, Data Science is not a new term. It was initially from statistics and outlined by John W. Tukey in his article *The Future of Data Analysis* in 1962. Professor Tukey pointed out the importance of articulating the distinction between exploratory data analysis and confirmatory data analysis as the very first step in establishing the field of Data Science (Tukey, 1962).

From the 1970s to early 2000, Data Science as an independent academic field or significant division began to have a role of play in major conferences and journals, such as the International Association for Statistical Computing (IASC), *Knowledge Discovery in Databases* (KDD), *Data Science Journal* (DSJ), etc.

In 2001, Leo Breiman argued that there are two distinct cultures in data analysis in his famous paper *Statistical Modeling: The Two Cultures*: one is the data modeling culture; the other is algorithmic modeling culture. The difference between these two cultures stems from the distinction between the mainstream models used by statisticians (data model) and machine learning practitioners (algorithmic model), which is recognized as a culture shift in Data Science (Breiman, 2001).

Data Science has grown widely into many fields in the past 10 years, including businesses and organizations worldwide. Workers from different industries also benefit from its emergences, such as governments, geneticists, engineers, and even astronomers. In terms of Big Data usage, Data Science is not limited to simply scaling up the data but has also boosted the development of new systems, algorithms, and computing paradigms. In general, Data Science has been spreading quickly across different fields by the emergence of cloud computing and those who want to make complete sense of Big Data.

4.2 Data Science Pipeline

4.2.1 *Data Science Divisions and Workflow*

Learning Objectives
- Understand the six divisions of Data Science.
- Understand the general workflow of Data Science.

Main Takeaways

Main Points
- A Data Science project's general workflow includes five main elements: data gathering, data processing, modeling, deployment, and monitoring.

Main Terms
- Divisions of Data Science: David Donoho categorized the activities of Data Science into the collection, representation, computing, visualization, modeling, and scientific researching.

(a) Divisions

David Donoho (2017), in his study *50 Years of Data Science,* gave a summary of the scope of Data Science. He categorized the activities of Data Science into six divisions:

- **Data collection, preparation, and exploration:** There are various ways to gather data through traditional experimental design and modern data gathering methods such as web crawling, sensor data, social media data, etc. These data are raw data, which means it is usually impossible to analyze them directly. Data preparation is required through pre-processing activity to make it ready, called "data cleaning". It is said that 80% of the effort devoted to Data Science is expended by diving into messy data to learn the basics of what is in them, to make the data ready for further exploration (Donoho, 2017).
- **Data representation and transformation:** Data sources are various, which induces that the gathered data are in an extensive range of formats. They can be numbers, images, audio, or even video. To make them readable by the computer, an appropriate transformation restructuring of the cleaned data needs to be implemented into a more revealing form.

  In general, data can be stored in the structural form in modern databases (such as SQL) or using mathematical structures for representing data of particular types, including text, image, video, etc. The basic idea of mathematical structures is extracting features of the particular data. For example, we can extract the color, shape, and theme features of an image figure.

- **Computing with data:** This division indicates the programming languages for data analysis and data processing. These can include popular languages like R, Python, MATLAB, etc.
- **Data visualization and presentation:** This division is about "exploratory data analysis" (EDA). It uses figures or tables to show what's in the data. Commonly used methods include histograms, scatterplots, time series plots, distribution figures, pie charts, and more.
- **Data modeling:** As per Leo Breiman's modeling cultures, Data Science can model data from two viewpoints: statistics-based generative modeling and machine learning-based predictive modeling.
- **Science about Data Science:** Tukey proposed that a "science of data analysis" exists and should be recognized as among the most complicated of all sciences (Donoho, 2017). Today, data scientists are doing such *science about Data Science* study when they try to identify common data analysis/processing workflows or encode documentation of individual analysis and results in a standard format for future meta-analysis.

(b) Workflow

As one work of *science about Data Science*, Figure 4.1 shows the general workflow of a Data Science project. It has five main elements or key steps: data gathering, data processing, modeling, deployment, and monitoring.

This workflow is a cycle; in other words, the Data Science project does not end when the model is deployed to production. There will always

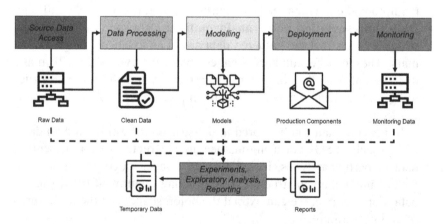

Figure 4.1: Workflow of a Data Science project.

be a need to repeat all the cycle steps because the input data may change with time.

(c) Possible Applications

Data Science workflow provides a general guideline on its applications in various fields, which include but not limited to:

- Healthcare
- Internet search
- Fraud detection
- Risk detection
- Targeting advertising
- Recommendation
- Pattern recognition
- Speech recognition
- Gaming
- Route planning and optimization

4.3 Trends and Challenges

4.3.1 *Trends and Challenges*

Learning Objectives
- Understand the main trends and challenges of Data Science.

Main Takeaways

Main Points
- Several future Data Science trends can be predicted through current situations like automation, AI explainability, cloud-based Big Data, graphing, and blockchain-based storage.
- There are some future development challenges, including real-time monitoring, data privacy, and accuracy for Data Science to conquer.

Main Terms
- **Graph database:** This is a graph database attaches equal importance to the relationship between data and data itself. Its purpose is to save data without limiting it to a pre-defined model.

(a) Trends

With the fast development of Big Data, AI, and other techniques, such as IoT and Blockchain, Data Science must usher in its new development as an interdisciplinary field. Here are several trends for Data Science.

- **Automation in Data Science:** Automation is already deployed in manufacturing facilities such as those producing self-driving cars, trucks, and more. It can be predicted that such deployment will alter the labor demand in current jobs, which is a big concern of the labor market. However, it will liberate human resources to focus on more creative and complex tasks that machines cannot do.
- **AI explainability/interpretability:** AI, especially deep learning, is recognized as a black box. While inputs and outputs can be viewed, even data scientists cannot explain how it works. However, experts can identify the decision-making process through transparent platforms in explainable/interpretable AI.
- **Cloud-based Big Data science:** Computing power on demand is very attractive to data scientists who want the resources, which helps cloud computing take Data Science by storm. In practice, cloud computing enables data scientists to access virtually limitless processing power and storage capacity from all over the world.
- **Graph databases:** As Big Data continues to march forward, complex questions about blended data sets, including structured and unstructured information, have excited many organizations. Graph databases provide the analytic ability for this level of data complexity at scale. Graph databases show how entities such as people, places, and things connect, which is a difference between their relational brethren. This technology can be applied to anti-money laundering, fraud detection, geospatial analysis, and supply chain analysis. Gartner predicts that graph databases' applications will grow at 100% annually in the near future to accelerate data preparation for more adaptive Data Science.
- **Blockchain-based data storage, sharing, and protection:** Data Science is for prediction, while blockchain is for data integrity. With blockchain, a new way of handling data is possible. The decentralized structure of blockchain has eliminated the need for the data to be centralized and paved the way for data analysis to be directly from an individual device.

Additionally, data generated through blockchain is validated, structured and immutable. Considering that the data derived from blockchain is ensured of integrity, it enhances Data Science.[1] Nevertheless, it is still too expensive to store and calculate data on the blockchain. Therefore, while it is a general trend to enhance blockchain's Data Science capability, it is challenging.

(b) Challenges

As an application tool, Data Science has its nature challenges in its practice.[2]

- **Finding the right data:** Taking data's large volume and velocity into account, one of the biggest challenges is making sense of all data and driving profitable business decisions. It cannot be denied that a large volume of data tends to move the focus away from actionability and even lead to data paralysis. Therefore, it is wise to correct the noise and make a robust analytical model. That is, data cleaning is necessary for accurate models.
- **Real-time modeling and monitoring:** People may feel faint-hearted when thinking about the entire process of adopting Data Science solutions to execution. Still, it is essential to enable your models to solve real-time challenges.
- **Agility:** Unfortunately, most analytical functions are structured to ignore adequate interaction with the end business user. In response, many experts have recommended that a business should be more agile during the decision-making process using analytical models.
- **Data security and privacy:** Analytics is all about handling a massive volume of data. However, it remains a puzzling challenge to ensure the security of data. Organizations need to ensure privacy and take necessary measures to impede data from improper use.
- **Lack of domain expertise:** Companies today are still struggling to build the right team while ensuring the proper infrastructure of hardware and software implementation, which induces the need for workers who can carry out complex analytics projects and reach a balance

---

[1]Vibhuthi Viswanathan (2019). Implications of Blockchain in Data Science. Retrieved from https://www.itproportal.com/features/implications-of-blockchain-in-data-science/.

[2]Srishti Deoras (2019). 10 Challenges That Data Science Industry Still Faces. Retrieved from https://analyticsindiamag.com/10-challenges-that-data-science-industry-still-faces/.

between analytics skills and professional knowledge. In general, there is a lack of talent that has comprehensive expertise in business, statistical, and programming.

4.4 Comparison: Big Data vs. Data Science

4.4.1 *Comparison*

Learning Objectives
- Understand the relationship between Big Data and Data Science.

Main Takeaways

Main Points
- To tell Big Data and Data Science apart, we can believe that Data Science supposedly uses theoretical and practical approaches to derive information from the Big Data.

Main Terms
- **Big Data approaches:** Scientific techniques to process data, extract information, and interpret results that contribute to the decision-making process. They often power predictive analytics, and the analysis of data sets is used widely to identify business trends, prevent diseases, combat crime, and much more.
- **Data Science approaches:** This is a multidisciplinary fusion of data reasoning, algorithm development, and techniques for pre-cleaning and sorting heterogeneous data obtained through Big Data and solving other complex analytical problems.

(a) Big Data vs. Data Science
Table 4.1 shows the comparison between Big Data and Data Science from multiple dimensions:[3]

(b) Major Differences
There are several major differences between Big Data vs. Data Science summarized as follows:

---

[3]Besant Technologies (2019). Big Data vs Data Science. Retrieved from https://www.besanttechnologies.com/big-data-vs-data-science#:~:text=Big%20data%20analysis%20caters%20to,the%20pile%20of%20big%20data.

Table 4.1: Differences between Big Data and Data Science.

Basis	Data Science	Big Data
Meaning	Tends to interpret data scientifically and search information from a given dataset	Circles around the sheer volumes of data that traditional data analysis methods can't handle
Concept	Scientific techniques for pre-cleaning, sorting, and mining heterogeneous data obtained through Big Data	Scientific techniques to process data, extract information and interpret results that contribute to the decision-making process
Formation	Internet users/traffic, live feeds, and data generated from system logs	Data filtering, preparation, and analysis
Application areas	Digital advertisements, Internet search, risk detection, text-to-speech recognition, and other activities	Biotechnology, e-commerce, telecommunication, health and sports, financial service, research and development, and security
Approach	Used by businesses to help make decisions by taking advantage of mathematics and statistics widely together with programming skills to design a model to test the hypotheses	Used by businesses to track their presence in the market, which helps them gain a high degree of agility and a comparative competitive advantage

- Organizations usually use Big Data to improve work efficiency, explore undeveloped markets and enhance competitiveness. In contrast, Data Science provides modeling techniques and methods to assess Big Data's potential accurately.
- Companies can collect and utilize Big Data to implement Data Science to obtain valuable information.
- To mine information from Big Data, Data Science should make more use of theoretical and practical methods. We generally regard Big Data as a data pool, which is inconceivable before deduction and induction.
- Big Data analysis is also called data mining because it can deal with many data sets. Data Science designs and develops statistical models to obtain knowledge from Big Data stacks through machine learning algorithms.
- Data Science pays more attention to the analysis of business decision-making process, while technologies like computer tools and software are more important in Big Data.

References/Further Readings

Breiman, L. (2001). Statistical Modeling: The Two Cultures. *Statistical Science*, **16**(3), 199–231.

Donoho, D. (2017). 50 Years of Data Science. *Journal of Computational and Graphical Statistics*, **26**(4), 745–766, doi: 10.1080/10618600.2017.1384734.

Press, G. (2013). A Very Short History of Data Science. *Forbes*. Retrieved from https://www.forbes.com/sites/gilpress/2013/05/28/a-very-short-history-of-data-science/#7eace5f355cf.

Tukey, J.W. (1962). The Future of Data Analysis. *The Annals of Mathematical Statistics*, **33**(1), 1–67.

4.5 Sample Questions

Question 1
Which of the following divisions is NOT belonging to Data Science?

(a) Data modeling
(b) Computing with data
(c) Insight's deployment

Question 2
Which of the following is NOT a way that data goes through the Data Science workflow?

(a) Data gathering
(b) Data computing
(c) Monitoring

Question 3
What Data Science division does identify common data analysis/processing workflows belong to?

(a) Science about Data Science
(b) Data modeling
(c) Data representation and transformation

Question 4
Which statement of trends of Data Science in the future is not correct?

(a) It is a general trend to enhance blockchain's Data Science capability because it is still too expensive to store and calculate data on the blockchain.
(b) Cloud-based Big Data Science provides the analysis ability for blended data sets, including structured and unstructured information.
(c) One of the advantages of Automation in Data Science is it will liberate humans to focus on more creative and complex tasks that machines cannot do.

Question 5
Which of the following are NOT challenges of Data Science?

(a) Transparency and accessibility
(b) Data security and privacy
(c) Real-time modeling and monitoring

Question 6
Which statement of the significant differences between Big Data and Data Science is incorrect?

(a) Companies can utilize Big Data to implement Data Science to obtain valuable information.
(b) Big Data pay more attention to analyzing the business decision-making process.
(c) Big Data is more like a data pool, which is inconceivable before deduction and induction.

Solutions

Question 1

Solution: Option **c** is correct.

David Donoho categorized Data Science activities into the collection, representation, computing, visualization, modeling, and scientific researching.

Question 2

Solution: Option **b** is correct.

A Data Science project's general workflow has five main elements or key steps: data gathering, data pre-processing, modeling, deployment, and monitoring.

Question 3

Solution: Option **a** is correct.

Data scientists try to identify common data analysis/processing work-flows or encode documentation of individual analysis and result in a standard format for future meta-analysis.

Question 4

Solution: Option **b** is correct.

As Big Data continues to march forward, complex questions about blended data sets, including structured and unstructured information, have arisen among businesses. Graph databases provide the analysis ability for this level of data complexity at scale.

Question 5

Solution: Option **a** is correct.

As an application tool, Data Science has its nature challenges in its practice, including Finding the correct data, real-time modeling, and monitoring, agility, data security and privacy, lack of domain expertise.

Question 6

Solution: Option **b** is correct.

Data Science pays more attention to the analysis of business decision-making process, while technologies like computer tools and software are more important in Big Data.

Part III

Artificial Intelligence and Machine Learning

Chapter 5

Artificial Intelligence

5.1 Introduction of Artificial Intelligence

5.1.1 *Definition and Evolution of Artificial Intelligence*

Learning Objectives
- Understand what Artificial Intelligence (AI) is.
- Understand the brief evolution of AI and the relationship between AI, Machine Learning, and Deep Learning.
- Understand why AI obtains significant effectiveness and progress over the last decade.

Main Takeaways

Main Points
- AI is about making agents (i.e., machines or computers) mimic cognitive functions requiring the human mind or human intelligence.
- AI evolves from early symbolic AI to knowledge-based expert systems, machine learning, and today's deep learning; AI is a general field. Machine learning is a subset of AI, and deep learning is a hot branch of machine learning.
- AI obtains significant effectiveness and progress over the last decade because of Big Data availability, dramatically improved advanced algorithms, and the powerful computing ability and cloud-based services.

Main Terms

- **Symbolic AI:** The dominant AI paradigm from the 1950s to the late 1980s.
- **Machine learning:** A subset field of AI, humans input data as well as the expected answers from the data, and the machine will "learn" by itself and outcome the hidden rules.
- **Deep learning:** It automates the feature engineering of the input data and allows algorithms to automatically discover complex patterns and relationships in the input data.

(a) What is Artificial Intelligence?

Early in the 1940s and 1950s, a handful of scientists from various fields, including mathematics, psychology, engineering, economics, and political science, began to discuss the possibility of creating an artificial brain. The term "Artificial Intelligence" was coined by John McCarthy at a Dartmouth conference in 1956, and following AI research was founded as an academic discipline.

The main unifying theme of AI is the idea of an "intelligent agent". In the widely referenced book written by Russell and Norvig (2002), AI is defined as:

> "The study of agents that receive precepts from the environment and perform actions".

In general, the term "AI" is about making agents (e.g., machines or computers) mimic cognitive functions that would require the human mind or human intelligence, such as learning and perception.

(b) An Evolution History of Artificial Intelligence

AI is a broad field that evolves from early symbolic AI to knowledge-based expert systems, machine learning, and today's neural networks and deep learning. Figure 5.1 shows the evolution history of AI.

Symbolic AI (Mid-1950s–Late 1980s): At the early stage, AI-trained machines used a set of production rules. The rules are similar to an *If-Then* statement. Teaching machines to play chess was one of AI's primary research focus areas. Chess has its playing rules. Many AI experts believed that AI could be achieved by having programmers handcraft a sufficiently large set of explicit rules for manipulating knowledge.

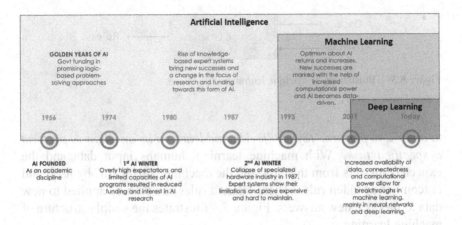

Figure 5.1: Evolution of AI.

Source: IMDA and Lee (2020).

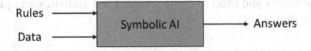

Figure 5.2: Illustration of Symbolic AI.

These rules are human-readable representations of problems and logic. "Symbolic AI" was developed during this period, and it was the dominant AI paradigm from the 1950s to the late 1980s. Figure 5.2 illustrates how Symbolic AI works.

Symbolic AI peaked during the "Expert Systems" booms of the 1980s. Expert systems are logical and knowledge-based approaches. Their power came from the expert knowledge they contained, but it also limited the further development of expert systems. The knowledge acquisition problem, knowledge base increasing, and updates issues are all the significant challenges of expert systems. In the 1990s and beyond, the term expert system mostly dropped from the IT lexicon. A new type of AI approach was required to take over rule-based technologies at that time.

Machine learning (1990s–Now): Machine learning, a subset field of AI, started to flourish in the 1990s. Unlike symbolic AI, machine learning does not require humans to understand the existing rules proficiently. It arises from this question: *could a computer go beyond 'what we know how*

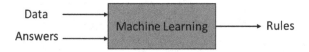

Figure 5.3: Illustration of machine learning.

Source: Francois (2017).

to order it to perform' (Symbolic AI), and learn on its own how to perform a specified task? With machine learning, humans input data and the expected answers from the data, and the machine will "learn" by itself and outcome the hidden rules. These learned rules can then be applied to new data to produce new answers. Figure 5.3 illustrates the simple structure of machine learning.

From the 1990s, AI changed its goal from achieving AI problem sets to tackling solvable problems of a practical nature. It shifted focus away from the symbolic approaches it had inherited from AI and toward constructing methods and models by leveraging the statistics and probability theory (Langley, 2011).

Deep learning (2011–Now): Following a series of ups and downs, often referred to as the "AI summers and winters", the interest in AI has alternately grown and diminished.[1] In the AI evolution roadmap, AI is a general field that covers machine learning. Deep learning is a hot branch of machine learning, which symbolizes the booming AI landscape from about 9 years ago.

Compared to machine learning, deep learning automates the feature engineering of the input data (the process of learning the optimal features of the data to create the best outcome) and allows algorithms to automatically discover complex patterns and relationships from the input data. Deep learning is based on artificial neural networks (ANNs), inspired by information processing and distributed communication nodes in biological systems, similar to human brains.

Figure 5.4 shows the information processing framework of the human brain and ANNs. ANN imitates the human brain's process by using multiple layers to progressively extract different levels of feature/interpretation from input data. In nature, deep learning algorithms *learn how to learn.*

---

[1]World Intellectual Property Organization (WIPO) (2019). WIPO Technology Trends 2019 — Artificial Intelligence.

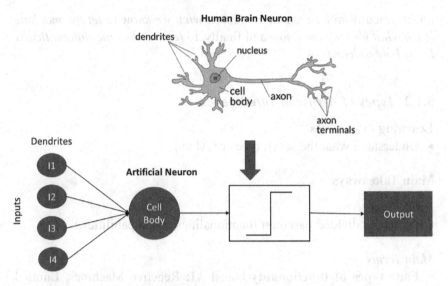

Figure 5.4: Human brain and neural network.

Source: What is neuron and artificial neuron in deep learning? MPLSVPN, November 2017.

Although AI research started early in the 1950s, its effectiveness and progress have been most significant over the last decade, driven by three mutually reinforcing factors:[2]

- **Big Data availability:** Various data sources including businesses, e-commerce, social media, science, wearable devices, government, etc.
- **Dramatical improvement of advanced algorithms:** The sheer amount of available data accelerates algorithm innovation.
- **More powerful computing ability and cloud-based services:** Make it possible to realize and implement advanced AI algorithms, like deep neural networks.

Significant progress in algorithms, hardware, and Big Data technology, combined with the financial incentives to find new products, have also contributed to the AI technology renaissance. Today, AI has

---

[2]Artificial Intelligence: A Primer, Garage Technology Ventures.

transformed from *let the machine learn what we know* to *let the machine learn what we may not know* and finally, to *let the machine automatically learn how to learn.*

5.1.2 *Types of Artificial Intelligence*

Learning Objectives
• Understand what the seven types of AI are.

Main Takeaways

Main Points
• AI can be divided based on functionalities and capabilities.[3]

Main Terms
• **Four types of functionality-based AI:** Reactive Machines, Limited Memory, Theory of Mind, and Self-Aware.
• **Three types of capability-based AI:** Artificial Narrow Intelligence (ANI), Artificial General Intelligence (AGI), and Artificial Super-intelligence (ASI).

AI is the process of imitating the human brain to build intelligent machines from vast volumes of data. Therefore, based on the machine's likeness to the human mind, and their ability to "think" and "act" like humans, AI can be classified into reactive machines, limited memory machines, theory of mind, and self-aware AI.[4]

• **Reactive machines:** It is the most basic types and also the oldest forms of AI systems that perceive the world directly and act on what it sees. These machines do not have memory-based functionality. In other words, they cannot "learn" from the previously gained experiences to guide their present actions. Therefore, they are purely reactive.
  A popular example of a reactive AI machine is IBM's Deep Blue, a chess-playing supercomputer who beat grandmaster Garry Kasparov in 1997. It did not take any pre-applied datasets or look for previous

---

[3]7 Types of Artificial Intelligence That You Should Know in 2020, Simplilearn, January 2021.
[4]7 Types of Artificial Intelligence, *Forbes*, June 2019.

matches. All it knows was how to play the game and the conditions. The computer moved chess coins based on its real-time intuition and won the game.[5]

- **Limited memory:** Limited memory AI systems are machines with two capabilities. They can be purely reactive machines capable of utilizing past data to make decisions. Limited memory machines are incredibly profound in our daily lives. The use of datasets characterizes them. For example, machines can be trained under deep learning domains by the extensive library of historical data saved in their memory dataset. By training using past historical data, pre-empt the machines to solve future data. The assumption underlined in this principle is that historical data serves as a reliable reference for the future. An application of this is in image recognition. Image recognition AI is trained using a large number of pictures. It can name different objects it comes into contact with by recognizing many pictures. The machine can also utilize its training images to draw references and understand the new images presented to them. With additional learning, the machine's analytics capabilities can be enhanced. This technology is widely adopted in Ai systems, ranging from chatbots, virtual assistance to self-driving vehicles.

- **Theory of mind:** The theory of mind AI system represents an advanced class of technology and exists only as a concept for now. This technology area remains crucial in its application of sorting human emotions, sentiments, and thoughts. Despite the progress in this technology line, it is not fully completed. To achieve a functional theory of mind AI, progress in other AI areas is just as important. The reason behind this is due to the complicated nature of human emotions. To comprehend human emotional needs, AI machines need to grasp many different factors that constitute human emotions.

- **Self-aware:** It is believed that self-awareness is the final stage of AI development which currently exists only hypothetically. As the terminology suggests, self-awareness refers to a state of self-awareness attained by the machine that is akin to our human level of self-awareness. This self-awareness level empowers the machine to display similar emotions akin to human beings. In addition to showing them, the device itself can also comprehend emotions, needs, beliefs, and

---

[5] 7 Types of Artificial Intelligence: Propelling the Technology Development, Analytics Insight, December 2020.

desires it came across during its interaction with others. The development of such technology is a double-edged sword.

On the one hand, it can lead to a more significant enhancement of our self-awareness. On the other hand, such a level of awareness attained by the machine breaches an ethical concern. To some, it meant that the machines could potentially outsmart human beings and seek to replace us eventually. However, this pessimistic scenario is still far-fetched and will not be realized in the short term.

The alternate classification of AI is more generally used in tech parlance, which is based on the capabilities of the AI system: ANI, AGI, and ASI.

- **Artificial narrow intelligence:** All the existing AI systems, including the most complex deep learning, belong to this type of AI. It refers to the machines that can only perform a specific task autonomously using human-like capabilities, no matter how complicated the job is. These machines can do nothing more than what they have been programmed to do and thus have a very limited or narrow range of competencies.

  According to the system mentioned above of classification, ANI corresponds to all the Reactive Machines and Limited Memory AI.

- **Artificial general intelligence:** AGI refers to a series of cognitive functions possessed by AI similar to human beings. These functions may include learning, perception, and understanding. The benefit of AGI lies in reducing training time. This is because machines are now capable of functioning independently and competently. Instead of this, machines will learn and draw links between information across different domains, with a remarkable resemblance to our human thought process.

- **Artificial superintelligence:** ASI refers to the highest artificial intelligence level. Apart from being the most advanced AI, ASI also can end the human race. ASI will not stop at duplicating human cognitive abilities. They are also likely to exceed our analysis, decision-making, and data processing capabilities.

5.1.3 *Theoretical Basics of AI*

Learning Objectives
- Understand the concepts of probability theory and information theory.
- Understand that optimization plays a fundamental role in AI and ML.

Main Takeaways

Main Points

- Probability theory is a mathematical framework for representing uncertain statements.
- Probability theory provides a means of quantifying uncertainty and axioms for driving new uncertain statements.
- Information theory provides a means of quantifying uncertainty in a probability distribution.

Main Terms

- **Uncertainty:** Non-deterministic qualities where machine learning techniques have to deal with.
- **Random variables:** Variables that can take on different values randomly.
- **Probability distributions:** The probability that random variables take on a specific state.
- **Information theory:** Branch of applied mathematics that quantifies how much information is present in a signal.

(a) What is Uncertainty?

Machine learning must always deal with uncertain quantities and sometimes stochastic (non-deterministic) quantities. Uncertainty and stochasticity can arise from many sources, and so nearly all activities require some ability to reason in the presence of uncertainty. Beyond mathematical statements that are true by definition, it isn't easy to think of any true proposition or event guaranteed to occur.

There are three possible sources of uncertainty:

1. Inherent stochasticity in the system being modeled,
2. Incomplete observability, and
3. Incomplete modeling.

In many cases, it is more practical to use a simple but uncertain rule rather than a complex but certain one, even if the true rule is deterministic. The modeling system has the fidelity to accommodate a complex rule. For example, the simple rule "Most birds fly" is cheap to develop and is broadly applicable. While a rule of the form, "Birds fly, except for very young birds that have not yet learned to fly, sick or injured birds that have lost the ability to fly, flightless species of birds including the casso-wary, ostrich, and kiwi ..." is expensive to develop, maintain and communicate.

Probability can be seen as the extension of logic to deal with uncertainty. Logic provides a set of formal rules for determining what propositions are implied to be true or false, given the assumption that some other set of propositions is true or false. Probability theory provides a set of formal rules for determining the likelihood of a proposition being true, given the likelihood of other propositions.

(b) Random Variables

A random variable is a variable that can take on different values randomly. We typically denote the random variable itself with a lowercase letter in plain typeface and the values it can take on lowercase script letters. For example, x_1 and x_2 are both possible values that the random variable x can take on. For vector-valued variables, we would write the random variable as x and one of its values as x. On its own, a random variable is just a description of the states that are possible; it must be coupled with a probability distribution that specifies how likely each of these states is.

Random variables may be discrete or continuous. A discrete random variable has a finite or countably infinite number of states. Note that these states are not necessarily the integers; they can also just be named states that are not considered to have any numerical value. A continuous random variable is associated with a real value.

(c) Probability Distributions

A probability distribution is a description of how likely a random variable or set of random variables is to take on each of its possible states. We describe probability distributions depending on whether the variables are discrete or continuous.

(d) Information Theory

Information theory is a branch of applied mathematics that revolves around quantifying how much information is present in a signal. It was initially invented to study messages using discrete alphabets over a noisy channel, such as radio transmission. In this context, information theory tells how to design optimal codes and calculate the expected length of messages sampled from specific probability distributions using various encoding schemes. We can also apply information theory to continuous variables in machine learning where some of these message length interpretations do not apply.

The basic intuition behind information theory is that learning that an unlikely event has occurred is more informative than learning that a likely event has occurred. A message saying "the sun rose this morning" is so uninformative as unnecessary to send, but a message saying "there was a solar eclipse this morning" is very informative.

We would like to quantify information in a way that formalizes this intuition.

- Likely, events should have low information content, and in extreme cases, events that are guaranteed to happen should have no information content whatsoever.
- Less likely events should have higher information content.
- Independent events should have additive information. For example, finding out that a tossed coin has come up as heads twice should convey twice as much information as finding out that a tossed coin has come up as heads once.

(e) Optimization

If we look at the mathematics behind the AI or ML models, it is not hard to realize that they all somehow come down to an optimization problem.[6] An optimization problem is selecting the best solution out of the many available alternatives under some constraints or restrictions. For instance, in machine learning, the least square estimation used in the ordinary linear regression is essentially trying to optimize the model's coefficients, which have the closest fit to the data set. The fundamental concept of AI and ML is to predict target parameters, and the optimization is to find the best estimate of the parameter.

For instance, in neural network training, optimization is used to find the best parameter configuration for each layer.[7] Understanding the optimization concept will help understand an AI algorithm's underlying

---

[6]joelbarmettlerUZH (October 10, 2019). ML Fundamentals: Optimization problems and how to solve them. Retrieved from https://medium.com/swlh/ml-fundamentals-optimization-problems-and-how-to-solve-them-572c6ddf0a0b.

[7]Aiden. G. (November 25, 2020). Optimization: The Intuitive Process at the Core of AI. Retrieved from https://medium.com/swlh/optimization-the-intuitive-process-at-the-core-of-ai-10b15df14949.

mechanisms. Here are some further readings about how optimization is applied in AI algorithms.[8,9]

References/Further Readings

Francois, C. (2017). *Deep Learning with Python*. Manning Publications Co., NY, USA.

Infocomm Media Development Authority (IMDA) & Lee, K.C. (2020). *Artificial Intelligence, Data and Blockchain in a Digital Economy*, 1st ed. World Scientific, Singapore.

Langley, P. (2011). The Changing Science of Machine Learning. *Machine Learning*, **82**(3), 275–279.

Russell, S., & Norvig, P. (2002). *Artificial Intelligence: A Modern Approach*. Prentice-Hall, Inc. New Jersey, U.S.

5.2 Sample Questions

Question 1
Which of the following statements is not correct?

(a) AI is a general field that includes machine learning and deep learning.
(b) Deep learning is a subset of machine learning.
(c) AlphaGo is designed using Symbolic AI techniques.

Question 2
Which of the following statements on ANI is correct?

(a) ANI can do more than what they have been designed to do
(b) ANI covers all the Limited Memory AI.
(c) Existing deep learning methods do not belong to ANI.

---

[8]Lewis, K. M., Varadharajan, S., & Kemelmacher-Shlizerman, I. (2021). VOGUE: Try-On by StyleGAN Interpolation Optimization. arXiv preprint arXiv:2101.02285.

[9]Adrian, Y. X. (July 28, 2020). Playing Doom with AI: Multi-Objective Optimization with Deep Q-learning Retrieved from https://towardsdatascience.com/playing-doom-with-ai-multi-objective-optimization-with-deep-q-learning-736a9d0f8c2.

Question 3

Which of the following AI products has not been realized?

(a) Self-aware robot
(b) Chatbots
(c) Self-driving vehicles

Question 4

Which is not a possible source of uncertainty in machine learning

(a) Incomplete observability
(b) Incomplete modeling
(c) High quality of data

Question 5

What is a random variable in machine learning?

(a) Random variable is a variable we cannot measure.
(b) Random variable is a variable that can take on different values randomly.
(c) Random variable is a variable we can observe but cannot describe.

Question 6

In AI, optimization problem is to _____.

(a) Search for the best data to fit the AI model.
(b) Search for the best variables to train the AI model.
(c) Search for the best estimate of an AI model's parameters to fit the data.

Question 7

Which is the following statement on information theory is correct?

(a) Information theory can only be applied to continuous variables.
(b) Learning an unlikely event has happened usually would attain more information comparing with a confirmed event.
(c) The information contained in an event is impossible to be zero.

Solutions

Question 1

Solution: Option **c** is correct.

AlphaGo is designed based on deep learning methods, not Symbolic AI.

Question 2

Solution: Option **b** is correct.

ANI is narrow AI, which covers all the Reactive Machines and Limited Memory methods, and it cannot do more than what it has been programmed to do. Existing deep learning methods belong to Limited Memory methods. Hence, they are ANI.

Question 3

Solution: Option **a** is correct.

Self-aware AI is still on the way.

Question 4

Solution: Option **c** is correct.

Noise in data is one possible reason for uncertainty. Hence, if the data is of high quality, it may not be a source of uncertainty.

Question 5

Solution: Option **b** is correct.

A random variable is a variable whose value may change randomly, but we still can observe it and represent it using a distribution.

Question 6

Solution: Option **c** is correct.

Optimization is used to select the best parameter of a model to fit the training data, that is, to find the best model that can best explain the data.

Question 7

Solution: Option **b** is correct.

Information theory can be applied to measure both discrete and continuous variables. Higher uncertainty contains more information, which confirmed event (uncertainty =0) contains no information in the information theory field.

Chapter 6

Machine Learning

6.1 Applied Math and Machine Learning Basics

6.1.1 *Machine Learning Basics*

Learning Objectives
- Understand the most important general principles of machine learning.

Main Takeaways

Main Points
- Machine learning algorithms can be categorized into four major types such as supervised, unsupervised, semi-supervised, and reinforcement learning.
- Common performance measures include accuracy, precision, recall, and F-measure.
- A model's capacity is its ability to fit a wide variety of input data.
- Underfitting occurs when the model cannot obtain a sufficiently low error value on the training set. Overfitting occurs when the gap between the training error and test error is too large.

Main Terms
- **Supervised learning:** Algorithms that are trained/taught using given data records.
- **Unsupervised learning:** Algorithms are tried to explore the given data and detect or mine the data's hidden patterns and relationships.

153

Learning is based on the similarity or distance among the given data points.

- **Performance measure:** Quantitative evaluation of a machine learning model's performance on completing its task.
- **Training and testing framework:** Widely used evaluation scheme for classification tasks.
- **Overfitting and underfitting:** Shortcomings that the model might have.
- **Generalization:** The ability to perform well on unseen inputs.

(a) Introduction

A machine learning algorithm is an algorithm that can learn from data. Mitchell (1997) provides a succinct definition: "A computer program is said to learn from experience E with respect to some class of tasks T and performance measure P, if its performance at tasks in T, as measured by P, improves with experience E."

(b) The Task, T

Machine learning enables us to tackle tasks that are too difficult to solve with fixed programs written and designed by human beings. From a scientific and philosophical point of view, machine learning is engaging because developing our understanding of it entails developing our knowledge of the principles that underlie intelligence.

In this relatively formal definition of the word "task", the process of learning itself is not the task. Learning is our means of attaining the ability to perform the task. For example, if we want a robot to walk, then walking is the task. We could program the robot to learn to walk, or we could attempt to write a program that specifies how to walk manually directly.

Machine learning tasks are usually described in terms of how the machine learning system should process an **example**. An example is a collection of **features** that have been quantitatively measured from some object or event that we want the machine learning system to process. We typically represent an example as $x \in R^n$ where each entry x_i of the vector is another feature. For example, an image's features are usually the values of the pixels in the image.

Many types of tasks can be solved by training an algorithm with machine learning. Some of the most common machine learning tasks include the following:

- **Classification:** Specifying which of k categories that the inputs belong to.
- **Regression:** Predicting a numerical value given the inputs.
- **Transcription:** Observing a relatively unstructured representation of some kind of data and transcribe the information into discrete textual form.
- **Machine translation:** Converting a sequence of symbols from one language to another.
- **Structured output:** Performing tasks where the output is a vector (or other data structure containing multiple values) with important relationships between the different elements.
- **Anomaly detection:** Sifting through a set of events or objects and flagging those that are unusual or atypical.
- **Synthesis and sampling** generate new examples similar to those in the training data. Synthesis and sampling via machine learning can be useful for media applications when generating large volumes of content by hand would be expensive, boring, or require too much time.

(c) The Experience, E

Machine learning algorithms can be broadly categorized into four major types: supervised, unsupervised, semi-supervised, and reinforcement learning by what kind of experience they are allowed to have during the learning process.

Supervised learning: The supervised learning algorithms are trained/ taught using given data records. The data are labeled, which means that the desired output for input is known.

For example, a credit card application can be labeled as either approved or rejected. The algorithm receives a set of inputs (the applicants' information) and the corresponding outputs (whether the application was approved or not) to foster learning. The model building or algorithm learning process minimizes the error between the estimated output and the actual output. Learning stops when the algorithm achieves an acceptable performance level, such as when the error becomes smaller than the minimum pre-defined mistake. The trained algorithm is then applied to unlabeled data to predict the possible output value, such as whether a new credit card application should be approved or not. This process could be used to onboard clients within banks. Such as the Know Your Customer (KYC) department.

There are multiple supervised learning algorithms, Bayesian statistics, linear regression, logistic regression, decision trees, random forests, support vector machines (SVMs), ensemble models, etc. Practical applications include risk assessment, fraud detection, image, speech and text recognition, etc. In the following section, three algorithms will be introduced in detail.

Unsupervised learning: Unlike supervised learning, in unsupervised learning, the algorithm is not trained/taught on the "right answer". The algorithm tries to explore the given data and detect or mine its hidden patterns and relationships. In this case, there is no answer key. Learning is based on the similarity or distance among the given data points. In the context of deep learning, the goal of unsupervised learning is to learn the entire probability distribution that generated a dataset, whether explicitly, as in density estimation, or implicitly, for tasks like synthesis or denoising.

Take bank customer segmentation as an example, where customers in a specific group exhibit similar characteristics. The learned homogenous groups can help the bank figure out the hidden relationship between customer demographics and bank product selection. This would provide valuable insights on customer targeting when the bank does product marketing to new customers. Also, unsupervised learning works well with transactional data. It can be used to identify a group of individuals with similar purchase behavior who can then be treated as a single homogenous unit during marketing promotions.[1]

Association rule mining, clustering like K-means, nearest-neighbor mapping, self-organizing mapping, dimensionality reduction like principal component analysis are common and popular unsupervised learning algorithms. Practical applications cover market basket analysis, customer segmentation, anomaly detection, etc.

Semi-supervised learning: Semi-supervised learning is similar to supervised learning as it is often used to address similar problems. The difference between semi-supervised learning and supervised learning is that in semi-supervised learning, a small amount of labeled data and many unlabeled data are provided simultaneously. Semi-supervised learning will be utilized when the labeling process is too costly for a fully labeled training process. A large amount of unlabeled data can be classified by

---

[1]A Primer on Machine Learning, UCI Division of Continuing Education.

semi-supervised learning algorithms with the labeled data. On top of that, a new model will further be trained using the new labeled data set. Semi-supervised learning is also known as a hybrid-type of learning as the data set is the hybridization of labeled and unlabeled observations. Other types of hybrid-type learnings include self-supervised learning (Kolesnikov *et al.*, 2019) and multi-instance learning (Bengio *et al.*, 2017).

An example would be an online news portal looking to do a web page classification or labeling. To be specific, the firm may want to classify its web pages into different categories such as Sports, Politics, Business, Entertainment, etc. However, manually doing so would be highly time-consuming and expensive. Semi-supervised learning is intended to take as many advantages of the unlabeled data as possible to improve the trained model's efficiency. Two typical practical applications of semi-supervised machine learning will be image classification and text classification.

Reinforcement learning: Reinforcement learning aims to find out the action which leads to the maximum reward or drive to the optimal outcome. A set of allowed actions, rules, and potential end states are provided to the machine beforehand. The machine's job is to explore different actions and observe resulting reactions. By the end, the machine learns to exploit the given rules to reach the desired outcome. In other words, it determines in certain circumstances what series of actions will lead to the optimized result.

Reinforcement learning is often utilized in gaming and robotics. It is akin to teaching someone to play a game. Although the rules and objectives are clearly defined, any single game's outcome relies on the player's judgment because the player is constantly adjusting his approach in response to the incumbent environment and the skills and reactions of his opponents.

Roughly speaking, unsupervised learning involves observing several examples of a random vector x and attempting to implicitly or explicitly learn the probability distribution $p(x)$ or some interesting distribution properties. In contrast, supervised learning involves observing several examples of a random vector x and an associated value or vector y, then learning to predict y from x, usually by estimating $p(y|x)$. The term supervised learning originates from the view of the target y being provided by an instructor or teacher who shows the machine learning system what to do. There is no instructor or teacher in unsupervised learning, and the algorithm must learn to make sense of the data without this guide.

(d) The Performance Measure, *P*

A machine learning model's ability to complete its tasks needs to be quantitatively measured with its performance. The performance measure, *P*, is specific to the task, *T* being carried by the machine learning model. We are usually interested in understanding how well a machine learning algorithm performs on data that it has not seen before. This would determine its effectiveness when deployed in the real world. We, therefore, evaluate these performance measures using a test set of data that is separate from the data used for training the machine learning system. Here we take the supervised learning problem as an example to illustrate the performance measure.

Supervised learning problems can be categorized into classification and regression. The widely used measurement scheme is the training-testing framework. It partitions the dataset into two subsets: the training set and the testing set. The former set is used to train the machine learning model, and the latter set is used to evaluate the trained model's classification performance. It is worth noticing that there is no overlap between the two data sets, meaning all the data in the testing set are unseen by the model.

In general, the more data assigned to the training set, the more learning there is, which produces a better model. Common partition ratio includes 70-30% or 80-20%. If the data size is vast, the 50-50% partition ratio can be used.

However, there are some instances with small data sizes. To ensure enough data to train the model, K-fold cross-validation is widely adopted to involve more training data. The basic procedures are as follows:

- Partition the dataset into K equal-size folds;
- Form K hold-out predictors, each time using one-fold as testing dataset and the rest K-1 as the training dataset;
- The final predictor is the average/majority vote over the K hold-out predictors.

In the K-fold cross-validation, all the data points are used to train the model and test it.

After gaining the trained model, it can predict the testing dataset and compare the predicted target value with the actual target value. The comparison is called performance measures.

For classification problems (i.e., the target is categorical type), we use binary target ($Y = 0$ or 1, Yes or No) to introduce several popular performance measures (Table 6.1).

Table 6.1:   Confusion matrix.

	Predicted $Y = 0$	Predicted $Y = 1$
Actual $Y = 0$	TN	FP
Actual $Y = 1$	FN	TP

This performance table is named the confusion matrix. We call "Actual $Y = 1$" a condition positive (P), or the number of real positive observations in the data. Opposingly, "Actual $Y = 0$" is a condition negative (N), or the number of real negative observations in the data. Based on this definition, the comparison between the predicted target value and the actual value results in four conditions: TN — True Negative, FN — False Negative, FP — False Positive, and TP — True Positive. Both TN and TP are correct classifications, whereas FN and FP are wrong classifications. Finally, we can produce the basic evaluation metrics:

$$Accuracy = \frac{TP + TN}{TP + TN + FP + FN}$$

$$Precision = \frac{TP}{TP + FP}$$

$$Recall = \frac{TP}{TP + FN}$$

$$F\text{-}measure = 2\frac{precision\,recall}{precision + recall}$$

For regression problems (i.e., the target is numeric type), the basic idea of performance measure is to calculate the difference between the predicted target value $\hat{y}_i$ and the actual target value y_i. Some common performance measures include:

- **Mean absolute error (MAE)** = $\frac{\sum_{i=1}^{n}|y_i - \hat{y}_i|}{n}$

- **Mean squared error (MSE)** = $\frac{\sum_{i=1}^{n}(y_i - \hat{y}_i)^2}{n}$

- **Root MSE (RMSE)** = the squared root of MSE

- **Mean absolute percentage error (MAPE)** = $\frac{\sum_{i=1}^{n}|(y_i - \hat{y}_i)/y_i|}{n}$

Example: Suppose the actual values of a target are 10, 22, and 50. The corresponding predicted values generated from a model are 12, 18, and 47, respectively. Compute the MAE, MSE, RMSE, and MAPE.

Answer:
MAE = [|10 − 12| + |22 − 18| + |50 − 47|]/3 = (2 + 4 + 3)/3 = 9/3 = 3.
MSE = [(10 − 12)^2 + (22 − 18)^2 + (50 − 47)^2]/3 = (4 + 16 + 9)/3 ≈ 9.67.
RMSE = $\sqrt{\text{MSE}}$ ≈ 3.11.
MAPE = [|−2/10| + |4/22| + |3/50|]/3 ≈ 0.1473 = 14.73%

(e) Capacity, Overfitting and Underfitting
The central challenge in machine learning is that the trained model must perform well on new, previously unseen inputs and not simply on training data. The ability to perform well on previously unobserved inputs is called **generalization**.

When training a machine learning model, we typically have access to a training set; we can compute some error measure on the training set, called the **training error**; and reduce this training error. So far, what we have described is simply an optimization problem. What separates machine learning from optimization is that we want the **generalization error**, also called the **test error**, to be low. The generalization error is defined as the error's expected value on new input. Here the expectation is taken across different possible inputs, drawn from the distribution of inputs we expect the system to encounter in practice.

We typically estimate the generalization error of a machine learning model by measuring its performance on a test set of examples collected separately from the training set.

The training and test data are generated by a probability distribution over datasets called the **data-generating process**. We typically make a set of assumptions known collectively as the i.i.d. assumptions. These assumptions are that each dataset's examples are independent of each other. The training set and test set are identically distributed, drawn from the same probability distribution. This assumption enables us to describe the data-generating process with a probability distribution over a single example. The same distribution is used to generate every training example and every test example. We call that underlying shared distribution the data-generating distribution, denoted *p_data*. This probabilistic framework and the assumptions enable us to study the relationship between training error and test error mathematically.

We can observe one immediate connection between training error and the test error because a randomly selected model's expected training error is equal to that model's expected test error. Suppose we have a probability distribution $p(x, y)$, and we sample from it repeatedly to generate the training set and the test set. For some fixed value w, the expected training set error is the same as the expected test set error because both expectations are formed using the same dataset sampling process. The only difference between the two conditions is the name we assign to the dataset we sample.

Of course, when we use a machine learning algorithm, we do not fix the parameters ahead of time, then sample both datasets. We sample the training set and then use it to choose the parameters to reduce training set error and sample the test set. Under this process, the expected test error is greater than or equal to the expected training error value. The factors determining how well a machine learning algorithm will perform are its ability to:

- Make the training error small
- Make the gap between training and test error small

These two factors correspond to machine learning's two central challenges: **underfitting** and **overfitting**. Underfitting occurs when the model cannot obtain a sufficiently low error value on the training set. Overfitting occurs when the gap between the training error and test error is too large.

We can control whether a model is more likely to overfit or underfit by altering its **capacity**. Informally, a model's capacity is its ability to fit a wide variety of functions. Models with low capacity may struggle to fit the training set. Models with high capacity can overfit by memorizing the training set's properties that do not serve them well on the test set.

6.2 Unsupervised Machine Learning

The unsupervised machine learning models' data are unlabeled. This means the input's desired output is unknown. Unsupervised machine learning is to mine the hidden patterns in a dataset. This section will introduce three unsupervised algorithms in detail: association analysis, clustering (hierarchical and k-means), and dimensionality reduction (principal component analysis, PCA).

6.2.1 *Association Analysis*

Learning Objectives
- Understand the concepts and applications of association analysis.
- Understand the techniques of the Apriori algorithm.

Main Takeaways

Main Points
- Association Analysis aims to discover items that frequently co-occur within a database.
- Apriori algorithm uses the Downward Closure Principle to speed up the learning process.

Main Terms
- **Support:** The percentage of times that X and Y appear together in the records database, i.e., $P(X \cap Y) \times 100\%$.
- **Confidence:** A conditional probability $P(Y|X) \times 100\%$.
- **Lift:** The ratio between X and Y appear together, and X and Y appear independently in the dataset of records, i.e., $P(X \cap Y)/(P(X) \times P(Y)) \times 100\%$.
- **Downward closure principle:** A principle used to accelerate the search for frequent itemsets by eliminating all non-frequent itemsets.

(a) Association Analysis
Association analysis aims to discover items that frequently co-occur within a database. For instance, a retail manager may want to understand the probability of a customer who bought bread also buy peanut butter and milk. Understanding this could assist the manager in product arrangement, shelf space planning, and the effective implementation of product promotion strategies. This process is widely known as the market basket analysis, originating from the study of customer transaction databases to determine the dependencies amongst different purchase items.

Association analysis transforms a vast amount of data into a set of mathematically supported statements. Each statement is known as an **association rule**. Generally, an association rule has the following format:

$$X \rightarrow Y \ (support, \ confidence),$$

where X is known as the antecedent and Y the consequent of the association rule. This rule indicates that X determines Y with specific rule support and confidence value.

(b) Support, Confidence, and Lift

There are many potential association rules in a dataset, but not all are valuable. Three measures are typically used to describe the relationship between the antecedent and consequent:

- **Support:** The percentage of times that X and Y appear together in the records database, i.e., $P(X \cap Y) \times 100\%$, where the symbol "$\cap$" refers to the intersection. Support is the relative frequency that the rules show up. In many cases, you may wish to seek a high level of support to ensure that this is a useful relationship. However, there may be instances where low support is useful if you are trying to find "hidden" relationships.
- **Confidence:** A conditional probability $P(Y|X) \times 100\%$, according to Bayes' Theorem, it is also can be written as $P(X \cap Y)/P(X) \times 100\%$. Confidence is a measure of the reliability of the rule.
- **Lift:** The ratio between X and Y appear together, and X and Y appear independently in the dataset of records, i.e., $P(X \cap Y)/(P(X) \times P(Y)) \times 100\%$.

$P(X)$ or $P(Y)$ is simply the probability of X or Y appears in the database of records.

During association analysis, two thresholds, minimum support and minimum confidence, are set to find interesting rules. Typically, an association rule with high support and confidence would be recognized as interesting or important. In general, a lift value larger than 1.0 implies that the association between the antecedent and the consequent is more significant than would be expected if the antecedent and consequent were independent. The larger the lift value, the more interesting the association rule.

(c) Apriori Algorithm

A classic technique used in association analysis is the Apriori algorithm (Agrawal *et al.*, 1996).

Given pre-defined minimum support and minimum confidence thresholds, the Apriori algorithm finds all association rules whose support values are greater than or equal to the minimum support threshold and confidence values greater than or equal to the minimum confidence threshold.

The key idea of Apriori is the progressive generation of frequent itemsets, starting from one item (one-itemsets) and so on, until frequent itemsets of all sizes are generated. The user determines the thresholds before conducting the analysis, and the algorithm is executed in two phases:

- The first phase involves the finding of all frequent itemsets. Frequent itemsets are those whose support satisfies the user's minimum support threshold.
- The second phase is to generate the association rules that meet a confidence requirement from the identified frequent itemsets. The idea is to filter the remaining rules and selects only those with high confidence.

(d) Downward Closure Principle

The Apriori algorithm can use the downward closure principle to accelerate the search for frequent itemsets. This principle states that *if a subset is not frequent, its superset must be infrequent.* Through this principle, identifying frequent itemsets is simplified as all non-frequent itemsets are automatically eliminated to ensure their support need not be evaluated.

For instance, to ensure that the following itemset {A, B, C} meets the minimum support threshold as a frequent itemset, its subsets of {A}, {B}, {C}, {A, B}, {A, C} and {B, C} must also be frequent itemsets that meet the support threshold. Applying this concept, one can reason that if any one of {A}, {B}, {C}, {A, B}, {A, C} or {B, C} is not frequent, {A, B, C} itself cannot be a frequent itemset — reducing the need to evaluate the support count of {A, B, C}. Using this principle, association analysis programs would identify frequent itemsets more effectively.

(e) Applications

Association analysis can be used to improve decision making in a wide variety of applications, such as market basket analysis, medical diagnosis, bio-medical literature, protein sequences, census data, fraud detection, customer relationship management (CRM) of credit card business, etc. (Rajak and Gupta, 2008).

6.2.2 Clustering

Learning Objectives

- Understand the concepts of hierarchical clustering and K-means
- Understand the advantages and limitations of clustering

Main Takeaways

Main Points

- Hierarchical clustering is to build a hierarchy of clusters. It can be done using an agglomerative approach or a divisive approach.
- K-means allocates every data observation to the nearest cluster while keeping the "means" as small as possible. The "means" here is the centroid of the data in the cluster.

Main Terms

- **Proximity matrix:** Measure the distance between two data observations in a dataset.
- **Linkage measurement:** Measure the distance between two clusters.

(a) Clustering

Cluster analysis (or simply clustering) is a class of exploratory techniques that aims to discover natural data groups. In the business and finance context, clustering is applicable in analyses such as market segmentation and credit scoring. During market segmentation, cluster analysis divides consumers into various groups to derive a mixture of selling strategies to maximize their revenue. In credit scoring, a bank or a credit card company may apply clustering techniques to identify potential fraud by analyzing the transaction size and volume and a debtors' personal information such as credit limits, annual income, and occupation.

Clustering does not reveal relationships between the variables (as in association analysis). Instead, it aims to group objects to identify groups with a high degree of internal (within-cluster) similarity and external (between-cluster) dissimilarity.

(b) Functions of Clustering

Clustering can work as an independent, unsupervised learning method. It can also layout pre-processing work for further analysis. There are three main functions of clustering:

- Identify objects that share common characteristics, which allow decision-makers to make sound decisions concerning the groups (e.g., the market segmentation example highlighted at the beginning).
- Serve as an exploratory tool for further data analysis or processing. Grouping observations intuitively means spotting outliers and crafting hypotheses concerning the underlying multivariate relationships.

- Identify the clusters' most representative record to ensure that subsequent analysis becomes more manageable.

(c) Hierarchical Clustering

Clustering algorithms can be categorized into two major types based on grouping data observations: **hierarchical clustering** and **partitioning clustering**. As seen in Table 6.1, hierarchical clustering's primary objective is to build a hierarchy of clusters, while partitioning clustering works to construct K non-overlapped partitions.

Hierarchical clustering can be done using an **agglomerative** approach or a **divisive** approach. The former is a "bottom-up" method. Initially, each observation is recognized as a cluster named Singleton. A pair of clusters are merged as one in each of the following steps to move up the hierarchy until all observations are grouped in one cluster. The latter one is the opposite, the "top-down" method. All the observations start in one cluster, and splits are performed recursively as one moves down the hierarchy. So the process is one cluster splits into two, then three, until Singleton. The results of hierarchical clustering are usually presented as a **Dendrogram**.

We use agglomerative hierarchical to illustrate the clustering process. In every step, agglomerative hierarchical clustering needs to decide between two clusters. As clustering is to assign observations into several heterogeneous groups, and each group is homogeneous inside, therefore, agglomerative hierarchical clustering merges those two clusters which are closest to each other. In other words, the two clusters which have the smallest distance are merged at each step.

A **proximity matrix** is constructed and updated in each step. The proximity matrix is to measure the distance between any two data observations. Then the two clusters which have the smallest distance are merged. In the first step, the distance is between two data observations, and we can use any distance measure to quantitate it, like Euclidean Distance, Mahalanobis Distance, Minkowski Distance, etc. While in the following steps, the distance is between two clusters. There are various linkage metrics being used to measure the proximity of two clusters:

- **Single linkage:** Minimum distance of all possible pairs of observations in the two clusters.
- **Complete linkage:** Maximum distance of all possible pairs of observations in the clusters.

- **Average linkage:** Average pair-wise distance among all pairs of observations in the two clusters.
- **Centroid linkage:** Distance between the centroids of the two clusters.
- **Ward's linkage:** Minimizes the total within-cluster sum of squares, which is termed as the error sum of squares (ESS) in clustering.

Regardless of which linkage metric was used, the two clusters with the smallest linkage proximity would be merged to form a new cluster.

The advantage of Hierarchical clustering is that it is easy to understand and interpret. However, the technique's nature limits its applications (Figure 6.1).

- First, we need to manually decide the clustering results, such as the number of clusters.
- Second, the input data must be numerical because of proximity measurement. This algorithm does not apply to mixed data types.
- Lastly, it is time-consuming. Therefore, hierarchical clustering is inefficient to process large data sets — making it more suitable to cluster small datasets.

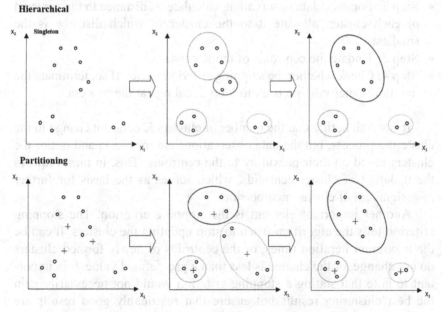

Figure 6.1: Hierarchical clustering and partitioning clustering.

(d) Partitioning Clustering: K-Means

K-means is a popular partitioning clustering technique. Unlike the hierarchical methods, it dissects the space spanned by the observations, using seeds selected before the clustering process begins.

The clustering process of K-means depends on the initial assignment rule. It usually randomly initializes the clustering or selects seeds that are well separated from each other. For example, the "+" points in Table 6.1 are the initialized seeds. A cluster of K-means refers to a collection of data points aggregated together because of certain similarities.

We define a target number K, which refers to the number of centroids or clusters. A centroid is an imaginary or actual location representing the cluster's center. Then every data observation is allocated to each cluster by reducing the in-cluster sum of squares. In other words, K-means allocates every data observation to the nearest cluster while keeping the "means" as small as possible. The 'means' here is the average of the data, the centroid.

The general flow of K-means is:

- **Step 1:** Define the cluster number K, initialize K centroid seeds of the clusters.
- **Step 2:** For each data observation, calculate its distance to the centroid of each cluster, allocate it to the cluster in which distance is the smallest.
- **Step 3:** Update the centroids of the K clusters.
- **Step 4:** Check whether the stopping criterion is met. If so, terminate the iteration; otherwise, go back to Step 2 and repeat the process.

It is worth noting that the number of clusters K does not change in the clustering process, but the data observations are moved in and out of the clusters based on their proximity to the centroids. This, in turn, requires the updating of cluster centroids, which serves as the basis for further re-assignment of cluster membership.

Another important element is the stopping criterion. The stopping criterion tells the algorithm when to stop updating the clusters. It can be the maximum iteration times, or the centroids of newly formed clusters do not change, or the change is less than a pre-defined value. It is important to note that setting a stopping criterion would not necessarily gain the best clustering results but ensure that reasonably good results are returned.

Compared to Hierarchical clustering methods, K-means is more efficient and easier to implement on large datasets. However, it still has some limitations:

- The clustering results are sensitive to initial centroids.
- It mainly detects spherical-shaped clusters and does not work well in detecting arbitrary-shape clusters.
- It is not ideal for datasets with mixed data-type (same for Hierarchical).
- Affected by outlier data observations as K-means uses centroids to group data.

6.2.3 *Principal Component Analysis*

Learning Objectives
- Understand the concepts of principal component analysis.

Main Takeaways

Main Points
- Principal component analysis (PCA) is a dimension-reduction tool aiming to reduce a large set of variables to a small set but still contains most of the original information.

Main Terms
- **Principal components:** Important information that is extracted from the original data. These components can either be constructed as linear combinations or as mixtures of the initial variables.

(a) Principal Component Analysis
For a high-dimension dataset, the number of its variables or simply the number of its columns is enormous. When working with this kind of data, we may encounter some problems. For example, we may need to understand the hidden correlations between variables because many variables may bring an overfitted model to the data. PCA is a popular algorithm to tackle this issue.

In general, PCA is a dimension-reduction tool that aims to reduce a large set of variables to a small set but still contains the most original information. It is a very flexible tool, and it can tolerate some common data issues, such as missing values, multicollinearity, and imprecise measurements.

(b) Principal Components

Principal components represent important information that is extracted from the original data. These components are new variables that are either constructed as linear combinations or as mixtures of the initial variables. These combinations are done so that new variables (i.e., principal components) are uncorrelated while having most of the information within the initial variables squeezed or compressed into the first several components. Suppose the dataset's dimension is p: PCA would attempt to put the maximum possible information in the first component, followed by the second component's maximum remaining information. This process continues until p principal components have been calculated, which is equal to the original number of variables.

To construct the principal components, we need to understand the correlations between all the possible pairs of variables, in other words, to know how the variables are varying with respect to each other. To identify these correlations, we compute the **covariance matrix**. The covariance matrix is a $p \times p$ symmetric matrix, which records the covariances associated with all possible pairs of the initial p variables.

The magic of PCA lies in its ability to leverage the power of eigenvectors and eigenvalues of the covariance matrix. Eigenvectors and eigenvalues come in a pair. The number of the eigenvectors is equal to the dimension p. Interestingly, the covariance matrix's eigenvectors are the axes' directions with the greatest variance (most information); what is referred to as Principal Components. The eigenvalues are simply the coefficients attached to eigenvectors, which give the amount of variance carried in each Principal Component. By ranking the eigenvectors in order of their eigenvalues, highest to lowest, we can get the principal components in order of significance.

Usually, we only use the first several principal components to represent the original dataset, as they contain most of the information (such as >90%). These principle components realize the dimension-reduction.

(c) Limitations

PCA is a useful pre-processing tool for further analysis, like multivariate data analysis. However, PCA's analysis results are not as readable and interpretable as the original dataset. The generated principal components are the combination of multiple initial variables. They may not have precise physical meanings.

6.3 Supervised Machine Learning

Supervised machine learning models are trained using given data records. The data are labeled, which means the desired output for input is known. The inputs are also named explanatory variables or independent variables, and the output is also called the target or dependent variable. The output can be either numerical (i.e., continuous value) or categorical (i.e., binary or nominal), and the models are estimation or prediction models accordingly. In this section, three supervised algorithms will be introduced in detail: Linear Regression (estimation model), Logistic Regression (prediction model), and Decision Trees (estimation and prediction models).

6.3.1 *Linear Regression*

Learning Objectives
- Understand the concepts and applications of linear regression.
- Understand how to construct a linear regression model and interpret the results.
- Understand how to use the regression function to do an estimation.

Main Takeaways

Main Points
- Linear regression is a linear approach to model the relationship between a numerical target and one or more explanatory variables; linearity refers to the fact that the target is expressed as a linear function of the coefficients and not about the linearity of the inputs.
- A positive (negative) coefficient indicates the positive (negative) impact of the target's input.
- The learned linear regression function can be used to do estimation for unseen input data.
- Linear regression can be used to do target estimation and relationship mining.

Main Terms
- **Linear regression:** A linear approach to model the relationship between a numerical target and one or more input variables.
- **Coefficients:** The mean change in the response variable for one unit of change in the predictor variable while holding other predictors in the model constant.

(a) What is Linear Regression?

Linear regression is usually recognized as a statistics-based machine learning method. Statistics is concerned with the probabilistic analysis and interpretation of data. As *the science of basing inferences on observed data and the entire problem of making decisions in the face of uncertainty* (Freund and Walpole, 1987), statistics attempts to generalize the properties of a population from sample data. Possessing similar characteristics to the population, its subset, a sample is collected to construct estimators for generating the population characteristics' numerical values. In statistics, linear regression is a linear approach to model the relationship between a numerical target and one or more input variables.

In a linear regression, i.e., $Y = \beta_0 + \beta_1 X_1 + \beta_2 X_2 + \ldots + \beta_k X_k + \varepsilon$, a target variable ($Y$) is usually formulated as a linear additive function of a list of input variables X. β_j in the regression model are the parameters of interest in the model building, it refers to the *j-th* coefficient which represents the direction and magnitude of variable X_j's influence on Y. ε is the error term, or the residual representing all the uncertainties underlying the relationship between the variables. The error term's inclusion implies that the target variable Y is a value to be estimated.

Depending on the number of input variables, linear regression can either be represented as simple linear regression or multiple linear regression. A simple linear regression model is a linear function with a y-intercept of β_0 and a slope of β_1. The difference between the actual value of Y and the estimated value on $\beta_0 + \beta_1 X_{1i}$ is ε_i. When the number of input variables becomes two or more, linear regression is multiple. And more axes need to be added to the graph if one wants to draw the possible relationships. The linear line is then replaced by a plane ($k = 2$) or hyper-plane ($k > 2$).

In linear regression, linearity refers to the fact that the target is expressed as a linear function of the coefficients (β), and not about the linearity of the inputs. Hence, $Y = \beta_0 + \beta_1 X_1^2 + \varepsilon$ and $ln(Y) = \beta_0 + \beta_1 X_1 + \varepsilon$ are linear models but $Y = b_0/[1 + b_1 e^{-\beta_2 X_i}]$ is not a linear model.

(b) Linear Regression Construction and Results Interpretation

All points on the linear function are the predicted values ($\hat{Y}$) for their corresponding observations (Y). The objective of performing regression analysis is to use sample data to estimate the numerical values of coefficients β, i.e., $\hat{\beta} = \{\hat{\beta}_0, \hat{\beta}_1, \ldots, \hat{\beta}_k\}$.

Once all the coefficients are estimated, the resulting regression equation is fitted. We can obtain the relationship between the inputs and the target by interpreting the signal of β. When the value of β_j is larger than 0, X_j is positively related to Y. On the other hand, if β_j is smaller than 0, X_j is negatively related to Y. Especially, when β_j is equal to 0, then X_j is not related to Y, which means X_j has no impact on the value of Y. The constant term β_0, which is not associated with any input) is required to characterize a linear function and may not possess any specific meaning.

(c) Estimation

The learned linear regression function $\hat{Y} = \hat{\beta} + \hat{\beta}_1 X_1 + \hat{\beta}_2 X_2 + \ldots + \hat{\beta}_k X_k$ can now be applied for making estimation on Y, given the specific values of Xs. It is rare that the estimated $\hat{\beta} = \beta$, because the estimated regression model is based on sample data.

Example: Suppose a liner regression model is built to estimate a company's monthly revenue (Y, \$'000) with X_1: advertising expenditure (\$'000), X_2: the size of salesforce (*No.*), X_3: dummy for the festive season (*1*: November to February, *0*: other months), and X_4: dummy for launching new products (*1*: Yes, *0*: No). Based on its time-series dataset with 85 observations, the regression coefficients are estimated: $\hat{\beta}_0 = 18.5$, $\hat{\beta}_1 = 4.2$, $\hat{\beta}_2 = 0.7$, $\hat{\beta}_3 = 25.0$, and $\hat{\beta}_4 = 55.0$. Suppose the company proposed a new product in December. What is the estimated revenue with a sales force of 98 personnel and an advertising expenditure of \$300,000?

Answer: $\hat{Y} = 18.5 + 4.2(300) + 0.7(98) + 25.0(1) + 15.0(1) = \$(18.5 + 1260 + 68.6 + 25 + 55) \approx \$1,427.1$.

(d) Applications of Linear Regression

Linear regression has many uses in daily life. It is useful in generating insights into consumer behaviors, evaluating business trends and making estimations or forecasts, analyzing marketing effectiveness, pricing, and promotions of certain sales events. Just like the company's revenue analysis shown in the above example. On top of that, linear regression can also be used in financial risk assessments. Most applications fall into one or two broad categories based on how one would like to use the learned regression function:

- Linear regression can fit the estimated model to a labeled data set. As shown in example 1, the fitted model can estimate the target value if

new explanatory variables are collected without an accompanying target value after developing such a model.
- Linear regression can be used to mine the hidden relationship between the target and the explanatory variables. The goal is to explain variation in the response variable attributed to variation in the explanatory variables. Linear regression analysis can quantify the strength of the relationship and determine whether some explanatory variables may have no linear relationship with the target at all.

6.3.2 *Logistic Regression*

Learning Objectives
- Understand the concepts and applications of logistic regression.
- Construct logistic regression for prediction and be able to interpret the results.
- Understand how to use the logistic regression function to make the prediction.

Main Takeaways

Main Points
- Logistic regression is to develop a predicting equation to explain the effect of input variables on a target variable's occurrence; the logistic regression target must be binary.
- Logistic regression uses logit function to measure the target variable's occurrence probability.
- The value, sign, and significant level of the coefficient explain the impact of input on the target's occurrence.
- The learned logistic regression function can be used to make a prediction.

Main Terms
- **Logit function:** A popular link function used to make the inputs explicitly "explain" the occurrence of target Y in logistic regression. It is also called the Sigmoid function.
- **Odds ratio:** The ratio of the odds of having the event with $X = 1$ to the odds of having the event with $X = 0$. It is often used to express the relative chance of an event happening under two different conditions.

(a) What is Logistic Regression?

Logistic regression is one of the most widely used predicted models after linear regression. Like linear regression, logistic regression modeling's objective is to develop a predicting equation to explain the occurrence of a target variable. The only difference between them is that the outcome or the explained variable of logistic regression is binary (e.g., yes/no, good/bad, success/failure, recover/relapse).

Logistic regression is modeled under the generalize linear model (GLM) framework. This framework enables the analyst to model the most commonly encountered business and economics processes. To model Y, three key steps must be followed:

- **Step 1:** Choose an appropriate distribution of Y from the exponential family (includes *Bernoulli, binomial, Poisson, normal, beta, exponential, gamma*, and *Weibull*).
- **Step 2:** Insert a meaningful and interpretable link function to connect the input (X) with Y's expected target value.
- **Step 3:** Construct the model using the maximum likelihood technique.

(b) Model Construction

Step 1: Choose Bernoulli distribution to describe Y

The most appropriate probability density function for Y is Bernoulli distribution:

$$f(y) = p^y (1-p)^{1-y}$$

where the parameter p satisfies $0 \leq p \leq 1$. Therefore, the probability that $Y = 1$ is $f(y=1) = p^1(1-p)^0 = p$. Similarly, the probability that $Y = 0$ is $1 - p$. State without proof, the mean and variance of Y are also p and $(1 - p)$, respectively.

In the case of logistic regression, one is supposed to have a sample of n independent observations of target and input values:

$$(x_{11}, ..., x_{k1}; y_1)$$
$$(x_{12}, ..., x_{k2}; y_2)$$
$$(x_{1n}, ..., x_{kn}; y_n)$$

where the subscript i refers to the i-th observation ($i = 1, 2, ..., n$). The observations are independently and identically distributed. There are

$1 < k < n$ inputs in the model, and the proposed model is "multiple" in nature. Given the Bernoulli distribution and the above discussion, the probability distribution of y_i is:

$$f(y_i; p_i) = p_i^{y_i}(1 - p_i)^{1-y_i}$$

Logit function:
Step 2: Select logit function as the link function to connect the inputs X with Y

An appropriate link function is used to make the inputs explicitly "explain" the occurrence of target Y. Since p_i governs the occurrence of Y_i and $p_i \in (0, 1)$, the influence of X on Y must be expressed as a function of p_i such that it is bounded within 0 and 1. Note that X may be metric or non-metric. The most appropriate function is known as the logit function, which is also named the Sigmoid function (see Figure 6.2):

$$p_i = \frac{1}{1+e^{-z}} = \frac{1}{1+e^{-[\beta_0+\beta_1 X_{1i}+...+\beta_k X_{ki}]}}$$

There are several interesting properties of the logit function that worth noting.

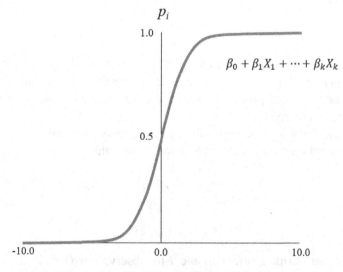

Figure 6.2: Logit function (sigmoid function).

- p_i is bounded within 0 and 1.
- The sigmoid shape of the logit function tells us that as the value of the linear product $z = \beta_0 + \beta_1 X_{1i} + \beta_2 X_{2i} + \ldots + \beta_k X_{ki}$ approaching 0, the value of p_i is approaching 0.5. This happens when none of the input variables effectively explains y_i. It is intuitive that if the input variables are incapable of explaining y_i, then the chance of $y_i = 1$ or $y_i = 0$ is half and half.
- If $\beta_0 + \beta_1 X_{1i} + \beta_2 X_{2i} + \ldots + \beta_k X_{ki}$ is very large, then the value of p_i is very close to 1. Likewise, if the value of $\beta_0 + \beta_1 X_{1i} + \beta_2 X_{2i} + \ldots + \beta_k X_{ki}$ is very small, then the value of p_i is very close to 0.

Prediction equation: Having selected the logit function as the link function, the maximum likelihood estimation (MLE) technique is employed to estimate the coefficients βs based on the sample data. The probability that Y takes on value 0 or 1 depends on $\frac{1}{1+e^{-[\beta_0 + \beta_1 X_{1i} + \ldots + \beta_k X_{ki}]}}$. With the values of Xs known and the coefficients βs estimated, we can predict Y's value.

After obtaining the estimated value of coefficients βs, we can use the prediction equation $\frac{1}{1+e^{-[\beta_0 + \beta_1 X_{1i} + \ldots + \beta_k X_{ki}]}}$ to predict. Because $\frac{1}{1+e^{-[\beta_0 + \beta_1 X_{1i} + \ldots + \beta_k X_{ki}]}}$ is a numerical value, a threshold should be chosen to transfer it to a value 0 or 1. Determining the value depends on different problems, but it should be no smaller than 0.5. Suppose we choose 0.5, then if $p_i = \frac{1}{1+e^{-[\beta_0 + \beta_1 X_{1i} + \ldots + \beta_k X_{ki}]}} \geq 0.5$, Y_i is classified as 1. Otherwise, it is classified as 0 ($p_i < 0.5$).

Example: Suppose a two-input logistic regression model is fully fitted, that is $\hat{\beta}_0 = 0.5$ and $\hat{\beta}_1 = 1.7$, how should y_i be classified, given $x_i = 1$? Assuming the classes of Y are 0 and 1.

Answer: $\hat{p}_i = \frac{1}{1+e^{-[0.5+1.7 X_i]}} = \frac{1}{1+e^{-[0.5+1.7]}} = \frac{1}{1+e^{-2.2}} \approx 0.90$. If the cut-off is 0.5, then y_i is classified as 1.

It is important to note that while the set-up is nonlinear, the logit is, in reality, a linear classifier. Consider a two-input logistic regression model and let the binary categories of Y be **1** · and **0** * (see Figure 6.3). The linear function $\beta_0 + \beta_1 X_1 + \beta_2 X_2$ is applied to separate the 1s from the 0s. This is the basis for classification with logistic regression.

In this case, we call the area above the graph of the linear function the **0 region** because there are more 0 than 1 in this region. Likewise, the area below the graph is called the **1 region**. Note that some observations are misclassified. The logit regression model aims to provide the "best"

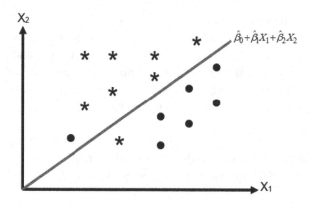

Figure 6.3:   Logistic regression model as a linear classifier.

estimated linear function that separates 1 and 0 with the lowest possible misclassification rate.

(c) Model Interpretation
Logistic regression models allow analysts to perform predictions and provide meaningful model interpretation.

Coefficient's sign and significant level: As seen above, logistic regression makes the inputs explicitly explain target Y (Y = 1). This explanation is given by the coefficient β. If $\beta > 0$, then the corresponding input variable increases the probability of occurrence of Y = 1. On the other hand, if $\beta < 0$, then the input variable decreases the probability. The larger the absolute value of the β, the stronger the impact of the input on the probability of occurrence.

The logistic regression model uses Wald-test to evaluate the significance of the impact on the probability of occurrence, which is the p-value. In statistics, usually, if $p < 0.05$, the corresponding variable is considered significant. Therefore, in logistic regression, if the p-value<0.05, the corresponding input variable is a significant factor that would affect the probability of Y's occurrence.

In a nutshell, the sign and the significance of a coefficient reflect how and how much the corresponding input variable would determine the occurrence of target Y.

Odds ratio: Taking $p_i/(1 - p_i)$ yields

$$\frac{p_i}{1 - p_i} = \frac{1}{1 + e^{-[\beta_0 + \beta_i X_{1i} + \dots + \beta_k X_{ki}]}} \div \frac{e^{-[\beta_0 + \beta_i X_{1i} + \dots + \beta_k X_{ki}]}}{1 + e^{-[\beta_0 + \beta_i X_{1i} + \dots + \beta_k X_{ki}]}} = e^{\beta_0 + \beta_1 x_{1i} + \dots + \beta_k x_{ki}}$$

$\frac{p_i}{1 - p_i}$ is called the odds, which quantifies the likelihood of observing an event for X = i compared with the chance of observing the non-event for X = i. Denote the odds of observing the event for X = 1 as $\frac{p_1}{1 - p_1}$ and for X = 0 as $\frac{p_0}{1 - p_0}$. As a result, the odds ratio is defined as the ratio of the probability of having the event with X = 1 to the probability of having the event with X = 0. In statistics, the odds ratio is often used to express an event's relative chance under two conditions.

If one of the x's, say x_j, is binary and labeled as 0 or 1, the odds ratio is:

$$\frac{p_1}{1 - p_1} / \frac{p_0}{1 - p_0} = \frac{e^{\beta_0 + \beta_1 X_{1i} + \dots + \beta_j + \dots + \beta_k X_{ki}}}{e^{\beta_0 + \beta_1 X_{1i} + \dots 0 + \dots + \beta_k X_{ki}}} = e^{\beta_j}.$$

As such, $e^{\beta_j} \left(j = 1, 2, \dots, k \right)$ is often termed as odds ratio for X_j, while all other input values remain unchanged. For example, gender (0: female; 1: male) may be related to the subscription to a rock music channel (0: no; 1: yes). Since a female gender is assigned a value of 0, female listeners are chosen as the reference category. If the estimated coefficient β is 0.4875, then one can conclude that male listeners are $e^{0.4875}$ or 1.63 times more likely to subscribe to the rock music channel when compared with female listeners.

(d) Applications of Logistic Regression
Like linear regression, logistic regression can also do prediction and explanatory relationship mining. It can be applied in multiple fields, including finance, healthcare, insurance, pattern recognition, weather forecasting, etc.

Take the credit card as a simple example: The bank may imply specific EMI options to minimize the portfolio's risk and determine the top five factors that can cause a customer to default.

6.3.3 *Decision Tree*

Learning Objectives
- Understand the concepts of the decision tree.
- Understand the techniques of CART and C5.0 tree.

Main Takeaways

Main Points
- Decision tree partitions a data set recursively into increasingly hetero-geneous subsets using a tree-like model.
- CART tree can solve regression (estimation) and classification (prediction) problems. It uses impurity measures to find the best split input and split value for each node splitting.
- C5.0 is a classification tree. It uses information theory to select the split input and split value.

Main Terms
- **Decision rule:** A decision path by navigating from the root node to the leaf node, according to the presenting input values of the observation. Each path from the root to the leaves is a decision rule.
- **Splitting:** The process of partitioning a node into two or more sub-nodes.
- **Pruning:** A method used to reduce decision trees' size by removing nodes. It is the opposite of splitting.

(a) What is a Decision Tree?
A decision tree is constructed by partitioning a data set recursively into increasingly heterogeneous subsets using a tree-like model (Zhang and Singer, 1999). It is one way to display an algorithm that only contains conditional control statements.

There are several basic terminologies used with decision trees:

- **Root node:** The entire sample data gets further partitioned into two or more heterogeneous subsets.
- **Parent node:** A node partitioned into sub-nodes.
- **Child node:** A sub-node belonging to a parent node.
- **Branch/sub-tree:** A sub-section of a decision tree.
- **Splitting:** The process of partitioning a node into two or more sub-nodes.
- **Leaf/terminal node:** Nodes with no child node.

- **Pruning** is a method to reduce decision trees' size by removing nodes (the opposite of splitting).

Typically, the data partitioning process is represented by a tree. A root node contains the entire data sample, with each remaining node containing a subset of the data sample in the node they are directly under. The partitioning process is repeated on each child node until the leaf node, whose values represent the target value, is reached.

Figure 6.4 demonstrates a scatter plot of the Iris flower dataset that a decision tree has partitioned.

The Iris dataset contains three types of flowers: Iris-setosa, Iris-versicolor, and Iris-virginica.

A decision involves an input variable and a split value within each non-terminal node. In each leaf node, the target class values can either be labeled as Iris-setosa, Iris-versicolor, or Iris-virginica. The tree branches correspond to divisions in the data space, and each node corresponds to a split on a particular input. Petal length and width are physical measurements taken on the flowers.

Based on the observation's presenting input values, all decisions would be made by navigating from the root node to the leaf node. Each path from the root to the leaves is a decision rule. Referring to the decision tree above, we can derive the following decision rules:

- If an Iris flower has a petal width ≥ 1.8 cm, it is an Iris-virginica.
- If an Iris flower has petal width < 1.8 cm, and petal length ≥ 2.9, it is an Iris-versicolor.
- If an Iris flower has petal width < 1.8 cm, and petal length < 2.9, it is an Iris-setosa.

(b) Decision Tree Construction
The inputs considered for decision tree induction may be metric and non-metric. The target can be either metric or non-metric. The tree can be a regression tree or a classification tree.

Nodes splitting: Constructing a decision tree (aka tree induction) involves the selection of "best" inputs and split points for splitting. In determining the splitting rule, the decision tree methodology looks at all possible splits for all inputs included in the analysis. Ideally, the data is split in a manner that produces 'pure' terminal nodes — all observations at each terminal node are assigned to the same target. Similar to logistic regression, not all inputs considered may be featured in the final decision tree, where inputs

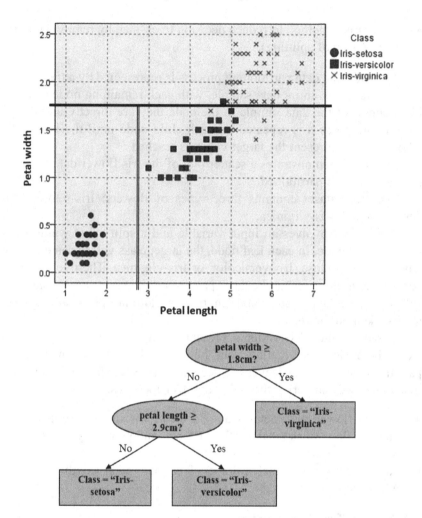

Figure 6.4: Scatter plot of the Iris dataset with data partitioning lines and the generated decision tree.

that are considered less important are omitted from the tree based on partitioning rules.

There are multiple ways to select the split input and value. Common impurity measurements include the Gini impurity index, Towing splitting criterion, information gain ratio, etc. Moreover, the splitting can be binary or multiple-way. The former is to split the parent node into two child nodes, and the latter is to split the parent node into at least three child nodes.

Tree size: A generated decision tree can be described using its height and depth.

- The depth of a node j in a decision tree is the length of the path from the root to j. Therefore, the depth of the root node is 0, and the depth of a tree is the longest path from its root to the furthest leaf node.
- The height of node j is the length of the longest path from node j to leaf node. Therefore, the height of a tree is the height of its root.

Example: The decision tree's height shown in Figure 6.4 is 2. And the depth of the node of Petal length is 1.

The size of a decision tree is the number of nodes in the tree. Suppose a tree's depth is d, and it is a binary splitting tree. Then the largest size of the tree is $2^{d+1} - 1$. Usually, the size would be larger if the tree is a multiple-splitting tree. A possible way to control a decision tree's size is to determine the desired tree depth before implementing tree induction.

Stopping and pruning: It is essential to prevent a decision tree from becoming too large or too complicated. An overgrown tree is undesirable as it captures minor and non-essential data features which result in over-fitting. This occurred when its fit of the training data set was not replicated when applied to the unseen observations. Hence, a complex tree, usually measured by tree depth, tree size, is well known to have a crucial impact on its accuracy (Breiman *et al.*, 1984). Nevertheless, this problem can be controlled by adopting specific stopping rules, such as pre-specify the tree size or tree depth.

However, stopping rules may not typically work as many threshold values are fixed without proper justification. Therefore, an alternative to control the tree size is pruning. Pruning helps reduce an overgrown tree to an appropriate size. They do so by generating a number of possible sub-trees for comparison, giving pruning an advantage over a stopping rule that can consider only a single node at a time.

(c) CART

The Classification and Regression Tree (CART) was developed in the early 1980s by Breiman (Breiman, 1984), where it is both an estimator and classifier. CART has the following characteristics:

- Construct trees where each internal node has exactly two outgoing branches — commonly known as a binary decision tree method.

- Identify and split through several methods. The algorithm uses impurity measures to quantify the "purity" of the nodes, which helps to determine if a terminal node was reached. A node is "pure" if the target values or categories within the node are homogenous, and further splits are not needed. CART also considers misclassification costs during the tree induction phase. In the case of metric targets, CART identifies splits that minimize the squared errors in estimation, where the estimate in each leaf node is based on the weighted mean of the target value.
- CART first generates three random subsets from the original data set. The first data subset acts as the training set for growing the tree. The second data subset serves as the testing set for providing information on the tree's performance. The feedback helps to prune the constructed tree. Finally, the third subset, also known as the validation set, re-constructs the optimum subtree's out-of-sample predictive accuracy.

To split nodes, CART uses impurity measures such as the Gini impurity index and entropy.

Gini impurity index: Without loss of generality, consider a classification problem where the target is binary. The Gini impurity index for a particular node A is computed as

$$I(A) = 1 - \sum_{c=1}^{k} p_c^2$$

where p_c is the proportion of observations in node A that belong to category c of the target ($k = 1, 2, 3, \ldots$). Note that the closer it is to 0, the purer or more homogeneous the node is. The maximum value of $I(A)$ is $(1 - 1/k)$ when there are equal proportions of observations for the k categories.

Example: A node A of CART contains two types of the target categories (shown in Figure 6.5), $c = 1$ (300 observations), $c = 2$ (200 observations). Then its impurity index is: $I(A) = 1 - \sum_{c=1}^{2} p_c^2 = 1 - [(300/500)^2 + (200/500)^2] = 1 - [(0.36) + (0.16)] = 0.48$.

Suppose parent node A is to be split into two child nodes B and C. Let the number of observations in A be n_A and B and C be n_B and n_C, respectively. The combined Gini impurity index of B and C is:

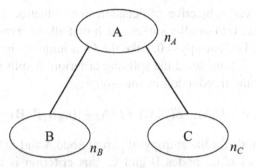

Figure 6.5: Target example.

$$I(B, C) = (n_B/n_A)I(B) + (n_C/n_A)I(C)$$

The Gini criterion for splitting is based on the reduction in Gini impurity indices $\Delta I(A, BC) = I(A) - I(B, C)$. A split input and a specific value are selected to split if its impurity reduction is the largest among all possible splits.

Example: Suppose a root node's (R) Gini impurity index is 0.4. Its two child-nodes A and B, whose Gini impurity indices are 0.2 and 0.1, respectively. There are total n=100 observations, and after the first split, half of the observations descend to node A, and the remaining half to node B. Then the combined Gini impurity index is $(n_A/n)I(A) + (n_B/n)I(B) = (0.5)(0.2) + (0.5)(0.1) = 0.15$. And impurity reduction is 0.4-0.15 = 0.25.

(d) Entropy
The second impurity measure is known as entropy, and it is used to measure the information content captured in a node (Applebaum, 2008):

$$E(A) = -\sum_{c=1}^{k} p_c \log_2(p_c)$$

With bits as its unit, this measure ranges from 0 (purest) to $\log_2(k)$, where k is the number of categories in Y. This suggests that a high value of entropy would represent a significant degree of impurity.

Entropy is also used to measure uncertainty in a data set. All data belong to a specific category of Y will indicate the selected node with no uncertainty, i.e., entropy = 0.

The underlying objective of decision tree induction is to iteratively partition the data into smaller subsets such that all observations belong to the same class, i.e., entropy = 0. Like the Gini impurity index, the reduction in entropy is considered the splitting criterion. A split is performed if there is a substantial reduction in entropy:

$$Gain(A, (B, C)) = E(A) - E(B, C) = E(A) - [(n_B/n_A)E(B) + (n_C/n_A)E(C)]$$

where $E(A)$ stands for the entropy of parent node A and $E(B, C)$ the combined entropy of child nodes B and C, this criterion is also known as information gain $Gain(A, X)$, X is the split. Information gain is the difference between original information in a parent node and its child node information. The input with the highest information gain is chosen as the input for splitting at node A.

(e) C5.0

As opposed to CART, C5.0 is purely a classification tree, with a commercial decision tree method, where details of its algorithm techniques are not yet released. Compared to other decision tree models, C5.0 usually constructs smaller trees. Moreover, with a more efficient memory, C5.0 can efficiently cope with vast data sets.

Gain ratio: C5.0 applies an extension to information gain known as a gain ratio for node splitting to construct a tree. The use of information gain for node partitioning tends to create too many possible partitions. To overcome this problem, the gain ratio of input X for splitting a node A is utilized:

$$Gain(A, X)/Split(X)$$

where $Gain(A, X)$ is information gain calculated using entropy reduction,

$$Split(X) = -\sum_{i=1}^{r} \frac{n_{iA}}{n_A} \log_2 \left(\frac{n_{iA}}{n_A} \right),$$

n_{iA} is the number of observations of category i in X, and n_A the total number of observations in node A. Similarly, the input with the highest information gain ratio is chosen as the input for splitting at node A.

Pruning: To prevent overfitting, C5.0 implements two pruning strategies.

The first strategy replaces a subtree with a leaf node if the replacement results in an error rate close to the original tree; the replacement works from the bottom of the tree up to the root.

The second strategy replaces a subtree with its most used subtree, where the subtree is raised from its current location to a "higher up" node in the tree — also known as subtree raising.

Boosting provides a significant improvement in C5.0. (Freund, 1995), where multiple classifiers can be generated instead of building one classifier. The component classifiers would be weighted according to the misclassification rate within the construction set, and unseen observations would be classified based on the combined weighted results.

References/Further Readings

Agrawal, R., Mannila, H., Srikant, R., Tiovonen, H., & Verkamo, A.I. (1996). Fast Discovery of Association Rules. *Advances in Knowledge Discovery and Data Mining*, **12**(1), 307–328.

Applebaum, D. (2008). *Probability and Information: An Integrated Approach.* Cambridge University Press, Cambridge.

Bengio, Y., Goodfellow, I., & Courville, A. (2017). *Deep Learning* (Vol. 1). MIT Press, Massachusetts, USA.

Breiman, L., Fridman, J., Olshen, R., & Stone, C.J. (1984). *Classification and Regression Tree.* Wadsworth & Brooks/Cole Advanced Books & Software, Pacific California.

Freund, Y. (1995). Boosting a Weak Learning Algorithm by Majority. *Information & Computation*, **121**(2), 256–285.

Freund, J.E. & Walpole, R.E. (1987). *Mathematical Statistics.* Google Scholar Digital Library.

Kolesnikov, A., Zhai, X., & Beyer, L. (2019). Revisiting Self-Supervised Visual Representation Learning. In *Proceedings of the IEEE/CVF Conference on Computer Vision and Pattern Recognition* (pp. 1920–1929).

Mitchell, T.M. (1997). *Machine Learning.* McGraw Hill.

Rajak, A. & Gupta, M.K. (2008). Association Rule Mining: Applications in Various Areas. In *Proceedings of International Conference on Data Management* (pp. 3–7), Ghaziabad, India.

6.4 Sample Questions

Question 1

Which of the following methods is not a performance measure of supervised machine learning?

(a) Overall accuracy
(b) Recall
(c) Confidence

Question 2

Suppose we use Apriori to analyze supermarket transactions, and we set the minimum confidence = 60%. Which of the following rules is meaningful?

(a) Bread → Jam, with confidence 50%
(b) Tissue → Window cleaner, with confidence 30%
(c) Beer → Diaper, with confidence 65%

Question 3

In hierarchical clustering, the Single linkage method determines the similarity between two clusters A and B based on the closest data points a and b, where _____

(a) a belongs to A and b belongs A as well
(b) a belongs to A, and b belongs to B
(c) a and b do not belong to any clusters

Question 4

Which of the following statements is correct?
At each step of the K-means clustering process, _____.

(a) The algorithm needs to keep track of the objects assigned to each cluster
(b) The algorithm needs to determine the number of clusters to generate
(c) The algorithm updates the centroids of the clusters

Question 5

K-means clustering is very sensitive to the initialization of the initial cluster _____.

(a) Shapes
(b) Centroids
(c) Sizes

Question 6

Which of the following statements about PCA is not correct?

(a) It can reduce the dimension of the data
(b) The generated principle components are easy to interpret
(c) It is an unsupervised learning method

Question 7

Which of the following function is linear?

(a) $Y = \beta_0 + \beta_1^3 X_1 + \beta_2 X_2$
(b) $Y = \beta_0 + \beta_1 X_1 + \beta_2 X_2$
(c) $Y = \beta_0 + \beta_1^{-\beta_2 X_1}$

Question 8

Which statement is correct for logistic regression?

(a) When using the logit function to transfer the continuous output into binary, the threshold can only be 0.5.
(b) Positive parameter means that the corresponding variable could increase the occurrence probability.
(c) The p-value of the parameter βi is 0.04, then the corresponding variable Xi is not significant.

Question 9

C&RT is performed to classify an observation: $X1 = 0$, $X2 = 5$, and $X3 = 1$. What is the decision?

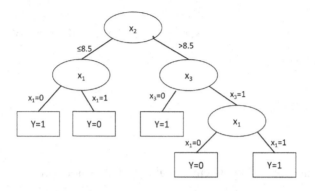

(a) Y = 1
(b) Y = 0
(c) Either Y = 0 or Y = 1

Question 10
What can you do if a full-grown decision tree is too huge and possibly over-trained? Choose the most appropriate answer.

(a) Apply pruning.
(b) Apply some stopping rules.
(c) Consider pruning and/or stopping rules.

Solutions

Question 1

Solution: Option **c** is correct.

Confidence is a performance measure of unsupervised machine learning.

Question 2

Solution: Option **c** is correct.

An association rule with high support and confidence would be recognized as interesting or important.

Question 3

Solution: Option **b** is correct.
Single linkage is a minimum distance of all possible pairs of observations in the two clusters.

Question 4

Solution: Option **c** is correct.
The general flow of K-means updates the centroids of the K clusters.

Question 5

Solution: Option **b** is correct.

The clustering results are sensitive to initial centroids.

Question 6

Solution: Option **b** is correct.

The generated principal components are the combination of multiple initial variables. They may not have precise meanings.

Question 7

Solution: Option **b** is correct.

In linear regression, linearity refers to the fact that the target is expressed as a linear function of the coefficients (β) and not about the inputs' linearity.

Question 8

Solution: Option **b** is correct.

Logistic regression makes the inputs explicitly explain target Y occurrence (Y = 1). This explanation is given by the coefficient β. If $\beta > 0$, then the corresponding input variable increases the probability of occurrence of Y = 1.

Question 9

Solution: Option **a** is correct.

In a decision tree, the partitioning process is repeated on each child node until the leaf node, whose values represent the target value, is reached.

Question 10

Solution: Option **c** is correct.

The problem can be controlled by adopting specific stopping rules, such as pre-specify the tree size or tree depth. However, stopping rules may not typically work as many threshold values are fixed without proper justification. Therefore, an alternative to control the tree size is pruning.

Chapter 7

Deep Learning

7.1 Introduction of Deep Learning

Learning Objectives
- Understand the concepts of deep learning.
- Understand the concepts of feed-forward and backpropagation.

Main Takeaways

Main Points
- Deep Learning is a sub-field of machine learning in Artificial Intelligence that deals with algorithms inspired by human brains' biological structure and functioning to aid machines with intelligence.
- Deep learning algorithms are based on neural network, which includes three types of layer such as input layer, hidden layer(s), and output layer.

Main Terms
- **Feed-forward:** Predict the possible output pattern using the assigned weight network from the input layer to the output layer.
- **Backpropagation:** Adjust the connection weights from the output layer to the input layer.

(a) Introduction of Deep Learning
Deep learning is a sub-field of machine learning in Artificial Intelligence that deals with algorithms inspired by human brains' biological structure

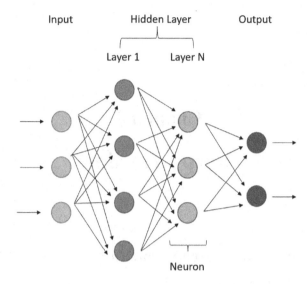

Figure 7.1: A simple version of DNN.

and functioning to aid machines with intelligence. It is also named deep neural network (DNN).

A simple version of DNN is represented as a hierarchical (layered) organization of neurons with connections to other neurons from the input side to the output side. As shown in Figure 7.1, DNN contains three layers: input layer, hidden layer, and output layer. It may have one hidden layer or multiple hidden layers. Based on the received input, the neurons on one layer pass it to other neurons on the next layer via the weighted connections between them and finally form a complex network that learns with some feedback mechanism. The feedback mechanism is a learning scheme that modifies the connection weights by considering the difference between the output of the DNN and the actual output of the input. The basic idea is to find a connection network that could make the difference as small as possible.

(b) Feed-forward and Backpropagation

Feed-forward and backpropagation is a simple deep learning algorithm named **Artificial Neural Network (ANN)**. Figure 7.2 gives an illustration of this process.

In the beginning, all the connections are randomly assigned weight values. Given an input, the feed-forward algorithm predicts the possible output pattern using the assigned weight network from the input layer to the

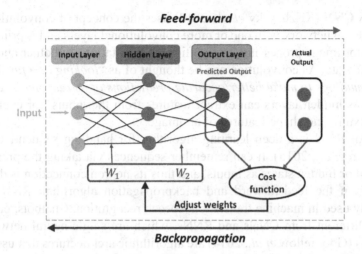

Figure 7.2: Feed-forward and backpropagation.

output layer. All the input nodes receive their respective values and generate a combination, like linear transmission, to the nodes in hidden layers. Upon receiving the input, hidden layers make information processing using an activation function to predict the output pattern using the assigned weights. There are various activation functions for calculating the hidden and output layers, for example, sigmoid function, softmax function, etc.

After gaining a prediction value from the feed-forward procedure, the backpropagation algorithm adjusts the connection weights from the output layer to the input layer. To do this, a cost function is adopted to measure the "error," that is, the difference between the actual output value and the predicted output value. It judges how wrong or bad the learned model is in its current form. The backpropagation process aims to reduce the current error cost by tweaking the weights of the previous layers. It needs to do this recursively throughout however many layers are in the network. Stochastic Gradient Descent is usually used to tweak the weights.

Feed-forward and backpropagation is a cycle learning process. There may be thousands, even millions of times, before finding the cost function's global minimum value.

(c) Popular Deep Learning Algorithms
Different connection types and learning schemes bring various DNNs, such as convolutional neural networks (CNNs), recurrent neural networks (RNNs), generative adversarial networks (GANs), etc.

A **CNN** (Krizhevsky *et al.*, 2012) uses the concept of convolution. It is a neural network with one or more convolutional layers and is primarily used for image processing, recognition, segmentation, and other autocorrelated data. As convolution can be thought of as *"looking at a function's surroundings to make better/accurate predictions of its outcome"*,[1] therefore, its hidden layers can extract features from the inputs, for example, the texture and shape features of an image.

An **RNN** is a deep learning algorithm for handling sequential data (Lipton *et al.*, 2015). It can remember sequences via taking the previous output or hidden states as inputs, and thus its neuron connection is different from the feed-forward and backpropagation algorithm. RNNs are widely used in machine translation, speech recognition, Chatbots, etc.

Different from CNNs and RNNs, which are single neural networks, **GANs** (Goodfellow *et al.*, 2014) are algorithmic architectures that use two neural networks, pitting one against the other (thus the "adversarial") to generate new, synthetic instances of data that can pass for real data. They are used widely in image generation, video generation, and voice generation.[2]

References/Further Readings

Goodfellow, I.J., Pouget-Abadie, J., Mirza, M., Xu, B., Warde-Farley, D., Ozair, S., ... & Bengio, Y. (2014). Generative Adversarial Networks. arXiv preprint arXiv:1406.2661.

Infocomm Media Development Authority (IMDA) & Lee, K.C. (2020). *Artificial Intelligence, Data and Blockchain in a Digital Economy*, 1st ed. World Scientific, Singapore.

Krizhevsky, A., Sutskever, I., & Hinton, G.E. (2012). Imagenet Classification with Deep Convolutional Neural Networks. *Advances in Neural Information Processing Systems*, **25**, 1097–1105.

Lipton, Z.C., Berkowitz, J., & Elkan, C. (2015). A Critical Review of Recurrent Neural Networks for Sequence Learning. arXiv preprint arXiv:1506.00019.

O'Shea, K. & Nash, R. (2019). *An Introduction to Convolutional Neural Networks Onwards Data Science*, May 2019. Retrieved from: https://arxiv.org/abs/1511.08458.

Zhang, H-P. & Singer, B. (1999). *Recursive Partitioning in the Health Sciences*. Springer, New York.

---

[1] An introduction to Convolutional Neural Networks Onwards Data Science, May 2019.
[2] A Beginner's Guide to Generative Adversarial Networks (GANs), Pathmind.

7.2 Sample Questions

Question 1
Which of the following is not a supervised learning algorithm in deep learning?

(a) Artificial neural network
(b) Convolution neural network
(c) Auto encoders

Question 2
Which of the following options does not match the corresponding description?

(a) Input layer: It contains input neurons that send information to the output layer.
(b) Hidden layer: It is used to send data to the output layer.
(c) Output layer: The data is made available at the output layer.

Question 3
Which of the following statements about cost function is wrong?

(a) A cost function describes how well the neural network performs with respect to its given training sample and the expected output.
(b) A cost function may depend on variables such as weights and biases.
(c) In deep learning, our priority is to maximize the cost function.

Question 4
Which of the following statements about feed-forward and backpropagation is wrong?

(a) Backpropagation is to update the neural network by learning from the feed-forward cost function.
(b) Feed-forward and backpropagation are two independent processes.
(c) Backpropagation can use stochastic gradient descent to tune the neural network weights.

Solutions

Question 1

Solution: Option **c** is correct.

Artificial neural networks and Convolution neural networks are supervised learning algorithms in deep learning. Auto Encoders are the unsupervised learning algorithms in deep learning.

Question 2

Solution: Option **a** is correct.

The input layer contains input neurons that send information to the hidden layer, not the output layer.

Question 3

Solution: Option **c** is correct.

In deep learning, our priority is to minimize the cost function. The smaller the cost function, the better the neural network's performance.

Question 4

Solution: Option **b** is correct.

Feed-forward and backpropagation work together to train a neural network model.

Part IV

Computer Network and Network Security

Chapter 8

Computer Network

8.1 Introduction

8.1.1 *Introduction to Computer Networks*

This introduction provides an overview of the different networks, components of a network, and functions of layers in a computer network.

Learning Objectives
- Learn about network hardware, software, and two essential models for network architectures.

Main Takeaways

Main Points
- Computer networks may be used in many settings, including business, home, and mobile settings, and address social issues.
- There are multiple types of network hardware (e.g., LANs, PANS, etc.) and software (e.g., various protocol hierarchies).

Main Terms
- **Computer networks:** A collection of autonomous computers interconnected by a single technology.
- **Protocol:** A set of rules that communicating parties agree upon and follow to communicate with each other.

(a) Uses of Computer Networks

This section will focus on what computer networks can be used for, including different uses in business and homes, mobile uses, and relevant social issues.

Business and home applications: The essential business applications of computer networks are **resource sharing**, where resources are no longer limited to physical resources but information. For example, when an employee is on a business trip to other places, he can remotely access the intranet's server resources through **virtual private network (VPNs)**, which breaks the **tyranny of geography**. This application mainly uses a client–server model. The **client–server model** is a network architecture that distinguishes clients from servers. In such models, the model would receive requests from the client, process them, and return the client's processed result. Figure 8.1 illustrates this model.

Computer networks also provide powerful **communication media tools** such as e-mail and video conferencing. This facilitates the communication between managers and employees. Through the Internet, companies can carry out various **electronic commerce (e-commerce)** activities to conduct multiple transactions with suppliers and customers on the Internet, such as aircraft manufacturers buying subsystems from multiple suppliers or shopping on Taobao.

Home applications of computer networks mainly include the following points:

- **Accessing remote information:** People usually browse web pages for information ranging from leisure to business, art to science, etc.

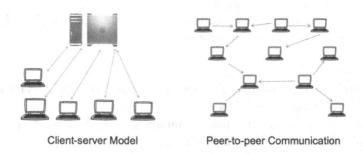

Client-server Model   Peer-to-peer Communication

Figure 8.1:   Client–server model and peer-to-peer communication.
Source: Tanenbaum and Wetherall (2010).

- **Communicating between individuals:** For example, **instant messaging**, which refers to a tool that can communicate online in real-time, is commonly known as an online chat tool (WhatsApp, FB Messenger, QQ, MSN, etc.). Taking a step further, participants can use peer-to-peer communication to share their resources and provide services and content to other users in the network. Such services are then accessed directly without passing through intermediaries. Both servers and clients can be participants in these networks. Figure 8.1 shows how it differs from the client–server model.
- **Entertainment:** For example, buying and downloading MP3 songs, watching interactive movies, and playing online games.
- **Ubiquitous computing:** For example, the use of electricity meters, gas meters, and water meters can be reported through the network, and the camera can directly transmit photos to computers or other equipment. Also, **radio frequency identification (RFID)** technology promotes the construction of the Internet of Things.

Mobile users: Based on wireless networks, computer networks mainly have the following applications for mobile users:

- **Mobile computers:** The demand for mobile Internet connections continues to drive laptops and other portable devices. Also, **cellular networks** enable our mobile phones to be covered by wireless networks.
- **Military:** In military activities, if the LANs are not reliable, the army needs to use its wireless network.
- **Wearable computers:** This kind of computer is made up of light equipment, composed of small mechanical and electronic parts such as watches. It is similar to an **head-mounted display (HMD)**, making the computer more portable. It can record users' state for health management and provide instant information, such as road guidance, peripheral information, etc.

Social issues: Another application of the Internet comes from its use in tackling political, social, and ethical issues.

One of the main issues is that it makes people's privacy more easily exposed. Common concerns such as employers spying on employees' e-mails and the government monitoring citizens' private information transmitted on the Internet may arise. There are also private sectors that track users' online activities, leading to the leakage of confidential information like credit card numbers. Phishing emails and viruses that steal our sensitive information also occur regularly.

Simultaneously, people's words, pictures, and videos published on the Internet may offend or hurt others. Even more extreme statements can lead to conflicts between different religions, races, or countries. Network operators may play a role in monitoring users and blocking certain content. However, they may mistreat other people, giving big companies better services and more freedom.

Computer networks have also raised new legal issues, such as the complexity of adjudicating criminals who come from different countries and commit crimes online.

(b) Network Hardware

A computer network can be defined as a group (or **set**) of autonomous computers interconnected by a single technology. There are two main classifications of networks: their transmission technology and their scale. There are two types of transmission technologies:

- **Broadcast links:** All machines share the communication channel on a broadcast network; short messages, sometimes called **packets**, are sent from one device to all others in the network, with a recipient specified in its address field. Machines ignore or process the packet based on this address field. The most common example of a broadcast link is a wireless network. These networks share communication over their coverage region, dependent on the transmission mechanism and the wireless channel specifications. **Broadcasting** refers to the mode of operation where a packet is addressed to *all* destinations using a special code in the address field. In contrast, **multicasting** refers to transmission to a subset of machines in a broadcast system. (Tanenbaum and Wetherall, 2010).
- **Point-to-point links:** These links connect individual pairs of machines. Packets may have first to visit at least one intermediate device to reach the destination on the network composed of such links. Since there are several possible routes, it is vital to find the optimum one. **Unicasting** refers to a **point-to-point** transmission mode with only one sender and one receiver.

When classifying network hardware by scale, we look at their interprocessor distance as a metric. Figure 8.2 classifies these networks by scale in ascending order:

Inter-processor Distance	1m	10m	100m	1km	10km	100km	1000km	10,000km
Processors located in the same...	Square meter	Room	Building	Campus	City	Country	Continent	Planet
Example	Personal area network	Local area network			Metropolitan area network	Wide area network		The Internet

Figure 8.2: Classification of networks by scale.

Source: Tanenbaum and Wetherall (2010).

Personal area networks (PANs): A PAN allows devices to communicate over short ranges. For example, **Bluetooth** and **RFID** are both short-range wireless networks. RFID is used on smartcards and library books. Bluetooth can connect devices like monitors, keyboards, printers to the PC, or digital music players to cars. A different type of PANs is medical devices such as pacemakers or hearing aids communicating with a user-operated remote control.

Local area networks (LANs): A LAN is a privately owned network limited to a relatively small space, such as a single building (home, office, or factory). Companies using LANs to connect devices to share resources such as printers are known as using **enterprise networks.** There can be wired and wireless LANs, with the latter being more popular. Each device has its own radio modem and antenna and communications with other devices via an access point (AP) in a wireless LAN. An AP is also known as a **wireless router**. The AP also functions as the connection between connected devices and the Internet. **WiFi** is an example of and the standard for wireless LANs.

Wired LANs perform better than wireless LANs because the packets can travel more efficiently along the wires rather than be transmitted omnidirectionally at the cost of efficiency and connection strength. Such LANs mainly consist of point-point links. **Ethernet** is an example of a wired LAN.

Metropolitan area networks (MANs): A MAN covers a city. Examples include the cable television network and **WiMAX**, which provides high-speed wireless Internet Access.

Wide area networks (WANs): A WAN covers a large geographical area such as a country or even a continent. An example of a Wired WAN is a company with multiple branch offices in different cities. In a wired WAN, computers in each branch office are known as **hosts**, while the rest of the network that connects these hosts is called the **communication subnet**, or just **subnet**. The subnet consists of two components: transmission lines and switching elements. **Transmission lines** are used to transfer data bits between machines. They can be made up of copper wire, optical fiber, or even radio links. In most WANs, transmission lines connect pairs of routers. **Switching elements**, also known as **switches**, are specialized computers that combine at least two transmission lines. They are responsible for choosing an outgoing line for data arriving on an incoming line. They are also commonly called **routers**.

A WAN may appear like a giant, wired LAN, but there are a few differences. Firstly, there is a greater separation between the communication and the application aspect of the WAN network. While a LAN is privately owned, in a WAN, it is common for different parties to own and operate the subnet and hosts. Secondly, routers in a WAN are usually connected to other kinds of networking technology. This means that many WANs are Internetworks, which will be described below. Thirdly, the subnet could be connected to different things.

A popular variant of a WAN is a **VPN**, where the branch offices are connected to the Internet instead of transmission lines. This provides flexible reuse of Internet connectivity but lacks control over the underlying resources.

Instead of the Internet, a WAN can also use an **Internet service provider (ISP) network**. Here, the subnet is operated by a different company, commonly known as a **network service provider**. Their customer base usually consists of offices. An ISP is a subnet operator that connects to other networks that are part of the Internet to allow customers to send packets to a wide range of receivers.

Popular WANs that use wireless technology include the cellular telephone network and the satellite network, where each computer on the ground sends and receives data via a satellite.

Internetworks: An Internetwork, or an **Internet**, is a collection of two or more interconnected networks. This "Internet" is used generically compared to the worldwide Internet, which is the most recognized Internet we usually refer to. Instead, the Internets merely refer to Interconnected networks that allow connected users to communicate with other users in a different network. The Internet uses ISP networks to connect enterprise networks, home networks, and many other networks.

How two networks with different hardware and software are connected is through a machine called a **gateway**. Gateways are differentiated by the layer at which they operate in the protocol hierarchy. Later in this chapter we will dive deeper into each layer.

(c) Network Software

Protocol hierarchies: Most networks are organized in stacks layer by layer. The number, contents, names, and functions of layers can vary from network to network. A **protocol** is a set of rules that communicating parties agree upon and follow to communicate. A list of protocols used by a particular system, one for each layer, is called a **protocol stack**. **Network architecture** is defined as a set of layers and protocols.

Figure 8.3 shows a five-layer network. Layers in the same levels across the two hosts are called **peers**, and they follow a set of protocols for communication.[1] As the name protocol hierarchies suggest, lower layers offer services to higher ones. Between each pair of adjacent layers is the **interface**, which defines which primitive operations and services the lower layer provides to the higher layer. For Host 1 to send a message to Host 2, Host 1 will first pass the data stream to the highest layer. This information is then passed down to the lower layers after performing some functions. When it reaches Layer 1, it passes the data stream to the **physical medium,** which contains cables. After the data stream reaches Layer 1 of Host 2, each layer then performs specified functions according to the protocol with its peer layer and passes it to the higher layers.

Design issues for layers: The following lists some of the key design issues for layers in network architecture:

- **Reliability:** A network needs to operate consistently despite its unreliable components.

---

[1] Protocol and Protocol Hierarchies (2020). Retrieved from https://www.tutorialspoint.com/ Protocol-and-Protocol-Hierarchies#:~:text=Most%20networks%20are%20organized%20 as,and%20adheres%20to%20specified%20protocols (accessed August 19, 2020).

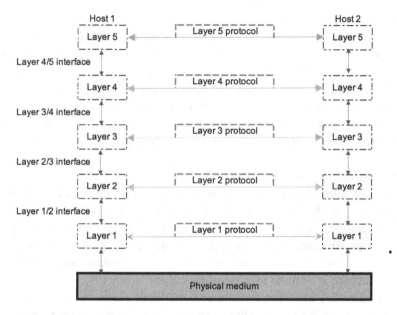

Figure 8.3: Layers, protocols, and interfaces in a five-layer network.

Source: Tanenbaum and Wetherall (2010).

- **Error detection** and **error correction** are mechanisms that use code to recover or retransmit incorrectly received information.
- **Routing:** Although there are multiple possible routes from a source to a destination, routing algorithms should choose the optimal one.
- **Scalability:** Problems may arise when networks grow larger and larger; thus, the layers should be designed such that the network continues to work well when it becomes larger.
- **Addressing:** Distinct mechanisms are required to identify the senders and receivers addressed in a specific message. This is known as **addressing** in the lower layers and **naming** in the higher layers.
- **Statistical multiplexing:** This concerns the resource allocation of bandwidth across hosts, where network bandwidth is shared dynamically, according to each host's short-term needs.
- **Flow control:** In networks with a fast sender but a slow receiver, the network may become congested, and data may be lost in the process. In this case, we can use flow control mechanisms at the receiver, such as increasing the buffer size to reduce congestion.

- **Confidentiality, authentication, and integrity:** Network security is paramount to defend against threats such as eavesdropping on communications (confidentiality), impersonating somebody else (authentication), and suspicious changes to messages (integrity).
- **Protocol layering:** As networks grow larger, new designs may also emerge that require the existing network to update. Protocol layering is a key mechanism used to support this change. It does this by splitting the problem into smaller steps and concealing implementation details.

Types of service offered by layers: There are two types of services offered by lower layers to higher layers, connection-oriented services and connectionless services. **Connection-oriented services** follow the telephone system, where the user establishes, and the user then terminates the connection. In contrast, **connectionless services** follow the postal system, where no connection is established or terminated.[2] The latter does not guarantee the reliability, but it is the more common service in most networks. In this case, reliability is implemented by acknowledging receipt of each message. Depending on the message, this may be worth the delays and additional costs, or it may also be undesirable.

Service primitives: A **service** refers to a set of **primitives**, or operations, that lower layers offer to higher layers across the interface. These primitives instruct the service to carry out or report specific actions taken on by a peer entity. The set of primitives depends on the nature of the service provided, and there are differences between the two types of services mentioned above.

The following lists six types of service primitives for a simple connection-oriented service:

1. **Listen:** This primitive is executed when a server is ready to receive an incoming connection and blocks waiting for an incoming connection.
2. **Connect:** This primitive establishes a connection with a waiting peer and awaits a response.
3. **Accept:** This accepts an incoming connection from a peer.
4. **Receive:** This blocks the server from waiting for an incoming message.

---

[2]GeeksforGeeks (2019). Difference between Connection-Oriented and Connection-Less Services. Retrieved from https://www.geeksforgeeks.org/difference-between-connection-oriented-and-connection-less-services/ (accessed August 19, 2020).

5. **Send:** This sends a message to the peer.
6. **Disconnect:** The connection is terminated, and no further messages can be sent. Both the client and the server send this packet to acknowledge the termination.[3]

(d) Reference Models and the Five Layers

The **open systems interconnection (OSI) reference model** is a general one that deals with connecting systems that are open for communication. Its protocols are not widely used, but each layer's features are essential.

The following is an overview of a general model that has been adapted from the OSI model, starting from the lowest layer:

- The **physical layer** is responsible for transmitting bits over a communication channel. This layer is above the physical medium.
- The **data link layer** focuses on how to send messages of a given length between directly connected computers with a given level of reliability.
- The **network layer** allows packets to be sent between distant hosts by combining several links into a network and several networks into Internetworks. They also choose a suitable path for the packets to be sent. As defined below, Internet Protocol (IP) is the primary protocol used here.
- The **transport layer's** purpose is to strengthen the network layer's delivery guarantees. The two main protocols are the TCP and UDP mentioned below.
- The **application layer** is the highest and determines the nature of communication to meet users' needs through programs that use the network. Examples of protocols are HTTP and DNS mentioned below.

The **transmission control protocol (TCP)/IP reference model** has widely used protocols, but the model itself is not as important. There are over 12 protocols, the most important of which include:

- **IP:** This is the most significant protocol responsible for IP addressing, host-to-host communication, data encapsulation, formatting, etc.[4]

---

[3]Studytonight (2020). Connection Oriented and Connectionless Services. Retrieved from https://www.studytonight.com/computer-networks/connection-oriented-and-connectionless-service (accessed August 19, 2020).

[4]javatpoint (2020). Computer Network. TCP/IP Model. Retrieved from https://www.javatpoint.com/computer-network-tcp-ip-model (accessed August 21, 2020).

- **TCP:** This protocol is a reliable connection-oriented protocol. It allows the byte stream of a host to be transmitted to the destination host without error and completes flow control.
- **User datagram protocol (UDP):** This is an unreliable and connectionless protocol widely used when prompt delivery is prioritized.
- **Domain name system (DNS):** This matches hosts' names to their IP addresses.
- **Hypertext transfer protocol (HTTP):** This protocol is used to fetch pages on the World Wide Web.
- **Real-time transport protocol (RTP):** This is used to deliver media such as movies or voice in real-time.

8.2 Five Layers

8.2.1 *The First Layer — Physical Layer*

The physical layer aims to transport bits from one device to another along the network. It is the most important layer, as communication between computers cannot happen without a physical layer.

Learning Objectives
- Learn about the theoretical basis of data transmission, transmission media, digital modulation, communication protocol, and communication systems.

Main Takeaways

Main Points
- The process of combining multiple signals into one signal over a shared channel is called **multiplexing**. It includes three forms such as FDM, TDM, and CDM.
- Two switching methods currently used to connect multiple communication devices are circuit and packet switching.

Main Terms
- **Multiplexing:** Combining multiple signals into one signal over a shared channel.
- **Digital modulation:** The process of converting between bits and signals.

- **Multipath fading:** The atmospheric layers may refract microwaves. The refracted waves may take longer to reach the destination than the direct waves.
- **Guard band:** A narrow frequency band between adjacent channels in multiplexing is used in FDM to separate the channel.

(a) Theoretical Basis of Data Transmission

Fourier analysis: Fourier analysis is how general functions can be represented as the sum of simple trigonometric functions. Jean-Baptiste Fourier proved that periodic function could be decomposed as the sum of sine and cosine components:

$$g(t) = \frac{1}{2}c + \sum_{n=1}^{\infty} a_n \sin(2\pi nft) + \sum_{n=1}^{\infty} b_n \cos(2\pi nft)$$

where f is the fundamental frequency ($= 1/T$), a_n is the sine amplitude of the nth harmonic, b_n is the cosine amplitude of the nth harmonic.

The values of a_n, b_n, and c are computed as follows:

$$a_n = \frac{2}{T}\int_0^T g(t)\sin(2\pi nft)dt$$

$$b_n = \frac{2}{T}\int_0^T g(t)\cos(2\pi nft)dt$$

$$c = \frac{2}{T}\int_0^T g(t)dt$$

The maximum data rate of a channel: The amount of thermal noise is calculated as the signal power ratio to the noise power, SNR. The signal-to-noise ratio is usually expressed in decibels (dB) given by

$$\text{SNR (dB)} = 10\log 10\ (S/N)$$

where S is the signal power, and N is the noise power.

Shannon's theorem gives a maximum data rate of a channel in bits per second. The Theorem can be shown as

$$c = w * \log 2(1 + S/N)$$

where c the achievable channel capacity *and* $(b/s)w$ is the bandwidth of the line.

This theorem suggests that if the channel's bandwidth increases, its capacity will be higher.

(b) Transmission Media
Guided transmission media:

- **Magnetic media:** Devices such as magnetic tape or removable media must move data from one device to another. Magnetic media is cost-effective.
- **Twisted pairs:** It is one of the oldest transmission media still in use today. A twisted pair is wiring where two wires are wrapped around each other (like a DNA molecule). Twisted pair is the widely used copper wire that connects most telephones to the telephone company. It can also be used for both analog and digital information communications. The use of twisted pairs is unique to different LAN standards.
- **Coaxial cable:** It is a type of cable that consists of a stiff copper wire as the core, surrounded by an insulating layer. A closely woven braided conductor encases the insulator. A plastic sheath again covers the outer conductor. Due to the construction and shielding of the coaxial cable, it has high bandwidth and excellent noise immunity. With better shielding and greater bandwidth, coaxial cable can span longer distances at higher speeds. Two types of coaxial cables with different impedance levels are commonly used: the 50-Ohm cable and 75-Ohm cable. The 50-Ohm cable is used primarily for data and wireless transmissions, and 75-Ohm is used for video signals.
- **Power lines:** It delivers electrical power to buildings. Once delivered to the buildings, electrical wiring brings the power to electrical outlets within the building for use.
- **Fiber optics:** It is used for long-distance and high-performance transmission in network backbones. Fiber optic cables bear similarities to coaxial cables but lack the trademark braid that coaxial have. The five main components of fiber optic cables are core, cladding, coating, strengthened fibers, and cable jacket. There are three key components of an optical transmission system: the light source, the transmission medium, and the detector. The light source transmits the data. The transmission medium is an ultra-thin fiber of glass that transmits maximum efficiency. The detector generates the electrical pulse based

on the light signal. **Multimode fiber** and **single-mode fiber** are two basic types of fibers. Single-mode is more expensive but more efficient than multimode. Compared with copper, fiber can handle much higher bandwidths and offers lower power loss. However, on the downside, fiber is relatively less pliable and can be easily damaged by overbending.

The electromagnetic spectrum and its uses for communication: Frequency starting from 3 to 30 kHz is known as **very low frequency (VLF)**. This range will easily get distorted by atmospheric changes. **Low frequency (LF)** ranges from 30 to 300 kHz. It is a good choice for long-distance communication because it will get reflected by the earth's ionosphere. **Medium frequency (MF)** is in the range of 300–3000 kHz. It is one of the most commonly used frequencies used in AM radio transmission, navigation systems, and emergency distress signals. **High frequency (HF)** is also known as short waves, ranging between 3 and 30 MHz. **Very high frequency (VHF)**, ranging from 30 to 300 MHz, is widely used in analog TV broadcasting and studying sea ice thickness. Figure 8.4 shows standard electromagnetic spectrum uses.

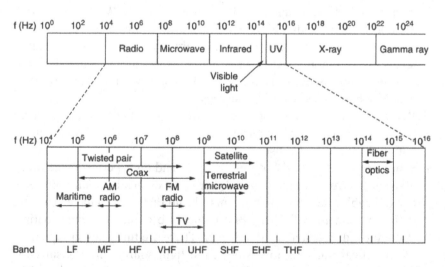

Figure 8.4: The electromagnetic spectrum and its uses for communication.

Source: Tanenbaum and Wetherall (2010).

Wireless Transmission:

- **The electromagnetic spectrum:** It is a continuous range of wavelengths. When electrons move, electromagnetic waves that can propagate through space are created.
- **Radio transmission:** Radio frequency (RF) waves are easy to generate, travel long distances, and penetrate buildings easily. This is due to their LF. Radio waves tend to travel in straight lines and bounce off obstacles in high frequencies. In the VLF, LF, and MF bands, radio waves follow the ground and can be detected for around 1000 km at the lower frequencies. In the HF and VHF bands, the radio waves must reach the ionosphere considering that the earth's ground wave tends to be absorbed.
- **Microwave transmission:** Microwaves travel in a straight line and do not pass through buildings well. Microwaves may be refracted by the atmospheric layers, causing the refracted waves to take longer to reach the destination than the direct waves. This effect is called **multipath fading**. Microwave communication is widely used for long-distance telephone communication, mobile phones.
- **Infrared transmission:** Unguided infrared waves are widely used for short-range communication. No government license is needed to operate an infrared system.
- **Light transmission:** Unguided optical signaling or free-space optics has been used for centuries. It is relatively easy to install and does not need a license.

(c) Digital Modulation
Digital modulation refers to transforming digital information (bits) into frequency (signals), as that is a necessary process to send digital information. Combining multiple signals into one signal over a shared channel called **multiplexing**.

Baseband transmission: Baseband transmission refers to send a digital signal over a channel without changing the digital signal to the analog signal. Using a positive voltage to represent a one and a negative voltage to represent a 0 is the most straightforward digital modulation form. The different encoding schemes of baseband modulation are non-return-to-zero (NRZ), NRZ invert (NRZI), Manchester encoding, and bipolar encoding.

Passband transmission: In Passband transmission, the amplitude, frequency, or phase of a carrier signal is modulated to transmit the bits. Each of these methods has a corresponding name. The types of passband transmission are amplitude shift keying (ASK), frequency shift keying (FSK), phase shift keying (PSK), and quadrature amplitude modulation (QAM). In **ASK**, two different amplitudes represent 0 and 1, while frequency and phase remain constant. Similarly, with **FSK**, more than one tone is used. The frequency of the signal is modulated to transmit bits. The simplest form of **PSK** is known as the **binary phase shift keying (BPSK)**, where the carrier wave uses only 2-phases separated by 180 degrees from each other. **Quadrature phase shift keying (QPSK)** involves 4-phases where each point on the 360-degree phase is equispaced to each other. With 4-spaces, the QPSK can double the data rate of BPSK. **QAM** is a combination of ASK and PSK. Both the amplitude and the phase are modulated to represent the signal levels.

Multiplexing: Multiplexing is the practice of sharing channels with multiple signals. It is more efficient for a single wire to carry multiple signals than to have a wire for every signal transmitted.

Frequency division multiplexing (FDM): FDM takes advantage of passband transmission to share a channel. It is a technique by which the spectrum is divided into a series of frequency bands, each used to send a separate signal. FDM is used in telephone networks, cellular, satellite networks, etc.

A narrow frequency band between adjacent channels in multiplexing, called **Guard band**, is used in FDM to separate the channel. However, it is also possible to efficiently divide the spectrum without using guard bands when sending digital data. In **orthogonal frequency division multiplexing (OFDM)**, the channel bandwidth is divided into many small frequencies (also called subcarriers) that independently send data (e.g., with QAM). These closely packed subcarriers are stored in the frequency domain. Thus, signals from each subcarrier extend into adjacent ones.

Time division multiplexing (TDM): In TDM, the users take turns in a round-robin fashion, each one periodically getting the entire bandwidth for a little bit of time. It is used widely as part of the telephone and cellular networks. TDM ensures that there will be no interference from simultaneous transmissions through allocating each user on a given frequency. TDM is very distinct from **statistical time division multiplexing**

(STDM). The prefix "statistical" signifies that the individual streams contribute to the multiplexed stream *not* on a fixed schedule but according to their demand statistics.

Code division multiplexing (CDM): CDM operates in a different way than FDM and TDM. It is a form of **spread spectrum** communication where a narrowband signal is spread over a wider frequency band.

This allows multiple users to share a common communication channel to send signals and can make it more tolerant to interference. **Code Division Multiple Access (CDMA)** is a standard technology used for the former purpose. CDMA allows each user (or station) to transmit their signals over the entire frequency spectrum at the same time. Each bit is then subdivided into m short intervals known as **chips**. There are usually 64 or 128 chips per bit. Each user is then assigned a unique m-bit chip sequence. This chip sequence is sent whenever the user wants to transmit 1 bit. To transmit 0 bit, the inverse of the chip sequence is sent instead. Thus, the data transmission rate is directly proportional to m (assuming no change in technology or breakthrough technique).

(d) Communication Protocol

Carrier sense multiple access (CSMA): CSMA is a network protocol. **1-persistent CSMA** requires that each station first listens to the channel and transmits immediately if the channel is idle. In the **non-persistent CSMA**, a station senses the channel when it wants to send a frame. If the channel is not idle, it waits a random period and then repeats the line. The **p-persistent CSMA** is applied to slotted channels. According to an Internet search, transmission with probability p happens at the end of the transmission when the transmitting station is sending a frame during a busy channel.

(e) Communication Systems

The mobile telephone system: The mobile phone system supports wide-area voice and data communication services.

- **First-generation(coco1G) mobile phones: Analog voice**
  In 1982, Bell Labs invented **Advanced Mobile Phone System (AMPS)**. Then the land area was divided into a small area called a cell. Each cell had a base station. The base station consists of a computer and transmitter/receiver connected to an antenna. All the base stations

are connected to an **Mobile Switching Centre (MSC)** or **Mobile Telephone Switching Office (MTSO)**. There was no worldwide standardization during the first generation.

- **Second-generation(2G) mobile phones: Digital voice**
  2G mobile phones switched from the analog system of 1G to a digital system. There are several advantages: (1) improves security; (2) provides capacity gains; (3) enables new services such as text messaging. There was also no worldwide standardization during the second generation, so various systems were developed. However, **global system for mobile (GSM) communications** is the dominant 2G system, which uses both FDM and TDM. The GSM **air interface** provides a link between the mobile and cell base stations. The **base station controller (BSC)** controls the cell base stations and connects the base stations and the Mobile Switching Centre (MSC). **Mobile assisted handoff (MAHO)** is a technique used in the GSM network where a mobile device helps the BSC transfer a call to another BSC.

- **Third-generation(3G) mobile phones: Digital voice and data**
  The ITU (International Telecommunications Union) issued IMT-2000 to support more diverse applications. The basic services that the **IMT-2000** network (IMT stands for International Mobile Telecommunication) was supposed to provide are (1) high-quality voice transmission; (2) messaging; (3) multimedia; (4) Internet access.

- **Fourth-generation(4G) mobile phones: Voice, data, signals and multimedia**
  4G comes in two main categories: **long-term evolution (LTE)** and **worldwide interoperability for microwave access (WIMAX)**. LTE is an extension of the 3G technology. It is based on **GSM/EDGE** and **UMTS/HSPA technologies**. WIMAX is a wireless broadband access standard mainly for mobile devices. With 4G, the transmission of voice, data, signals, and media will be carried out through IP, promising faster connection speeds across the board than 3G.

- **Fifth-generation(5G) mobile phones: Internet of things**
  5G has very little lag, with reaction times faster than the human brain. It is expected to provide faster speeds, greater capacity, and the potential to support new features and services.

Switching: Two switching methods currently used to connect multiple communication devices are circuit and packet switching. Circuit switching, which traditional telephone systems are built on, used to be the norm, but packet switching is becoming more popular with the rise of IP technology.

- **Circuit switching** is a switching method that creates an end-to-end path between two stations within a network before starting the data transfer. There are three phases: circuit establishment, transferring the data, and circuit disconnect. It is a good choice for continuous transmission over a long duration. Another advantage is that the data transmission delay is negligible. However, circuit switching requires more bandwidth and takes a lot of time to establish the physical links.
- **Packet switching** breaks data into small pieces (or packets) and then transmitted to the network line. Like circuit switching, the transmission delay is also minimal in packet switching. Unlike circuit switching, the data can be transferred directly. It is a cost-effective implementation. However, packet missing may occur in huge data transmission.

8.2.2 *The Second Layer — Data Link Layer*

The data link layer is the second layer above the physical layer. One of the data link layer tasks is to take the packets (such as IP) from the network layer and encapsulates them into frames, then transfer the data between adjacent nodes in the network.

Learning Objectives
- Learn about the design principles for the data link layer.

Main Takeaways

Main Points
- Main functions of data link layer: framing, error control, and flow control.
- The difference between error-correcting codes and error-detecting codes.
- The functionality of the data link layer.

Main Terms
- **Error detection:** A technique used to detect noise or other impairments present in the data transmission.

- **Cyclic redundancy checks (CRC):** A technique used to detect digital data errors.
- **Truncated binary exponential backoff:** The algorithm to determine the time needed for repeated retransmissions of the same block of data.
- **Zero-bit insertion:** A bit-stuffing technique in which a zero bit is inserted after a series of one bit to highlight a sequence change or break.
- **Acknowledgements (Acks):** Acks are signals passed between devices to signify an acknowledgment of a message's receipt.

(a) Design Principles

The data link layer is the protocol layer that manages data movement in and out of a communication channel. It is divided into two sub-layers: logical link control (LLC) sub-layer and media access control (MAC) sub-layer. The three primary functions of the data link layer are to (1) provide an interface to the network layer that is well defined, (2) handle transmission errors, and (3) control the flow of data.

Design issues for the layers: The data link layer can be designed to offer various services. The actual services offered can vary from protocol to protocol. Three reasonable possibilities are:

1. Unacknowledged connectionless service:
   - No Acks, no connection
   - Error recovery up to higher layers
   - For low error-rate links or voice traffic
2. Acknowledged connectionless service:
   - Acks improve reliability
   - For unreliable channel (wireless systems)
3. Acknowledged connection-oriented service:
   - The equivalent of reliable bit-stream
   - Connection establishment
   - Packets delivered in-order
   - Connection release
   - Inter-router traffic

(b) Error Detection and Correction

There are three main types of errors: single-bit errors, multiple-bit errors, and burst errors. There are two basic strategies for dealing with errors.

Error-correcting codes involve enough redundant data to allow the receiver to deduce the original message is one solution. **Error-detecting codes** include enough redundant information such that the receiver knows that an error has occurred. Retransmission is then requested.

Error-correcting codes: Error-correcting codes are widely used on wireless links. The four main error correction codes are hamming codes, binary convolution code, reed-solomon code, and low-density parity check (LDPC).

There are two principal ways:

Backward error correction (Retransmission): It is a method used in data transmission in which the receiver detects the errors. If the receiver detects an error in the incoming frame, it requests the sender to retransmit the frame.

Forward error correction: It is an error detection technique to detect and correct errors without retransmission. If the receiver detects some error in the incoming frame, it executes an error-correcting code that generates the actual frame.

Error-detecting codes: Error detection refers to the techniques used to detect noise or other impairments present in the data transmission. Over high-quality copper and fiber cable, the error rate is much lower, so error detection is usually more efficient for dealing with the occasional error.

There are three main techniques for detecting errors in frames: Parity, Checksums, and CRC.

1. **Parity check** is done by appending an extra bit, called the **parity bit**. This scheme is suitable for single-bit error detection only.
2. **A checksum** is based on addition. It is efficient and straightforward but provides weak protection in some cases because it does not detect the deletion or addition of zero data nor swapping parts of the massages.
3. The **CRC**, also known as a **polynomial code**, is a powerful and easy to implement the technique. It is an error detection mechanism in which a unique number is appended to a block of data to detect any changes introduced during storage or transmission. Polynomial codes are based upon treating bit strings as representations of polynomials with 0 and 1 only.

Polynomial arithmetic is done modulo 2, according to the rules of algebraic field theory. In Polynomial arithmetic, the sender divides the data to be transmitted by a predetermined divisor to obtain the remainder. This remainder is called CRC. If the remainder is zero, the message is assumed to be correctly received and accepted. If the remainder is not zero, it indicates that the message is corrupted and is therefore rejected. CRC is an efficient method to ensure a low probability of undetected errors using a suitable division.

CSMA/CD: CSMA is a network protocol where a node senses the network signals on the medium to check for lack of traffic before transmitting any data. **Carrier sense multiple access with collision detection (CSMA/CD)** is a network protocol for carrier transmission operating in the medium access control (MAC) layer. In this protocol, CSMA is improved by terminating any transmission when a collision is detected, reducing the time required to resend the transmission.

Truncated binary exponential backoff: Truncated binary exponential backoff refers to the algorithm to determine the time needed for repeated retransmissions of the same block of data.

Ethernet requires each transmitter to wait an integral number of slot time (51.2 μs). As for 10 Mb/s Ethernet, it takes slot-time to transmit 512 bits (64 bytes). If no collision occurs during the Ethernet transmission, no collision will occur for the following data.

(c) Data Link Protocols

Point-to-point links are needed for the Internet, dial-up modems, leased lines, and so on. A standard protocol called **point-to-point protocol (PPP)** is used to send packets over such links. PPP is byte-oriented rather than bit-oriented. The protocol field is two bytes long and identifies the protocol data unit (PDU) that the PPP frame has encapsulated. Synchronous PPP uses bit stuffing (same as HDLC). Asynchronous PPP uses a technique called byte stuffing. The requirements and non-requirements are shown in Table 8.1.

PPP provides three main features:

1. a framing method that is used to cover multiprotocol datagrams;
2. a link control protocol (LCP) to create, configure and test the data-link connection and
3. a way to establish and configure different types of network-layer protocols. Generally, this means that a different **network control protocol (NCP)** for each network layer supported is needed.

Table 8.1: List of PPP requirements and non-requirements.

PPP design requirements	PPP non-requirements
Simple	Lack of error correction/recovery
Packet framing	Lack of flow control
Bit transparency	Out of order delivery is not a problem
Data-compression negotiation	No need to support multipoint links
Network protocol multiplexing	
Error detection	
Network layer address negotiation	
Connection liveness: detect, signal link failure to the network layer	

Byte stuffing: The stream of bits from the physical layer may be divided into data frames in the data link layer. A pattern of bits, called **flag byte**, marks one frame's end and the beginning of the next one.

A frame contains the following parts:

- **Frame header:** Source and destination address of the frame.
- **Payload field:** Message to be delivered.
- **Trailer:** Error detection and error correction bits.
- **Flags:** 1-byte flag at the beginning and the end of the frame.

Two approaches, byte stuffing and bit stuffing are used to transmit the data. The data link layer on the receiving end removes the escape bytes before giving the network layer data. This technique is called **byte stuffing**. Byte stuffing is also called character stuffing. The PPP protocol uses an "escape" style of byte stuffing.

Bit stuffing: Each frame begins and ends with a unique bit pattern called a flag byte, 01111110. The sender data link layer will automatically stuff a 0 bit into the outgoing stream when it encounters five consecutive ones in the data stream. The receiver will automatically destuff the 0 bit before sending the data to the network layer when it sees five consecutive incoming ones. This technique is called **bit stuffing**.

Zero-bit insertion: Zero-bit insertion is a bit-stuffing technique in which a zero bit is inserted after a series of one bit to highlight a sequence change or break. It is used to achieve transparent transmission

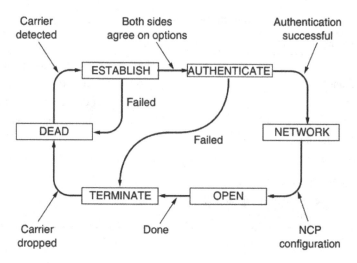

Figure 8.5:   State diagram for bringing a PPP link up and down.
Source: Tanenbaum and Wetherall (2010).

in SONET/SDH. If the sender encounters five consecutive **1 bits**, an extra 0 is added after these bits. When the receiver checks for five consecutive ones, the zero will be removed if the next bits after five consecutive 1 bits equals zero.

PPP link up and down: PPP is responsible for establishing, configuring, testing, maintaining, and terminating transmission links. ISPs adopted it to provide dial-up Internet access. Users use modems to connect to an **ISP**, and the ISP connects users to the Internet. **LCP** is used to agree upon the encapsulation format options automatically. **NCP** is used for transmitting multi-protocol data between two point-to-point devices (as shown in Figure 8.5).

(d) Ethernet
The main advantages of LAN:

- **Sharing of resources:** With the help of LAN, computer hardware resources and software applications can be shared.
- A **LAN** is very adaptable.
- **Securing of the system:** Keeping data on the server is more secure. It is a reliable type of communication.

Topology refers to the pattern of interconnection between the nodes of the network. The basic topologies of a LAN are Star, Tree, Ring, Hybrid.

Ethernet performance: The performance of Ethernet under conditions of heavy and constant load:

Assume that k stations always ready to transmit, and each station transmits during a contention slot with probability p. A station that acquires the channel in that slot with probability A:

$$A = kp(1 - p)^{k-1}$$

A is maximized when $p = 1/k$. Since each slot has duration of 2τ, the mean contention interval is $2\tau/A$. If the mean frame takes T s to transmit:

$$\text{Channel efficiency} = \frac{T}{T + 2\tau/A}$$

Hence, the longer the cable, the longer the contention interval.

Fast ethernet features: Fast Ethernets are implemented as **full-duplex networks**, so **CSMA/CD** plays a minor role in practices. Ethernet (**IEEE 802.3**) Frame Format defines the MAC sub-layer of the data link layer for wired Ethernet networks. Inter frame time gap is reduced to 0.96 μs from 9.6 μs if the length of cables is limited to 100 meters.

Gigabit ethernet: The features of Gigabit Ethernet are: (1) provide a higher rate of transmission up to 1 Gbps; (2) support both the modes full-duplex (does support CSMA/CD) and half-duplex (support CSMA/CD).

Gigabit Ethernet offers broad technological flexibility and scalability on bandwidth, cable length, and so on, so it is simple to upgrade from 1GbE to 10GbE. 10GbE is a telecommunication technology that extends Gigabit Ethernet by 10-fold. It works only in the full-duplex mod and extends Ethernet's traditional use in LAN to WAN and MAN.

(e) Network Bridges
A bridge is a network device that connects multiple LANs to form a larger LAN.

The benefits of Network bridges are:

- reduces network traffic with minor segmentation
- helps in extension of physical network
- reduces collisions
- improves reliability
- connects LAN having different speeds (such as 10Mb/s and 100Mb/s)

Bridges' drawbacks are the complex network topology and that it cannot help build a communication network between the networks of different architectures.

A transparent bridge is the most widely used type of network bridge that observes incoming network traffic to identify MAC addresses. The IEEE-defined transparent bridging is an industry-standard in 802.1D.

Transparent bridges use the backward learning algorithm. When a bridge starts, its routing table is empty:

1. The bridge does not know where any address is.
2. The incoming frame carries a source address. The bridges look at the frame's source and remember which LAN it came from.
3. If an incoming frame has a destination address remembered, send it only there.

Sliding window protocol: Sliding window protocol is a method of flow control for network data transfers. Sliding means moving to a new set of messages. The essence of all sliding window protocols is that at any instant of time, the sender maintains a set of sequence numbers corresponding to frames it is permitted to send. Data transmission is mainly run in both directions. A method to achieve full-duplex data transmission is to consider both the communication as a simplex communication pair. Each link comprises a "forward" channel (for data) and a "reverse" channel (for acknowledgments). The capacity of the reverse channel is almost entirely wasted.

A better idea is to use the same link for data in both directions. **Piggybacking** can provide better utilization of bandwidth. It is a technique that temporarily delays outgoing acknowledgments to be hooked onto the next outgoing data frame.

A **one-bit sliding window protocol** is also called a stop-and-wait protocol. It is a sliding window protocol with a window size of 1. In this protocol, the sender transmits a frame and waits for its acknowledgment before sending the next one. However, it is inefficient. Frames may be sent more than three times if multiple premature timeouts occur.

Go-back-n protocol is a sliding window protocol used to ensure reliable and sequential data frame delivery. In such a protocol, the sender window size is set to an arbitrary number N, but the receiver window will be 1. The protocol will keep sending N frames (known as the window) before receiving ack for the first frame. If the ack is not received, the protocol will resend everything from the first frame.

The go-back-n works well if errors are rare. However, it will waste many bandwidths on retransmitted frames if the line is poor. The **selective repeat protocol** allows the receiver to accept and buffer the frames following a damaged or lost one. In this protocol, both sender and receiver maintain a window of outstanding and acceptable sequence numbers, respectively. In selective repeat protocol, the sender window size starts at 0 and grows to some predefined maximum. The receiver window size is permanently fixed in size and equal to the predetermined maximum.

8.2.3 *The Third Layer — Network Layer*

The network layer's main task is to provide a reliable end-to-end service between the source and the destination. The station splits the message into several packets and then transmits. However, the packets' delivery does not need to be in order during transmission.

Learning Objectives
- Understand the design issues, Congestion Control Algorithms, and network-layer protocols.

Main Takeaways

Main Points
- Main functions of Network layers: routing, fragmentation, Internetworking, logical addressing.
- IP addressing scheme: IPv4 (32-bit IP address) and IPv6 (128-bit IP address).

Main Terms
- **Congestion:** Too many packets present in the network causes packet delay and loss that degrades performance.

- **Nonadaptive algorithms:** The algorithms do not make base routing decisions on any measurements or estimates of the current network topology and traffic condition.
- **Sink tree:** The union of optimal routes from all sources to a given destination.
- **Address resolution protocol (ARP):** A protocol that converts a dynamic IP address to its corresponding physical network address in a LAN.

(a) Network Layer Design Issues

The network layer is the lowest layer that deals with the end-to-end transmission. It offers services to the transport layer at the network layer/transport layer interface. The network layer can provide two types of service to its users: datagram network and virtual-circuit network.

The datagram is a connectionless service, and a virtual circuit is a connection-oriented service. For connectionless service, no advance setup is needed. Packets (called **datagrams**) are injected into the network (called a **datagram network**) individually and routed independently of each other. The path between the source and destination may be different for different packets. In the connection-oriented approach, a virtual-circuit network is needed. Each packet carries an identifier that determines which virtual circuit it belongs to (as shown in Table 8.2).

Table 8.2:   Comparison of a datagram and virtual-circuit networks.

Issue	Datagram network	Virtual-circuit network
Circuit setup	Not required	Required
Addressing	Each packet contains the full source and destination address	Each packet contains a short VC number
State information	Routers do not hold state information about connections	Each VC requires router table space per connection
Routing	Each packet is routed independently	The route chosen when VC is set up; all packets follow it
Effect of router failures	None, except for packets lost during the crash	All VCs that passed through the failed router are terminated
Quality of service	Difficult	Easy if enough resources can be allocated in advance for each VC
Congestion control	Difficult	Easy if enough resources can be allocated in advance for each VC

Source: Tanenbaum and Wetherall (2010).

(b) Routing Algorithms

The network layer's primary function is routing packets from the source machine to the destination machine. The network layer's software for deciding which output line an incoming packet should be transmitted is called a **routing algorithm**. Routing algorithms can be grouped into two major categories: non-adaptive and adaptive.

Non-adaptive algorithms are also known as **static routing algorithms**, which do not make base routing decisions on any measurements or estimates of the current network topology and traffic condition. **Adaptive (or dynamic) algorithms** adjust the route based on the traffic and topological conditions when routing to pick the best route. There are three categories of adaptive algorithms, which differ based on their information gathering method when they change their route and their optimization metric: centralized routing, isolated routing, distributed routing.

The optimality principle: It states that if router J is on the optimal path from router I to router K, then the optimal path from J to K also falls along the same route. To see this, consider the part of the route from I to J as r_1, and the rest of the route as r_2. If a route better than r_2 exists, it can be concatenated with r_1 to improve the route from I to K. This contradicts the earlier statement that r_1r_2 is optimal. The union of optimal routes from all sources to a given destination is a tree called **sink tree**. All routing algorithms aim to determine the sink trees for all the routers.

The optimality principle states that when considering the optimal path from routers X to Z, if router Y is on that path, then the optimal path from Y to Z (and X to Y) is also along the same route. A sink tree describes the optimal routes from all sources.

Shortest path algorithm: The idea is to find the shortest paths between a given pair of routers in the given graph.

Dijkstra's algorithm is a label-setting shortest path algorithm. Once a node is scanned, its labels are set permanently and never changed again.

Flooding: Flooding is a non-adaptive algorithm where every incoming packet is sent out through every outgoing line except the one it arrived on, thus generating many duplicate packets. One method is to have a decrementing counter that counts down with each hop, discarding when the counter reaches zero. Another approach is to have routers keep track of which packets have been flooded and stop sending them again. The benefit of flooding is that every node is guaranteed to have the packet. Thus, it is a suitable broadcasting mechanism. Flooding can also be a good baseline to judge other routing algorithms to choose the shortest path from source to destination.

Distance vector routing: Both distance vector and link-state routing are the preferred dynamic routing algorithms currently in use. Distance vector routing employs tables that each router must maintain, detailing the best-known route to each destination and the links used to get there. The tables are periodically updated by exchanging data with the router's neighbors. The result is that every router knows the best connection to every destination.

Link state routing: Link state routing refers to an algorithm where each router exchanges its neighborhood's knowledge to each router to learn the entire network topology. There are five steps:

1. Learning about the neighbors
2. Setting link costs
3. Building link-state packets
4. Distributing the link-state packets
5. Computing the new routes

Hierarchical routing: As networks grow in size, the router routing tables grow proportionally. The routing must be hierarchical and organized into multiple levels. For massive networks, it needs a multi-level hierarchy: the regions should be group into clusters, the clusters into zones, the zones into groups, and so on.

Broadcast routing: Broadcast routing refers to sending a packet to all destinations simultaneously. Various methods have been proposed for doing it. One that requires no special features from the network is for the source to send a distinct packet to each destination, but this method is not desirable in practice. Each packet contains either a list of destinations or a bit map indicating the desired destinations in multi-destination routing.

Multicast routing: Multicasting refers to sending a message to well-defined groups that are numerically large but small compared to the network as a whole. The routing algorithm used is called **multicast routing**.

Anycast routing: Anycast routing is an algorithm that advertises unique IP addresses on multiple nodes. Services like DNS or CDN use it.

(c) Congestion Control Algorithms

Congestion refers to a situation where too many packets present in the network causes packet delay and loss that degrades performance. The network may experience a **congestion collapse** if the network is not well designed.

The relationship between congestion control and flow control is a very subtle one. Both of them are traffic control methods. The main difference between congestion control and flow control is that congestion control is a global issue involving all the hosts' and routers' behavior. In contrast, flow control controls the traffic between a specific sender and a specific receiver.

Traffic-aware routing: Traffic-aware routing is an algorithm that tailors routes to traffic patterns that change during the day as network users wake and sleep in different time zones. This way, it can make the most of the existing network capacity.

Admission control: Admission control is widely used in virtual-circuit networks to keep congestion at bay. The idea behind this is not to set up a new virtual circuit unless the network can carry the added traffic without becoming congested. Decreasing the load is a helpful way when it is not possible to increase capacity.

Load shedding: If traffic-aware routing and admission control cannot make the congestion disappear, load shedding will be used. **Load shedding** refers to when the network has to throw away packets that it cannot deliver. The key problem is which packets should be dropped. There are two policies called **wine** (old is better than the new) and **milk** (new is better than the old).

(d) Quality of Service

Overprovisioning refers to a strategy to build a network with enough capacity by allocating more routers than is necessary for the network to function. This solution is inefficient and costly to implement.

Four issues must be addressed to ensure the quality of service:

1. Needs that application require from the network
2. Network traffic regulation
3. Methods to reserve resources to guarantee performance at
4. How traffic scalable the network is

(e) Network Layer Protocol

In the network layer, the Internet can be viewed as a collection of networks, and **Autonomous systems (ASes)** are the extensive networks that make up the Internet. These are constructed from high-bandwidth lines and fast routers. **Tier 1 networks** are the biggest of these backbones, to which everyone else connects to reach the rest of the Internet. Attached to the backbones are **ISPs**. The glue that holds the whole Internet together is the network layer protocol, **IP**. IP has been in heavy use for decades.

Except for IP, there are still four common communication protocols of TCP/IP (the **Transmission Control Protocol/IP**) in the network layer:

ARP is a protocol that converts a dynamic IP address to its corresponding physical network address in a **LAN**.

Reverse address resolution protocol (RARP) is a protocol used to translate interface addresses to protocol addresses.

The internet control message protocol (ICMP) is a protocol that network devices (e.g., routers) use to generate error messages due to network issues that stop IP packets from getting through.

Internet group management protocol (IGMP) is a protocol used by hosts and adjacent routers to establish multicast group memberships.

The relay system has two primary functions. One is to trip the circuit, and the other is to re-close the circuit.

- The relay system of physical layer: repeater.
- The relay system of physical layer: bridge.

- The relay system of physical layer: router.
- BRouter: A device that can forward data between networks (the bridge) and route data to individual systems within a network (the router).

IP address: An IP address refers to a network interface, not a host. Every host and router on the Internet has an IP address that can be used as the **source** and **destination address** fields of IP packets. When IP was first standardized in September 1981, the specification required that each system attached to an **IP-based Internet** be assigned a unique, **32-bit Internet address value**. There are two versions of the IP address in use currently: IPv4 and IPv6.

An IP address format is customarily divided into network ID (to identify the host's network) and host ID (to identify the host in a particular network). A host must have two IP addresses if it is on two networks. Routers have multiple interfaces and thus multiple IP addresses. Therefore, IP addresses are classified into various classes.

Followings are the five classes of IPv4 addresses:

1. **Class A:** It is mainly used for massive networks, such as government and big corporations.
2. **Class B:** It is mainly for medium-sized networks, such as multinational companies.
3. **Class C:** It is mainly for medium to small-sized networks, such as companies and colleges.
4. **Class D:** It has no segregation of host and network addresses. It allows multicast.
5. **Class E:** It is reserved for future use and research purpose. There is no defined use for class E.

However, there are some limitations of IPv4. IPv4 address space is not sufficient. IPv6 is a replacement design that provides 128-bit addresses expressed in hexadecimal notation. There are eight chunks of 16 bits each of IPv6 address, and a colon separates each chunk (:) (as shown in Table 8.3).

The difference between IPv4 and IPv6 is shown in Table 8.3.

Address resolution protocol: ARP is a general-purpose address translation protocol for IP networks.

Table 8.3: Comparison of IPv4 and IPv6.

	IPv4	IPv6
Address length	32 bits	128 bits
Address representation	In decimal	In hexadecimal
End-to-end connection integrity	Unachievable	Achievable
Address configuration	Manual and DHCP configuration	Auto-configuration and renumbering
Message transmission	Broadcasting	Multicasting and Any casting
Checksum field	Available	Not available
Packet format	An IPv4 packet is comprised of a header and data. The header contains information essential to routing and delivery.	An IPv6 packet has three parts: a basic header, one or more extension headers, and an upper-layer PDU. An upper-layer PDU is a combination of the upper-layer protocol header and its payload.

The important terms associated with ARP are:

(1) **ARP cache:** It contains tables used to store IP addresses.
(2) **ARP cache timeout:** It indicates how long the MAC IP address can be kept in its ARP cache.
(3) **ARP request:** ARP request packet contains the following: the physical address of the sender, the IP address of the sender, and the IP address of the receiver.

ARP response/reply: An ARP request is a broadcast, and an ARP response is a Unicast. There are four typical cases when an ARP is used:

- The sender is a host:
    1. It needs to send a packet to another host on the same network. Use ARP to find another host's physical address.
    2. It needs to send a packet to another host on another network. Use ARP to find the router's physical address.

- The sender is a router:
    3. It needs to send a datagram to a host on another network. Use ARP to find the next router's physical address.
    4. It needs to send a datagram to a host in the same network. Use ARP to find this host's physical address.

Open shortest path first (OSPF) — An interior gateway routing protocol: The OSPF is one of the Interior Gateway Protocol (IGP) used to find the shortest path from one router to another. It drew on a protocol called Intermediate-System to Intermediate-System (IS-IS). OSPF supports both point-to-point links and broadcast networks. There are five types of message:

1. **Type 1:** Hello group. Use to discover who the neighbors are.
2. **Type 2:** Database Description group. Announces which updates the sender has.
3. **Type 3:** Link-State Request group. Requests information from the partner.
4. **Type 4:** Link-State Update group. Provides the sender's costs to its neighbors.
5. **Type 5:** Link-State Acknowledgment group. Acknowledges link-state update.

Border gateway protocol (BGP) — The exterior gateway routing protocol: BGP is a dynamic routing protocol used between ASes to manage how packets get routed from the network to the network.

Internet multicasting: Internet multicasting is an IP-based technique used to support multicasting, using class D IP addresses. The range of IP addresses 224.0.0.0/24 is reserved for multicast on the local network. These are some local multicast addresses:

224.0.0.1 All systems on a LAN
224.0.0.2 All routers on a LAN
224.0.0.5 All OSPF routers on a LAN
224.0.0.251 All DNS servers on a LAN

8.2.4 *The Fourth Layer — Transport Layer*

The transport layer is the fourth layer. The transport layer's primary function is to transport data between processes on source machines to those on destination machines within certain reliability levels.

Learning Objectives
- Learn about the elements of transport protocols, congestion control, and Internet transport protocols.

Main Takeaways

Main Points
- **The elements of transport protocols:** Addressing, flow control, error control, multiplexing, and crash recovery.
- **The internet transport protocols:** A connectionless protocol (UDP) and a connection-oriented protocol (TCP).

Main Terms
- **Error detection:** a technique used to detect noise or other impairments present in the data transmission.
- **Max-min fairness:** An equilibrium where bandwidth flow cannot increase in a flow without a decrease somewhere else.
- **UDP:** an unreliable, connectionless protocol, which can be used on client–server interactions and multimedia.
- **TCP:** a protocol that can provide a reliable end-to-end byte stream over unreliable Internetwork.
- **Socket address:** A combination of IP address and port number.

(a) The Transport Service
The transport layer is an end-to-end layer, from source to destination. The services provided by the transport layer are like those of the data link layer, but the primary difference lies in where the code runs. For transport codes mainly run on the machines themselves. They mostly run on the routers for those of the network layer. The services provided by the transport layer include the following: end-to-end transmission, addressing, reliable delivery (including error control, sequence control, loss control, duplication control), flow control, congestion control, and multiplexing.

(b) Elements of Transport Protocols

A transport protocol is used to implement the transport service between two transport entities. The transport layer aims to offer efficient, reliable, and cost-effective data transmission services.

Addressing: An addressing scheme must deliver the information from one application process to another. These processes may run simultaneously while doing so. Each process has a specific port number to identify the correct process out of the various running processes.

Error control and Flow control: Error control ensures that the data is delivered with the desired level of reliability (usually set as no errors). Flow control is used to keep a fast transmitter from transmitting more than a slow receiver can handle.

The data link layer also provides an error detection mechanism, where the checksum is used by the receiving host to check for introduced errors in the system. It ensures node-to-node error-free delivery. However, the transport layer checksum covers a segment while crossing an entire network path. It is an end-to-end check. The transport layer deals with several types of errors due to the following: corrupted bits, non-delivery of TPDUs, duplicate delivery of TPDUs, and delivery of TPDU to a wrong destination.

Unlike the data link layer, flow control at the transport layer is also performed end-to-end instead of node-to-node. If the receiver is overloaded with too much data, the receiver discards the packets and asks for the retransmission of packets. This increases network congestion and thus, reduces the system performance. The transport layer uses the sliding window protocol that makes the data transmission more efficient. The sliding window protocol is byte-oriented rather than frame-oriented.

Multiplexing: Multiplexing involves sharing several conversations over connections, virtual circuits, and physical links. It plays a role in several layers of the network architecture. Multiplexing allows for the simultaneous use of different applications over a network that is running on a host. The transport layer uses multiplexing to improve transmission efficiency. Multiplexing can occur in two ways, namely upward and downward multiplexing.

Crash recovery: If the hosts and/or routers are prone to crashes or when connections are long-lived, crash recovery becomes a more pressing problem. If the transport entity is entirely within the hosts, recovery from network and router crashes is straightforward.

(c) Congestion Control
The network will become congested if the transport entities transmit too many packets too quickly. The Internet relies heavily on the transport layer for congestion control.

Desirable bandwidth allocation: The goal is to find a reasonable allocation of bandwidth to the transport entities using the network and avoid congestion. An efficient allocation will use all the available bandwidth but avoids congestion. **Max–min fairness**, which is an equilibrium where bandwidth flow cannot increase in a flow without a decrease somewhere else, is the ideal state of fairness for network usage.

Regulating the sending rate: Two factors may limit the sending rate. One is flow control (insufficient buffering at the receiver), another is congestion (low capacity in the network).

Wireless issues: The protocols that implement congestion control (like TCP) should remain independent from the underlying network and link-layer technologies. However, there are some problems with wireless networks; they always lose packets due to transmission errors, while sometimes packet loss is used as a congestion signal.

(d) The Internet Transport Protocols
There are two main protocols in the transport layer, a connectionless protocol (UDP) and a connection-oriented protocol (TCP). The protocols complement each other.

User datagram protocol: UDP is an unreliable, connectionless protocol, which can be used on client–server interactions and multimedia. UDP does not provide error control or flow control, so UDP is used for prompt delivery, which is more important than accurate delivery. In UDP, applications can send encapsulated IP datagrams even without an established connection. UDP transmits segments consisting of an 8 byte header. All

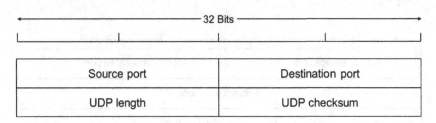

Figure 8.6: The UDP header.

Source: Tanenbaum and Wetherall (2010).

necessary header information is stored in the first 8 bytes (as shown in Figure 8.6).

Source port: It is a 2-byte long field. The source port is primarily needed when a reply must be sent back to the source.

Destination port: It is a 2-byte long field.

UDP length: The UDP length field includes the 8-byte header and the data. It is a 16-bits field.

UDP checksum: It is also provided for extra reliability.

TCP: TCP can provide a reliable end-to-end byte stream over unreliable Internetwork. In TCP, a logical connection must be established before communication. All TCP connections are full-duplex (meaning that data can flow both ways) and point-to-point (meaning that each connection has precisely two endpoints).

TCP estimates **round-trip time (RTT)** between a client and server dynamically to know how long to wait for an acknowledgment, and it does not support broadcasting and multicasting.

TCP service is obtained by having both the sender and receiver create endpoints, called **sockets**. Each socket has a specific number (address). This address contains the host's IP address and a 16-bit number local to that host called port. A socket address is a triple: {protocol, local-address, local-process}, where a port number identifies the local process. A connection must be explicitly established between a socket on the sending

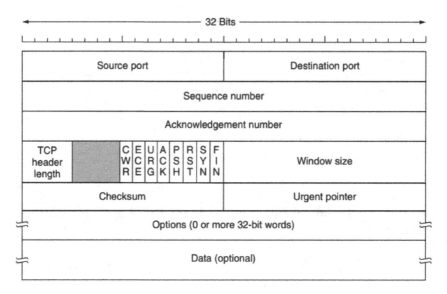

Figure 8.7: The TCP header.

Source: Tanenbaum and Wetherall (2010).

machine and a socket on the receiving device to obtain TCP service. The connection is a byte stream rather than a message stream.

TCP header contains the following fields:

- **Source port and destination port:** These fields are used to identify the connection's local endpoints. The connection identifier is called a five-tuple and contains five pieces of information, including the protocol (TCP), source IP and source port, destination IP, and destination port (as shown in Figure 8.7).
- **The sequence number and acknowledgment number:** The former indicates the byte sequence number of the byte of the data in the TCP packet segment, the latter specifies the next in-order byte expected, not the last byte correctly received. Every byte of data is numbered in a TCP stream, so both are 32 bits.
- **TCP header length:** It tells the number of 32-bit words in the TCP header.
- **A 4-bit field that is not used.**
- **Eight 1-bit flags:** *Congestion Window Reduced* (*CWR*) and *ECN-Echo* (*ECE*) are used to signal congestion when *explicit congestion notification* is used. If the *Urgent pointer* is in use, the *Urgent* (*URG*) is set

to 1. The *Acknowledge* (*ACK*) bit is set to 1 to indicate that the Acknowledgment number is valid. The *Push* (*PSH*) bit indicates Pushed data. The *Reset* (*RST*) bit is sent from the receiver when the packet received was not expected. It can be used to reset connections (e.g., during a host crash), reject invalid segments, and refuse connections. The *Synchronization* (*SYN*) bit is used to establish handshakes between hosts (or connections). The *Finished* (*FIN*) bit is used to release a connection.

- **Window field:** It tells how many bytes may be sent starting at the byte acknowledged.
- **Checksum:** It is also provided for extra reliability. It checksums the header, the data, and a conceptual pseudo-header in the same way as UDP.
- **Option field:** It is designed to provide a way to add extra facilities not covered by the regular header. A widely used option is the one that allows each host to specify the **maximum segment size (MSS)** it is willing to accept.

To release a TCP connection, either party can send a FIN segment to mean it has no more data to transmit. When the FIN is acknowledged, that direction is shut down. The connection will be released when both directions have been shut down.

TCP timer management: TCP uses more than one timer to do its work. One of the most important timers is the **retransmission timeout (RTO).**

TCP congestion control: TCP plays the central role in controlling congestion and reliable transport on the Internet. The TCP congestion window is used to manage the data traffic volume. The window's size is the number of bytes the sender may have in the network at any time.

TCP slow start is an algorithm used to detect the available bandwidth for packet transmission and balance the amount of data a sender can transmit with the amount of data the receiver can accept (the lower of the two values is the maximum amount of data that can be transmitted). It is a kind of sliding window.

TCP slow start can prevent a network from becoming overloaded. It slowly increases the amount of data transmitted until it reaches the maximum amount of data that the sender and receiver are allowed.

TCP slow start works as follows:

1. The sender transmits the packet, which contains the congestion window (*cwnd*), to a receiver.
2. The receiver acknowledges the packet and responds with its window size.
3. The sender will increase the next packet's window size after receiving the ACK until the limit is reached.

8.2.5 *The Fifth Layer — Application Layer*

The application layer has many support protocols that help applications such as the World Wide Web and multimedia function. This section will discuss the DNS, explore the types of Web pages and applications and protocols like HTTP that allows communication between the client and the server. We will also briefly touch on streaming multimedia and content delivery such as peer-to-peer networks.

Learning Objectives
- Understand how support protocols in the application layer work to allow applications to function.
- Understand the challenges and solutions of these support protocols.

Main Takeaways

Main Points
- When a client accesses a Web page, the Web browser used makes a TCP connection to the IP address for the HTTP protocol. It then submits an HTTP request and receives a response. Hyperlinks on the requested Web page are fetched in the same way.
- Two architectures designed for content distribution using the bandwidth are the Content Distribution Network (CDN) and the P2P network.
- For streaming stored media, compression algorithms are used to encode and decode the data for quick transfer and reduce bandwidth usage.

Main Terms
- **DNS:** A naming database is mainly used to map hostnames to IP addresses.

- **HTTP:** HTTP is a simple request-response protocol that usually runs over TCP. It specifies what the client will send and receive from the server.
- **Peer-to-peer (P2P) networks:** P2P networks are an alternative for content distribution, where many computers pool their resources and form a content distribution system.

(a) Domain Name System

There needs to be a protocol that maps hostnames to IP addresses in the application layer. The **DNS** is a distributed, hierarchical naming database invented in 1983, mainly used for this purpose. When a user accesses a website, the browser performs a DNS query against a server, providing the hostname.[5] Other Internet activities apart from web browsing also rely on DNS to connect users to remote hosts by providing information quickly. Access providers such as enterprises, governments, or universities usually have assigned ranges of IP addresses and domain names. They may also run DNS servers to manage the mapping of names to addresses.

Briefly, a DNS is used in the following explanation. A **resolver** is a library procedure called by an application program to map a host name onto an IP address. It sends a query containing the host name to a local DNS server, which searches and returns the IP address.

DNS name space: To avoid confusion, there is a naming hierarchy in DNS. This hierarchy is managed by an organization known as the Internet Corporation for Assigned Names and Numbers (ICANN). The **top-level domain** appears after the domain name period and comes in two types: generic and countries. Table 8.4 lists some generic top-level domains.

Some internationalized country domains allow host names using non-Latin alphabets such as Arabic, Chinese, and Cyrillic ones. To obtain a second-level domain, such as company-name.com, one just must check with registrars appointed by ICANN if the name is available and pay an annual fee. Some earn significant profits by registering domains and selling them to interested parties at a much higher price. There are also

---

[5]DNS Types: Types of DNS Records, Servers and Queries (2020). Retrieved from https://ns1.com/resources/dns-types-records-servers-and-queries (accessed September 4, 2020).

Table 8.4: Top-level domains.

Domain	Use
com	Commercial
net	Network providers
edu	Educational institutions
org	Non-profit organizations
int	International organizations
mil	Military
biz	Businesses
name	People
pro	Professionals
xxx	Sex industry

restrictions on who can obtain a name. For example, there are restrictions for the military and educational institutions but none for network providers or commercial use.

A domain name is made of multiple components known as labels. The label on the left denotes another subdomain to the right. Each domain is named by the upper-level paths and separated by periods. The maximum number of characters for each label is 63 characters, and there can be up to 127 subdomains.[6] The entire domain name should not exceed 253 characters.[7] Taking the science department at Harvard as an example, the domain name might be science.harvard.com. The domains control and permit how the subdomains are allocated. For instance, in Japan, the domains ac.jp and co.jp are used instead of *edu* and *com,* while in the Netherlands, all organizations are under *nl.* Companies can register under several top-level domains.

Domain names are case-insensitive. They can be either absolute or relative, with the former always ending with a period. Absolute domain names give the full path to the domain while relative domain names do

---

[6]What is the Domain Name System? — Definition from WhatIs.com (2020). Retrieved from https://searchnetworking.techtarget.com/definition/domain-name-system#:~:text=The%20domain%20name%20system%20(DNS,uses%20to%20locate%20a%20website (accessed September 3, 2020).

[7]Port 80 is one of the most commonly used port numbers in the TCP suite. Web/HTTP clients such as Web browsers use port 80 to send and receive requested pages from a HTTP server.

not. Thus, they are used within a specific parent domain and must be interpreted in that context.

Domain resource records: A **resource record** is the basic data element in the DNS. Each domain may have a set of resource records associated with it, typically the website's connections with the outside world. To be more specific, the function of DNS is to map domain names onto resource records. The most common resource record is its IP address.

Resource records are encoded in binary and sent across a network in text format. Each record is a five-tuple in the following format:

Domain_name	Time_to_live	Class	Type	Value

- *Domain_name*: This tells us the corresponding domain for the record. Since there are usually many records for each domain, this is used as the primary search key for queries.
- *Time_to_live*: This specifies the duration in seconds of the time taken for any DNS changes to affect users across the Internet.[8] Simply put, it indicates the stability of the record. A longer *time_to_live* denotes more stable information and vice versa.
- *Class*: This field is always *IN* for Internet information. Non-Internet information can use other codes, but these are rarely seen in practice.
- *Type*: There are 23 types of DNS records which will be elaborated below (Singh, 2020).
- *Value*: This can be a number, domain name or ASCII text,[9] depending on the resource record type.

Table 8.5 summarizes the meanings and values of the more common types of DNS records:

The A (Address) record type is the most important. It holds a 32-bit IPv4 address that the DNS returns for a hostname. The MX (Mail

---

[8]Klensin J. (2004). RFC 3696 — Application Techniques for Checking and Transformation of Names (2020). Retrieved from https://tools.ietf.org/html/rfc3696 (accessed September 7, 2020).

[9]ASCII is a 7-bit character set containing 128 characters. It contains the numbers from 0 to 9, the upper- and lower-case English letters from A to Z, and some special characters. The character sets used in modern computers, in HTML, and on the Internet, are all based on ASCII.

Table 8.5: Main DNS resource record types.

Type	Meaning	Value
SOA	Start of authority	Parameters for this zone
A	IPv4 address of a host	32-Bit integer
AAAA	IPv6 address of a host	128-Bit integer
MX	Mail exchange	Priority, domain willing to accept email
NS	Name server	Name of a server for this domain
CNAME	Canonical name	Domain name
PTR	Pointer	Alias for an IP address
SPF	Sender policy framework	The text encoding of mail sending policy
SRV	Service	Host that provides it
TXT	Text	Descriptive ASCII text

Source: Tanenbaum and Wetherall (2010).

exchange) record type is a common type that provides information about the name of a host prepared to accept mail for the specified domain. The NS (Name Server) record specifies a name server for the domain or sub-domain. It is used as part of the process to look up names and copy the database for a domain.

Name servers: The DNS namespace is divided into **zones** that do not overlap to prevent problems with a single source of information. The zones are decided upon by its administrator based on the name servers' demand and location. These name servers are hosts that hold the zone's database. Each zone usually has a primary name server and at least one secondary name server.

As explained briefly on how a DNS is used via a resolver, **name resolution** refers to the process of searching a domain name and finding an address. If the name can be found, it returns the authoritative resource records. An **authoritative record** comes from the authority that manages the record and is always correct. On the other hand, **cached records** may be outdated.

The **root name server** is at the top of the hierarchy, and these name servers contain information about each top-level domain. There are 13 root DNS servers in the world that are replicated and located world-wide for reliability and performance purposes.

Down the hierarchy, local servers continue to send queries. There are three types of DNS queries:

- **Recursive query:** When a hostname is searched, the DNS resolver is obligated to provide an answer — either the relevant resource record or an error message.
- **Iterative query:** When a hostname is searched, the DNS resolver provides the best answer. If the relevant resource record cannot be found, the resolver will direct the DNS client to the name server closest to the required zone to continue the name resolution by issuing more queries.
- **Non-recursive query:** This is a query in which the resolver already knows the answer and returns a record without needing additional rounds of questions.

Email protocol: Email protocols are a set of rules to help transfer the information between two computers. There are four different mail protocols: SMTP, POP3, IMAP, and HTTP.

Simple mail transfer protocol (SMTP) is a connection-oriented application layer protocol. It transfers the client's email (only text) on and across the network.

Post office protocol version 3 (POP3) is a protocol used by email clients to receive emails from a web server. Mail is usually downloaded to the user agent computer instead of remaining on the mail server. Once the emails are downloaded, they disappear from the server. It is a simple protocol but can support only one mail server for each mailbox.

Internet message access protocol (IMAP) is a protocol used by email clients to receive emails from multiple mail servers. It supports multiple mail clients connecting to a single mailbox at the same time. Mail does not need to be downloaded first before managing or reading. There is still a record of all emails on the server. The main difference between SMTP and POP3/IMAP is that SMTP is used for sending email while POP3/IMAP are nodes to join and leave with minimal or no disruption be used to retrieve and manage email.

HTTP is a request-response protocol used to send and receive mails on Internet browsers. Yahoo! And Hotmail use HTTP for accessing emails through the Internet. It is a simple but powerful protocol. The three basic HTTP features are connectionless, media-independent, stateless (the server and client are aware of each other only during a current request).

(b) World Wide Web

Architectural overview: The World Wide Web, also known as the Web, is an architectural framework for accessing content linked and spread out over millions of machines on the Internet. The web **browser** is a program that fetches pages requested, interprets, and displays the page. Pages are fetched by sending requests to one or more servers, responding with the page content. This request-response protocol runs over TCP and is called the **HTTP**. This content can be static or dynamic. A **static page** is the same every time it is displayed. In contrast, a **dynamic page** contains a program or is generated by a program on-demand, thus presenting itself differently each time it is displayed.

For a browser to display a page, mechanisms are needed to name and locate distinct pages. A **Uniform Resource Locator (URL)** is assigned to every page and essentially serves as its worldwide name. There are three components in a URL: the protocol, the DNS name of the host, and the pathname. Using http://www.sci.harvard.edu/index.html as an example, the protocol is http, the DNS hostname is www.sci.harvard.edu, and the pathname is *index.html.*

On the client-side, the following happens when a link, such as the URL given above, is clicked[10]:

1. The web browser determines the URL by seeing what was clicked.
2. The browser requests DNS for the IP address of the server www.sci. harvard.edu.
3. DNS replies with an IP address.
4. The browser makes a TCP connection to the IP address on port 80[11] for the HTTP protocol.
5. The browser sends over an HTTP request for the page */index.html.*
6. The server sends the page as an HTTP response.
7. If the page contains URLs needed for display, the browser fetches the relevant URLs in the same manner.
8. The browser displays the page.

---

[10]*Ibid.,* p. 650.
[11]Same as Footnote 7.

9. Once there are no further requests to the same servers for a period of time, the TCP connections are released.

For certain websites such as news or e-commerce, the server needs to determine whether users who request the page have previously visited and track what users have added into their cart for e-commerce. A cookie is a mechanism used to solve this problem. A **cookie** is a small named string that the server associates with a browser that contains information about the client requesting the page. Cookies can track user behavior on web pages and is a key concern for many about privacy. Most browsers allow users to block **third-party cookies**, cookies from a different site than the page being fetched.

Static web pages: As mentioned previously, static pages are the same each time they are fetched and displayed. Most pages are written in **HyperText Markup Language (HTML)**. **HTML** describes the formatting of documents, allowing users to design pages that include text, video, hyperlinks, etc. Forms that allow users to submit information can also be written in HTML. **Cascading Style Sheets (CSS)** enables users to control tagged content's appearance without editing the HTML file, keeping them small.

Dynamic web pages and web applications: The web applications that we use in our everyday lives, such as shopping on e-commerce, navigating maps, looking at our email, and collaborating on documents, all require dynamic pages. In web applications, user data is stored on servers in Internet data centers. The dynamic content needed for these applications is generated by programs running on the server or in the browser. Generally, when a user submits a request, a program will run on the server, which consults a database to generate the relevant page and return it to the browser.

There are two standard Application Programming Interfaces (APIs) for server-side dynamic web page generation, developed for Web servers to invoke programs. These allow developers to extend different servers with Web applications. The APIs are:

- **Common gateway interface (CGI):** CGI is used to handle dynamic page requests. It is a part of the server that communicates with other programs on the server. It allows the server to call up a program while passing user-specific data such as those submitted in forms in HTML form (Gundavaram, 1997). The data is then processed, and the server gives the response back to the Web browser.

- **Hypertext preprocessor (PHP):** PHP is an open-source scripting language used for Web development embedded into HTML.[12] A similar way to generate dynamic HTML pages is through **JavaServer Pages (JSP)**, which uses Java instead of PHP.

On the client-side, such as pages responding to cursor movements, scripts embedded in HTML need to be executed on the client machine. **Dynamic HTML** generally refers to the technologies used to produce such interactive Web pages. The most popular scripting language for the client-side is **JavaScript**, which has different PHP uses.

To create the Web application's seamlessness and responsiveness, several technologies, including the scripting language we discussed above, are used in a combination known as **Asynchronous JavaScript and Xml (AJAX)**. Web applications such as Gmail and Google docs are written with AJAX. The combination of technologies is:

1. HTML and CSS are used to display information as pages.
2. Document Object Model (DOM)[13] to modify parts of pages when viewed.
3. Extensible Markup Language (XML)[14] allows programs to exchange data with the server.
4. An asynchronous way to carry out #3.
5. JavaScript to bind these functionalities together.

Hypertext transfer protocol: HTTP is a simple request-response protocol that usually runs over TCP. It specifies what the client will send and receive from the server. For example, the following is a typical request-response circle[15]:

Table 8.6 shows a browser contacts a server by establishing a TCP connection to port 80 on its machine. There are two types of connections.

---

[12] PHP: What is PHP? — Manual (2020). Retrieved from https://www.php.net/manual/en/intro-whatis.php (accessed September 5, 2020).

[13] DOM is a representation of an HTML page that all programs can access.

[14] XML is a language for specifying structured content.

[15] What is HTTP (2020). Retrieved from https://www.w3schools.com/whatis/whatis_http.asp (accessed September 5, 2020).

Table 8.6: Browser requests and responses.

Browser request	Server response
HTML page	HTML file
Style sheet	CSS file
JPG image	JPG file
Javascript code	JS file
Data	Data in XML or JSON

Persistent connections make it possible for **connection reuse**, where additional requests and responses can be exchanged by establishing a TCP connection once. In contrast, **parallel connections** are when one request is sent per TCP connection, but several TCP connections are run in parallel. Though the latter has much better performance, it is discouraged due to overhead and congestion problems.

Methods are operations that HTTP supports, in addition to requesting a Web page. The following list summarizes the main built-in request methods and their descriptions[16]:

- **GET:** Requests the server to send the page.
- **HEAD:** Reads a Web page's header.
- **POST:** Uploads data to the server, such as contents of a form.

Each response to a request contains a status line and additional information like the Web page. We often run into Error 404: Page not found. These three-digit codes specify whether the request was satisfied and the reason if it was not. Table 8.7 summarizes the types of code.

HTTP **headers** allow the client and server to pass additional information with a request, response, or both. For example, the *User-Agent* is a request header that tells the server about the client's browser implementation. This allows servers to tailor specific responses to the browser. The *If-Modified-Since* and *If-None-Match* headers are used with caching, which will be discussed below. These headers allow clients to request for a page to be sent only if the cached copy is no longer valid. There are

---

[16]HTTP request methods. (2020). Retrieved from https://developer.mozilla.org/en-US/docs/Web/HTTP/Methods (accessed September 6, 2020).

Table 8.7:　Status codes.

Code	Meaning	Examples
1xx	Information	100 = server agrees to handle client's request
2xx	Success	200 = request succeeded; 204 = no content present
3xx	Redirection	301 = page moved; 304 = cached page still valid
4xx	Client error	403 = forbidden page; 404 = page not found
5xx	Server error	500 = internal server error; 503 = try again late

Source: Tanenbaum and Wetherall (2010).

many other headers such as *Host, Authorization, Location, Cookie* used for a wide variety of purposes.

Since many users frequently revisit pages, there should be a mechanism to quickly fetch data from the browser instead of the underlying storage layer. A **cache** is a high-speed data storage layer that typically stores temporary data to serve data faster.[17] **Caching** allows for the efficient reuse of previously fetched data. In HTTP, built-in support helps clients determine when they can safely reuse cached pages. The browser has to store pages. To ensure the cached copy is identical to the page if it was fetched again, HTTP uses two strategies — page validation and a conditional GET.

- **Page validation:** Headers like *Expires* or *Last-Modified* can be used to consult whether the cached copy is still valid.
- **Conditional GET:** This strategy asks the server if the cached copy is still valid, which will respond to confirm the validity or send the full response.

Caching can also be done outside the browser. This is called **proxy caching**. HTTP requests can be routed through a series of caches.

The mobile web: The Mobile Web is simply Web access from mobile devices. When it first started, it was common to see user experience problems while browsing the Web on mobile devices such as scaling, limited input capabilities, network bandwidth, and computing power. Although

---

[17]What is Caching and How it Works | AWS (2020). Retrieved from https://aws.amazon.com/caching/ (accessed September 6, 2020).

most of these have been solved, there is still a gap between mobile and desktop browsing. Some approaches used to make pages function well on the mobile Web include:

- Running the same Web protocols for mobile devices and desktops
- Websites creating mobile-friendly content and delivering the relevant type using servers to detect browser software in the request header
- XHTML Basic, a stripped-down version of HTML
- Content transformation, or **transcoding**, where a computer acts as the middleman between the mobile and the server by transforming content from the server into mobile Web content.

Web search: Perhaps the most successful Web application is search. When users go to the URL of the search engine, they enter search terms through a form. The search engine then queries its database for relevant pages, images, or other resources, returning the results as a dynamic page. Search engines can do this through a process known as **web crawling**, where the content of different pages is downloaded and indexed so relevant information can be retrieved when needed. This is possible since pages are usually linked to other pages. Web crawlers follow specific rules in deciding which pages to crawl, such as their relative importance (based on the number of visitors, how many other pages link to that page, etc.), and revisit webpages (to make sure the most updated content is indexed) and *robots.txt* requirements,[18,19] Data indexed are then processed using algorithms.

(c) Streaming Audio and Video
Apart from Web applications, audio and video are other exciting network developments. Advancements in Internet bandwidth and growth in computers' power paved the way for voice data carried over Internet networks, called **voice over IP** or **Internet telephony** and video. Streaming and conferencing applications need to be designed to reduce network delay. Audio and video need real-time presentation, which means they need to

---

[18]Also known as the robots exclusion protocol, *robots.txt* is a file hosted by the page's server that specifies the rules for any bots accessing the hosted website or application.
[19]What Is a Web Crawler? | How Web Spiders Work. (n.d.). Retrieved from https://www.cloudflare.com/learning/bots/what-is-a-web-crawler/ (accessed September 6, 2020).

be played at a predetermined rate. **Jitter** is the variation in delay, rather than absolute delay, that causes audio or video to be interrupted.

Digital audio: Digital audio is a digital representation of an audio wave that can recreate it. Audio waves are converted digitally via an **Analog-to-Digital Converter (ADC)**. To lower bandwidth needs, encoding and decoding algorithms are used to compress and decompress audio data. The most popular formats of compression algorithms are the **MPEG audio layer 3 (MP3)** and **Advanced Audio Coding (AAC) in MPEG-4 (MP4) files**.

There are two ways to compress audio:

1. **Waveform coding:** Fourier transform is used to transform the signal into its frequency components.
2. **Perceptual coding:** Signals are encoded based on **psychoacoustics**.[20] Frequency masking and temporal masking are used. MP3 and AAC are based on perceptual coding.

Digital video: The most straightforward digital representation of a video is a sequence of frames that each consists of **pixels.** Low-resolution video maybe 320 by 240 pixels, while High-Definition TeleVision (HDTV) can be 1280 by 720 pixels. Videos also need to be compressed for quicker transmission.

The **Joint Photographic Experts Group (JPEG)** is a standard for compressing continuous-tone photographs. It can provide incredible compression ratios of 10:1 or higher. JPEG encoding is complicated with many mathematical details which will not be explored here. It is also **symmetric** — this means that encoding takes roughly as long as decoding.

The **Motion Picture Experts Group (MPEG)** standards define the primary algorithms used to compress video. To synchronize audio and video output with the two encoders working independently, timestamps are included in the receiver's encoded output. MPEG compression makes use of spatial and temporal redundancies in movies. MPEG and JPEG's key difference is that MPEG can be used when the camera is panning or zooming and the background is not stationary.

---

[20]Psychoacoustics refer to how sound is perceived by people.

There are three types of frames in a MPEG output:

1. **Intra-coded (I) frames:** I-frames are compressed still pictures.
2. **Predictive (P) frames:** P-frames are the differences with previous frames. They are more compressible than I-frames.
3. **Bidirectional (B) frames:** B-frames are the differences between previous and forward frames. They are the most compressible.

Streaming stored media: Video on Demand (VoD) has become increasingly popular in recent years. One can download it through a simple MP4 download to watch a movie through the browser. However, the whole video must be transmitted over the network before being watched. A **metafile**, which is a very short file containing key descriptions about the movie, can be used to solve this problem. A browser will now submit an HTTP metafile request to the server and receive a metafile response. It will then hand off this metafile onto a media player, which sends a media request using a protocol like the **Real-Time Streaming Protocol (RTSP)** and receives a response via TCP or UDP. In this case, the movie does not have to be downloaded entirely before it can be played.

RTSP provides remote control to start and stop media flow through commands to the server such as *DESCRIBE, SETUP, PLAY, RECORD, PAUSE,* and *TEARDOWN*. TCP is often used as it can pass through firewalls more easily as compared to UDP, especially when it is run over the HTTP port. It also provides more reliability.

A media player's significant functions include managing the user interface, dealing with transmission errors, decompressing the content, and eliminating jitter. Apart from managing the user interface, the other three functions are associated with the network protocols.

Streaming live media: IP TeleVision (IPTV) refers to live streaming by television stations. **Internet radio** is the broadcasting of radio stations such as the BBC. There are two approaches to live streaming. The first one is to record programs to the disk. Users can pull up programs from the servers' archives and download them for consumption. The second approach is to broadcast live over the Internet. When streaming from a file, buffering can be reduced since the media can be sent faster than the playback rate. However, live streaming is always transmitted at the same rate as the media is generated. This means that there should be a sufficiently large buffer to deal with network jitter. This is usually 10–15 s.

Since live streaming events may have many viewers, it seems natural and efficient to use **multicasting**. The server sends each media packet once using IP multicast to a group address. The network then delivers a copy of the packet to each member. Packets are sent over a UDP transport since TCP is used between a single sender and receiver. Since UDP does not provide reliability, packets may be lost. Forward Error Correction (FEC) and interleaving are two strategies used to counter this, but we will not go into detail about them.

However, multicasting is not used in real life. This is because IP multicasting is not widely available across network boundaries. Only when used within a provider network will UDP and multicasting work for streaming. Usually, each user will establish a TCP connection through which the media is streamed, just like streaming stored media, as discussed above. Streaming with TCP can be disguised as HTTP to pass through firewalls and allow the media to reach nearly all users on the Internet. One particular disadvantage is that the server must send different copies of the media to each client, which is feasible for a moderate number of clients. For large streaming sites like Netflix with many clients, they do not stream media using TCP to each client from a single server as there is insufficient bandwidth. Instead, they use servers spread globally, and users can connect to the nearest server.

Real-time conferencing: Video conferencing has become the norm in 2020. With the advent of voice-over IP, the monopolized telephone service industry has been disrupted. In 2003, people could call regular phone numbers or computers with IP addresses with Skype. Compared with streaming stored or live media, real-time conferencing requires low latency for an effective conversation.

UDP is better than TCP to minimize latency as it would not have the delays associated with TCP retransmissions. Short packets are also used to reduce latency, despite being less efficient in bandwidth. Since it is real-time, the encoder and decoder must operate quickly. A small buffer also reduces latency at the expense of more loss due to jitter. There is two quality of service mechanisms used to reduce jitter and sometimes latency:

1. Differentiated services (DS): Packets are marked to distinguish their class and manner of handling within the network. For voice-over IP packets, they are marked with *low delay*. This means they are prioritized.

2. Ensure sufficient bandwidth by making a reservation with the network.

Another issue regarding real-time conferencing is the setup and termination of the calls. Two protocols, H.323 and SIP, are used to do that. Both protocols allow for several parties to call using both computers and telephones.

H.323 is a full protocol stack that is the telephone-industry standard and inflexible, making it challenging to adapt to future applications. It more closely serves as an architectural overview of voice-over IP than as a protocol, as seen in Figure 8.8.

At the center of the model is the **gateway**, connecting the Internet to the telephone network. A LAN may have a **gatekeeper** that controls the endpoints in its zone.

To see how the protocols work together, an example of a PC terminal calling a telephone will be used. Briefly, the PC first requests bandwidth through a series of exchanges with the gatekeeper. It then establishes a TCP connection and sends requests to the gatekeeper, which will be forwarded to the gateway. The gateway makes a regular phone call to the PC, and a connection is established after some messages are sent. The PC releases the bandwidth by contacting the gatekeeper to terminate the call (as shown in Figure 8.9).

On the other hand, **Session Initiation Protocol (SIP)** is a single module modeled on HTTP that handles setup, management, and session termination. It is an Internet protocol that handles the setup by exchanging ASCII text lines. It works well with other Internet protocols but not

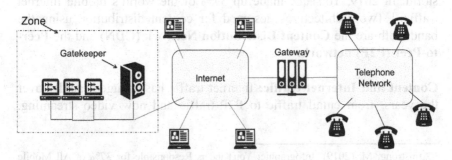

Figure 8.8: H.323 architectural overview for voice-over IP.

Source: Tanenbaum and Wetherall (2010).

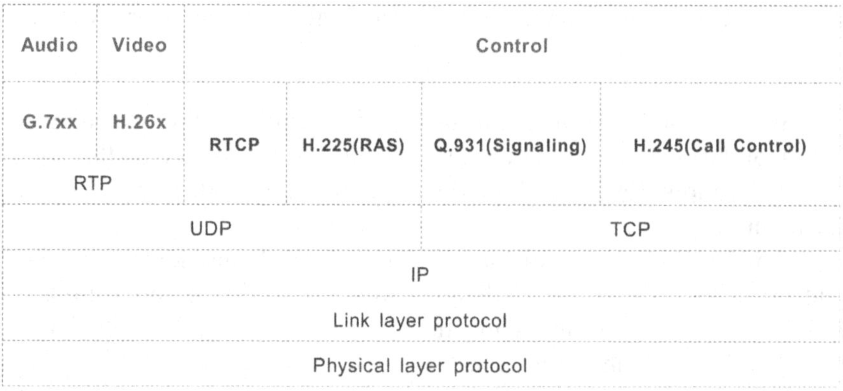

Audio	Video	Control			
G.7xx	H.26x	RTCP	H.225(RAS)	Q.931(Signaling)	H.245(Call Control)
RTP					
UDP				TCP	
IP					
Link layer protocol					
Physical layer protocol					

Figure 8.9:   H.323 protocol stack.

Source: Tanenbaum and Wetherall (2010).

existing telephone system signaling protocols. To set up a call, the caller can either create a TCP connection and send an *INVITE* message, a SIP method to request a session initiation, or send the *INVITE* message in a UDP packet. The callee will respond with a reply code just like the HTTP status codes. For example, the callee will send the message 200 to accept the call. The caller then responds with the *ACK* method, acknowledging the session initiation. Any party can request to terminate the session using the *BYE* method, which the other side must acknowledge. There are also other methods like *OPTIONS, CANCEL and REGISTER.*

(c) Content Delivery

Apart from communication, content may have overtaken the Internet by storm. In 2019, YouTube made up 37% of the world's mobile Internet traffic.[21] Two architectures designed for content distribution using the bandwidth are the **Content Distribution Network (CDN)** and the **Peer-to-Peer (P2P) network.**

Content and Internet traffic: Internet traffic has changed rapidly over the years, from email traffic to P2P traffic and now video streaming.

---

[21]Armstrong, M. (2019). Infographic: YouTube is Responsible for 37% of All Mobile Internet Traffic. Retrieved from https://www.statista.com/chart/17321/global-downstream-mobile-traffic-by-app/ (accessed September 6, 2020).

Traffic volume and bandwidth requirements of the type of traffic stress the network. Internet traffic is also highly skewed, meaning the traffic at popular sites and unpopular sites are drastically different. While unpopular sites can use DNS to be run on the same computer, popular sites pose more challenges and cannot be handled on a single computer. Content distribution systems must be built.

Server farms and web proxies: We have discussed communication between a single server and multiple client machines. For large Web sites, powerful servers can be built with a **server farm**, where a group of computers acts as a single server.

The primary difficulty with server farms is having the multiple servers appear as a single Web site rather than different sites running in parallel. Some solutions to tackle this difficulty will be discussed below. It is essential that any of the servers can handle client requests. Thus, they should each have a copy of the Web site while being connected to a common back-end database.

One solution is using DNS to spread client requests across the server farm. This method is the core of CDNs. Whenever a DNS request is made, the DNS server returns a rotating list of the servers' IP addresses. Different clients will then contact other servers to access the same Web site.

Another solution is based on the **front end**, typically a link-layer switch or an IP router that handles packets. Requests and responses are carried as a TCP connection, and the front end will distribute the packets for a request to the same server. Requests are broadcasted by the front end, and each server answers a fraction of incoming requests based on predetermined rules.

On the client-side, better-caching techniques improve performance by reducing network load and shortening response time. **Web proxies** are used to share cache among users. This means that pages visited by a user can be returned to another user without fetching from the server, even though it is the other user's first time visiting the page. As discussed above, caching is only effective for static pages. Like the definition of a proxy, the Web proxy fetches requests on behalf of the users.

Organizations typically operate one Web proxy for all users. Each user will first consult their browser cache before moving on to the proxy cache. Other proxies may be added, with each proxy or browser making requests via its **upstream proxy**. Other benefits of web proxies are filtering content and providing anonymity to the user from the server.

Content delivery networks (CDNs): Having discussed server farms and web proxies, we will discuss a larger-scale approach for Web sites globally. For CDNs, clients request copies of the Web page in a nearby cache. These copies are placed in a set of nodes at different locations. The data distribution is like a tree, starting from the CDN origin server then distributes a copy of the page to its nodes in various geographical areas. Clients all around the world then fetch the pages from the nearest node. CDNs are highly scalable and do not overload the origin server.

Organizing clients for this distribution tree is not a straightforward problem. Using proxy servers is infeasible as users use different Web proxies. **Mirroring** is one approach where the origin server replicates the content over the nodes and allows the user to choose a nearby mirror to access the content manually. This is usually used for static pages. **DNS redirection** is the most feasible approach where the browser uses DNS to resolve the page URL to an IP address, and the name server run by CDN will return a response of the IP address of the node closest to the client. Companies usually use a CDN provider's services rather than setting up their own to distribute content.

Peer-to-peer (P2P) networks: P2P networks are an alternative for content distribution, where many computers pool their resources and form a content distribution system. These can simply be home computers. Unlike CDNs, there is not a centralized control system. They are self-scaling without the need for infrastructure. Their upload capacity grows with the download demands made by the users. One major challenge regarding P2P networks is how to use the bandwidth well when its users have different download and upload capacities.

The **BitTorrent protocol** allows peers to share files efficiently. A **torrent** is a content description used to verify the data's integrity downloaded from peers. It contains a tracker's name, which is the server with a list of other peers downloading and uploading content, also known as a **swarm.** It also includes a list of **chunks** that make up the content. This makes the torrent file at least three orders of magnitude smaller than the content, allowing for quick transfers. **Seeders** are peers within the swarm that possess all the chunks, while **leechers** or **free riders** are nodes that consume resources without contribution. To incentivize favorable uploads and disincentivize leechers, a **choking algorithm** is used.

Although P2P file sharing is decentralized, there is still a centralized tracker for each swarm. To find out which peers have sought-after content, we need solutions to create P2P indexes that are entirely distributed and work well. Four solutions were invented in 2001, namely Chord, CAN, Pastry and Tapestry. These solutions are collectively known as **Distributed Hash Tables (DHTs)**. DHTs are also called **structured P2P networks** as they impose a stable structure on the communication between nodes. DHT techniques are widely researched and used commercially, such as in Amazon's Dynamo.[22] DHTs are decentralized and distributed data structures that store data items associated with labels. It holds key-value pairs <key, value> by assigning keys to different nodes. Nodes all use the same hash function and are distributed across the network (for data communication). This distribution allows nodes to enter and leave with minimal disruption. DHTs are s an excellent way to store and access big data on multiple computers.

References/Further Readings

Gundavaram, S. (1997). CGI Programming on the World Wide Web. Retrieved from https://www.oreilly.com/openbook/cgi/ch01_01.html (accessed September 28, 2020).

Singh, S.P. (2012). The Use of DNS Resource Records. *International Journal of Advances in Electrical and Electronics Engineering*. Retrieved from https://citeseerx.ist.psu.edu/viewdoc/download?doi=10.1.1.640.444&rep=rep1&type=pdf (accessed September 4, 2020).

Tanenbaum, A.S. & Wetherall, D. (2010). *Computer Networks*, 5th ed. Pearson Education (US), Boston, MA, United States.

8.3 Sample Questions

Question 1
What is the function of a network layer?

(a) It handles the routing of packets and controls the subnet's operation.
(b) It allows the option for greater reliability of packets sent.
(c) It masks transmission errors.

---

[22] Amazon's Dynamo — All Things Distributed (2020). Retrieved from https://www.allthingsdistributed.com/2007/10/amazons_dynamo.html (accessed September 7, 2020).

Question 2
Which of the following layers transport bits from one device to another along the network?

(a) The physical layer
(b) The data link layer
(c) The transport layer

Question 3
High frequency ranges from ____ to _____.

(a) 3 kHz to 30 kHz
(b) 300 kHz to 3000 kHz
(c) 3 MHz to 30 MHz

Question 4
Which of the following are PPP design requirements?

I. Network protocol multiplexing
II. Packet framing
III. No flow control

    (a) I and II
    (b) I and III
    (c) I, II, and III

Question 5
The network layer provides a reliable _____ service.

(a) node-to-node
(b) end-to-end
(c) process-to-process

Question 6
Which of the following about IPv4 and IPv6 is correct?

I. Checksum field is available in IPv4
II. IPv6 supports multicasting
III. IPv6 provides 128-bit addresses

(a) I and II
(b) I and III
(c) I, II, and III

Question 7
Which of the following about datagram network and virtual-circuit network is correct?

I. Datagram network does not need circuit setup, while circuit setup is needed in a virtual-circuit network
II. In a datagram network, each packet is routed independently
III. Congestion control is easy in datagram networks

(a) I and II
(b) I and III
(c) I, II, and III

Question 8
The network layer concerns with _____.

(a) bits
(b) frames
(c) packets

Question 9
What are the functions of the transport layer?

I. Multiplexing
II. Congestion control
III. Flow control

(a) I and II
(b) I and III
(c) I, II, and III

Question 10
The transport layer is which layer?

(a) Third layer
(b) Fourth layer
(c) Fifth layer

Question 11
Which of the following is true?

(a) The engineering and science departments, which share the same LAN in a building, must have the same domain.
(b) The engineering department is split over multiple buildings, and so the LANs should have different domains.
(c) The engineering and science departments, which share the same LAN in a building, can have distinct domains.

Solutions

Question 1

Solution: Option **a** is correct.

Option b is the function of the transport layer, and Option c is the function of the data link layer.

Question 2

Solution: Option **a** is correct.

One of the data link layer tasks is to take the packets (such as IP) from the network layer and encapsulates them into frames, then transfers the data between adjacent nodes in the network. The transport layer's primary function is to provide data transport from a process on a source machine to a destination machine with a desired level of reliability. The network layer's main task is to provide a reliable end-to-end service between the source and the destination.

Question 3

Solution: Option **c** is correct.

Question 4

Solution: Option **a** is correct.

No flow control is one of PPP non-requirements.

Question 5

Solution: Option **b** is correct.

Question 6

Solution: Option **c** is correct.

Question 7

Solution: Option **a** is correct.

Refer to the comparison of a datagram and virtual-circuit networks figure.

Question 8

Solution: Option **c** is correct.

Question 9

Solution: Option **b** is correct.

The services provided by the transport layer include: end-to-end transmission, addressing, reliable delivery (including error control, sequence control, loss control, duplication control), flow control, congestion control, and multiplexing.

Question 10

Solution: Option **b** is correct.

Question 11

Solution: Option **c** is correct.

Domain naming does not have to follow physical networks. Instead, they follow organizational boundaries.

Chapter 9

Network Security

9.1 Introduction

Learning Objectives

- Understand the threats and targets of network security.
- Understand several effective ways to handle the threats and achieve the targets.

Main Takeaways

Main Points

- **Two categories of attack:** Passive and active attacks. Examples of passive attacks are eavesdropping and traffic analysis. Examples of active attacks are impersonation, interruption, tampering, replay, and denial of service.
- **Five targets of network communication security:** Preventing the leak of messages, preventing analysis of communication amounts, detecting changed message flows, detecting rejected message service, and detecting forged initialization connections.

Main Terms

- **Network security:** Refers to the network system hardware, software, and data in the system that are protected.
- **Information security:** Refers to protecting information systems and information resources from all kinds of threats, interference, and destruction to ensure information security.

267

- **Communication security:** Communication security is based on the signal level of security, does not involve specific data information content.

9.1.1 *Network Security Overview*

In daily work and life, **network security** is very common. Network security means that the network system's hardware and software and the system's data are protected from damage, change, and leakage due to accidental or malicious reasons. The system should run continuously and reliably; the network service should not be interrupted. If you want to protect a network resource, the easiest way is to assign it a name and set a corresponding password.

To deal with various factors that can cause a network to be vulnerable, network security involves a broad range of practices, which include:

- **Deploying active devices:** Such as using anti-virus software to prevent the installation and operation of malicious programs, blocking suspicious email and websites, etc.
- **Deploying passive devices:** For example, usage devices and software that report unauthorized network activity or authorized user activity could endanger network security as the specific action (blocking or continuing) is still determined by the user.
- **Using preventative devices:** Detect whether there are security vulnerabilities in the system so as to prevent network security incidents.
- **Ensuring users follow safe practices:** Even with the above devices and software used to maintain network security, it is important to strengthen network security education for users because users' dangerous actions can cause network security problems.

9.1.2 *Importance of Network Security*

Regardless of the industry or business type, all organizations need to review their network environment and network security issues. Although there is no perfect network security environment, a secure and stable network security system should protect the user's data and enhance its trust in the organization's system.

Network security prevents spyware from breaking into enterprise systems to steal information and protects Shared data. The network security infrastructure builds multiple protection levels against Man-in-the-Middle (MITM) attacks by breaking up information into parts, encrypting them separately, and sending them over separate paths.

When the system is connected to the Internet, there is a massive amount of traffic which leads to stability problems. If the vulnerability of the system is exploited, the network system of the enterprise may be subject to network attack. Network security improves network reliability by continuously monitoring any suspicious behavior that might disrupt the system to prevent delays and outages.

9.1.3 *Negative Impacts When Networks Go Wrong*

For individuals, if their network is hacked, they may go bankrupt. For example, **vandalism** may occur. This usually involves planting misleading information in the system. This is one of many strategies used by hackers. Once false information is planted, its integrity is questioned, and its customer feels misled.

For companies, cybersecurity incidents can also damage their intellectual property. Hackers can gain unauthorized access to corporate or personal information. If a hacker tries to steal a plan or solution, the company will not continue implementing new designs and products. It can destroy the company or bring its operations to a standstill in severe cases.

Companies could also lose revenue. Most cyber-attacks can cause systems to crash, shutting down companies for some time. The longer the network goes down, the more revenue is lost, and the company may lose credibility.

9.1.4 *How Network Security Works*

Network security generally revolves around two processes such as authentication and authorization. The former is similar to the key of our house. Only the correct key can open the door. In other words, authentication ensures access only to users who belong to the network and prevents outsiders' entry.

The second is authorization, which determines how each user in the network has access. It's like being in a "shared" house, whereby you can only access your bedroom as well as public rooms. Administrators need access to the entire network in a network, while other users are assigned access based on their identity and responsibilities.

Several essential technologies exist to make sure that network security is adequate, including firewalls, anti-virus, and anti-malware software, access control data loss prevention, and intrusion prevention systems:

- **Firewalls:** Firewalls use specific rules to control traffic flow, thus creating a barrier between a trusted internal network and an untrusted external network. Firewalls can be hardware as well as software, or both. For example, Cisco provides unified **Threat Management (UTM)** devices and next-generation firewalls to prevent attacks.
- **Anti-virus and anti-malware software:** "Malware" is short for "malicious software", such as spyware and viruses. A computer infected with malware does not necessarily cause immediate problems and can lie dormant for days or even weeks. Good anti-malware software scans malware as it enters and continues to follow up to detect anomalies and remove them in time.
- **Access control: Network access control (NAC)** means that the operator can control each user's access rights and each device. To protect against potential attacks, the operator can enforce security policies to determine which programs each specific user can access. So not every user has access to the entire network.
- **Data loss prevention:** Businesses need to ensure that their employees do not transfer sensitive information outside the company, so they use data loss prevention (DLP) technology to prevent unsafe upload and download.
- **Intrusion prevention systems: Intrusion prevention systems (IPS)** actively prevent attacks, virus outbreaks from spreading, and re-infecting by scanning network traffic.

9.1.5 *Information Security Overview*

Information security refers to protecting information systems and information resources from all kinds of threats, interference, and destruction to ensure information security. It means preventing unauthorized or inappropriate access to or illegal use of data and reducing such incidents' negative impact. Information security focuses on balancing the confidentiality, integrity, and availability of data and implementing effective policies.

9.1.6 *Communication Security Overview*

Communication security is based on the signal level of security, does not involve specific data information content. It is one of the most important issues in the network. Thus, understanding communication security requires a deeper understanding of network security and information security.

Typically, communication security is faced with two categories of attacks: passive and active attacks. Passive attacks attempt to learn or use information from the system but do not affect the resources. Active attacks attempt to alter resources or affect an information system's operation. Two types of passive attack are **eavesdropping** and **traffic analysis**. Eavesdropping refers to learning the information resources' content by observing its transmission; this can be easily prevented using encryption. Traffic analysis is to observe patterns of the information, such as its frequency and the length of messages, to derive useful information about the nature of the communication. Passive attacks are difficult to detect, but encrypting information is usually sufficient to thwart passive attacks' success. Examples of active attacks are **impersonation, interruption, tampering, replay attack, denial of service**. Impersonation refers to the case where one entity pretends to be another entity to obtain particular privileges or information. Interruption refers to intentionally interrupting other people's communications on the network and disrupt communications. Tampering refers to deliberately tampering messages (such as modify, delete, or insert data of the messages) transmitted over the network. Replay attack involves capturing messages and retransmitting the message to produce an unauthorized effect. Denial of Service is an attack that sends bogus messages to overwhelm the server and prevents the normal usage of the communication system by legitimate users.

Therefore, the targets of communication security include five points: preventing the leak of messages, preventing analysis of communication amounts, detecting changed message flows, detecting rejected message service, and detecting forged initialization connections.

9.1.7 *Ways to Guarantee Communication Security*

One effective way to counter passive attacks is by **encryption**. Encryption refers to the process of encrypting the original data conversion. Any form of data can be encrypted, including video, documents, images, etc. Encryption schemes are generally divided into **symmetric encryption and asymmetric encryption**. Compared with symmetric encryption, asymmetric schemes use different keys for encryption and decryption, respectively. In other words, asymmetric encryption uses the public key to encrypt the data and the private key to decrypt it.

Another effective way is to establish a firewall, a system composed of software and hardware. A firewall is a specially programmed router used to implement an access control policy between two networks. Access control policies are developed by the organization using the firewall to best suit the organization's needs. Firewall systems can be divided into the host-based system and network-based system. The former's firewall is directly deployed on the host, and barriers are established by controlling traffic and resources. Since the latter can be anywhere in LAN or WAN, it may be a software device running on general hardware, a hardware device running on dedicated hardware, or a virtual device on a virtual host.

X.800 divides security services into five categories.

1. The **authentication** service is concerned with assuring that communication is authentic. This is guaranteed from two aspects: The data is from the source that it claims to be from (data authentication), and the user is who he/she claims he/she is (user authentication).
2. The **access control** service can limit access to users based on their privileges. The pre-condition is that the user must be authenticated to use the system first before access rights can be tailored to the individual.
3. **Confidentiality** is concerned with protecting the information resources from being learned by unauthorized users or outsiders. Another aspect of confidentiality, which sits closer to **privacy**, is to protect data from being analyzed by unauthorized users or outsiders.

4. Data **integrity** is a service that ensures any modification on the data can be detected. When a connection-oriented protocol such as the TCP is integrated with integrity service, it can assure that messages are received with no duplication, insertion, modification, reordering, or replays. On the other hand, a connectionless protocol such as UDP can only protect against message modification.
5. **Nonrepudiation** prevents the users from denying a transmitted message. When a message is sent, the receiver can always prove that the sender has indeed sent the message and vice versa.

Another security service that is worth mentioning is the provision of **availability** service. This is related to an active attack called denial of service. Availability is the property of a system or its resources to continue being accessible to its legitimate (or authorized) users.

9.2 Web Security

Learning Objectives
- Understand what Web security is and why it is essential.
- Understand several technologies to achieve web security.

Main Takeaways

Main Points
- Website security includes website and web application security issues, source code, visitor access, and security software.
- Insufficient web security affects business reputation and causes revenue loss.
- Secure naming, SSL, and Mobile Code Security are the most common technologies to keep a website safe.

Main Terms
- **Web security:** Refers to a series of defense mechanisms to prevent a website from being hijacked by intruders, such as hacking the server and tampering with the website or web application.
- **Secure naming:** Its basic idea is to decouple the names/DNS names of the services from the identities that the services are running.

- **Secure sockets layer (SSL):** SSL can help secure data transmission over the Internet. It uses data encryption to ensure that data cannot be intercepted or eavesdropped on as it travels over the network.

9.2.1 *Web Security Overview*

Web security refers to a series of defense works to prevent a website or web application from being hijacked by intruders. As enterprise network vulnerabilities can cause huge losses, ensuring enterprise web security is crucial.

- **Web security issues:** As the website or web application often needs to deal with users' private data, such as social security numbers, identity numbers, and contact information, security problems such as data theft and leakage may occur.
- **Source code:** Poor source code are more prone to security hazards. In general, the more complex the management of a website or the more dynamic the site, the more likely it is to be vulnerable.
- **Visitor access:** Parts of a website may require access rights to function. Simultaneously, it is more difficult to identify truly authorized visitors, so how to restrict access to unauthorized, malicious visitors can be a challenge.
- **Security software:** Network security software protects websites by providing security management services, usually managed security-as-a-service (SaaS) models.

9.2.2 *Threats of Web Security*

A hacked website may cause a loss of reputation and credibility. Also, a breach of customer data could bring lawsuits and fines.

Most hacker attacks are targeted at customers' data. The aim is commonly to monetize the data or deny the company's access to its own customers' data before paying a certain amount of ransom (as commonly is the case in a ransomware attack). Denial of service attacks has paralyzed many sites. In this type of attack, crackers flood the site with traffic, making it unable to respond to legitimate queries. Usually, the attack is initiated by many computers that the hacker has penetrated via a denial-of-service (DDoS) attack. These attacks are so common that they will not even release news, but they may cost the attacked site thousands of dollars in business losses.

According to Google, it sent more than 45 million security alerts to registered website owners in 2018. Also, they sent nearly 6 million messages to web admins about illegal manual operations. In a report by firewall provider Sukuri, they intercepted more than 17 million attacks in 2019, up nearly 52% from a year earlier.

A hacked website or server is detrimental to a company's reputation and revenue. For example, many organizations' homepages were attacked and replaced by the new homepage of Cookie Choice. The websites that were cracked included Yahoo!, US Army, CIA, NASA, and the New York Times website. In most cases, cookies are just some interesting texts, and these sites are fixed within a few hours.

When a website is attacked, Google and other search engines restrict access to the site, resulting in a massive loss of corporate customers and, ultimately, a loss of revenue and credibility. Websites may also be blacklisted by search engines. Google "quarantines" at least 10,000 websites a day, which users see marked "this website may harm your computer" in search results.

Compared to website protection, website cleaning is more expensive. After the attack, companies usually spend a lot of energy protecting their back door. This will lead to the fact that once the loophole is exploited, it will take more energy to fill it.

Spam: We usually encounter situations where spam emails are sent to our inbox, or occasionally see spam pop-ups when we browse online. However, sometimes spam can be malicious. It is widespread for emails to appear on websites in the form of comments. The bot can add a link to another website in the website's comment section to try to establish a backlink. Although these types of comments are annoying and do not look good on the site, they are not always harmful. However, malware may be contained on the site and may cause harm to website visitors.

Also, Google's crawler can usually detect malicious URLs and impose a hosted spam penalty on them. This can ruin a website's SEO (Search Engine Optimisation) ranking.

Viruses and malware: Malware is a collective term for "malicious software" to make it clear. As many as 230,000 malware samples are created every day. These types of viruses are usually used to access private data or use server resources. Criminals also invade website permissions to make money through advertising or affiliate links. With malware, operators and website visitors are at risk. Someone visiting the site may accidentally visit a link with a malicious file. It is the operator's responsibility to maintain the web site's security and prevent this from happening.

DDoS attacks: DDoS attacks will prevent users from accessing certain websites. Hackers use fake IP addresses to overload the server. This will cause the website to go offline. This will cause the website to go offline. The website host will need to restore the server and run it as soon as possible.

9.2.3 *Secure Naming*

Secure naming is a technology used in some mature companies such as Google. Its basic idea is to decouple the names/DNS (Domain Name System) names of the services from the identities that the services are running as. A simple example is the service frontend (resolvable by the front end on DNS server) holding the certificate with identity frontend-prod-team. In Kubernetes, the identity frontend-prod-team is the service account of the workloads running the frontend service.

DNS spoofing (also known as DNS cache poisoning) can also pose a threat to computer security. It introduces corrupted domain name system data into the DNS resolver's cache, causing the name server to return incorrect result records, such as IP addresses. This causes the traffic to be diverted to the attacker's computer (or any other computer).

The DNS Security Extensions (DNSSEC) is a secure protocol that can digitally sign data, effectively alleviating this problem. Signing at each level during the DNS lookup helps to secure the lookup.

9.2.4 *Secure Sockets Layer*

Secure sockets layer (SSL) is a security technique used to establish a standard for encrypted links between a server and a client, usually a mail server and mail client, or a website and browser.

Sensitive information (such as bank card numbers, ID numbers, etc.) can also be transmitted over SSL. Because browsers and Web pages send plain text data to each other, this data is vulnerable to theft.

9.2.5 *Mobile Code Security*

The essence of the security problems that mobile code can cause is the need to access system resources while running code that comes from another, even untrustworthy, host. Security problems caused by mobile code can be divided into malicious code problems and malicious host problems.

One of Java's more important features is that it allows untrusted code to run in a restricted environment, thereby preventing code from performing malicious actions.

ActiveX was created by Microsoft as a framework for its older component Object Model (COM) and object linking and embedding (OLE) technology for downloading content from the web but has since been defunct. **JavaScript** has no formal security model, each vendor handles security differently, and its implementation is chronically vulnerable.

In addition to extending Web pages through code, the market for browser extensions, plug-ins, and plug-ins is booming. These are computer programs that extend the capabilities of the Web browser. Plug-ins typically provide the ability to interpret or display specific types of content, such as PDF or Flash animations. Extensions and add-ons provide new browser features, such as better password management or ways to interact with pages, such as marking them or allowing the easy purchase of related items.

The Open Web Application Security Project (OWASP) identified the top ten web vulnerabilities.[1] These vulnerabilities include injection, broken authentication, sensitive data exposure, XML external entities, broken access control, security misconfiguration, cross-site scripting, insecure deserialization, using components with known vulnerabilities, and insufficient logging and monitoring. The OWASP standard is commonly used as a guideline by web developers to ensure safe and secure web

---

[1]OWASP (2017). OWASP Top Ten Web Application Security Risks. OWASP. Retrieved from https://owasp.org/www-project-top-ten/.

applications. Essential steps in protecting websites or web applications from attacks include using up-to-date, open-source, and credible security configurations, algorithms, and patches, setting proper authentication and access control schemes, and practice secure software development practices.

References/Further Readings

Breiman, L. (2001). Statistical Modeling: The Two Cultures. *Statistical Science*, **16**(3), 199–231.

Donoho, D. (2017). 50 Years of Data Science. *Journal of Computational and Graphical Statistics*, **26**(4), 745–766, doi:10.1080/10618600.2017.1384734.

Kalman, G. (2014). 10 Most Common Web Security Vulnerabilities. Total Engineering Blog. Retrieved from https://www.toptal.com/security/10-most-common-web-security-vulnerabilities.

Press, G. (2013). A Very Short History of Data Science. *Forbes*. Retrieved from https://www.forbes.com/sites/gilpress/2013/05/28/a-very-short-history-of-data-science/#7eace5f355cf.

Tukey, J.W. (1962). The Future of Data Analysis. *The Annals of Mathematical Statistics*, **33**(1), 1–67.

9.3 Sample Questions

Question 1
Which of the following is **NOT** a reason why website security is important?

(a) Hacked websites target the customers.
(b) Website security is expensive.
(c) The number of hacked sites rises rapidly.

Question 2
Which of the following about blacklisted websites is **TRUE**?

(a) When seeing warnings of blacklisted websites, consumers get panic.
(b) Businesses can negotiate with searching engines to be deleted from the website.
(c) Business revenue might suffer when its website is blacklisted.

Question 3
Which of the following issues are associated with the targets of network security?

(a) Preventing the leak of messages
(b) Interception and interruption
(c) Increasing the revenue of the business

Question 4
Which of the following describes firewall most accurately?

(a) Firewall is a system composed of software.
(b) Host-based firewalls can be positioned anywhere within a LAN or WAN.
(c) Firewalls are categorized as a network-based or a host-based system.

Solutions

Question 1

Solution: Option **b** is correct.

It is website security that is expensive.

Question 2

Solution: Option **c** is correct.

For option a, consumers are grateful for the warning, but website business owners may panic. For option b, search engines, such as Google, detect suspicious websites according to their analysis and algorithm, which cannot be negotiated.

Question 3

Solution: Option **a** is correct.

For option b, interception and interruption are threats to network security. Option c is not relevant to this question.

Question 4

Solution: Option **c** is correct.

For option a, the firewall is a system composed of software and hardware. For option b, network-based, not host-based, firewalls can be positioned anywhere within a LAN or WAN.

Global Fintech Institute - World Scientific Series on Fintech

(Continued from page ii)

Applications and Trends in Fintech II: Cloud Computing, Compliance, and Global Fintech Trends
        David Lee Kuo Chuen (Global Fintech Institute, Singapore & Singapore University of Social Sciences, Singapore), Joseph Lim, Phoon Kok Fai and Wang Yu (Singapore University of Social Sciences, Singapore)